The Fundamentals of

Islamic Creed

BY

Abu Ja`far Ahmad Salamah al-Azdi, al-Tahawi

COMMENTARY BY

Ali ibn abi al-`Izz al-Adhru`i`

ABRIDGED BY

Abdul Mun`am Salih al-`Ali al-`Izzi`

TRANSLATED BY

Syed Iqbal Zaheer

Contents

Publisher's Note   i

Foreword   v

Preface   xv

Tawḥīd   1

Nothing resembles Him   14

Nothing can frustrate Him   17

The Everlasting   19

His Will prevails   22

Intellects cannot grasp Him   25

Mankind do not resemble Him   25

The Self subsisting   27

Creator without the need   29

Eternal of Qualities   31

The Creator before creation   34

Nothing like unto Him   38

He predetermined   40

His Will is executed   45

Muhammad is His slave   49

Last of the Prophets   53

The Qur`an is Allah's Speech 59

The Beatific Vision 72

Denial of the Beatific Vision 85

Allah's Attributes are unique 91

Our Lord is without parts and limbs 93

The Night Ascension 98

The Pond 107

The Intercession 108

The primordial compact 115

Allah's fore-knowledge 116

The Divine Decree 117

The Tablet and the Pen 125

The Pen has dried 127

Perfectly determined decree 131

The `Arsh and the Kursiyy 134

He does not need them 136

He took Ibrahim as a friend 144

Angels, Prophets, Books 145

Those who face our Qiblah 150

The Qur`an was not created 151

The apostates 152

Salvation lies between hope and fear 161

The Favorites 171

Those who committed major sins 180

Prayers behind the corrupt 181

Judging the people 186

The rulers	188
Holding the scribes in honor	193
The angel of death	194
Punishment in the grave	195
Resurrection, the Bridge	199
Paradise will not perish	205
Human abilities	210
Deeds are people's acquisition	213
That imposed which is within ability	218
Supplication for the dead	222
Allah responds	226
The Companions	231
Abu Bakr	233
`Umar	235
`Uthman	236
`Ali	241
The ten given glad tiding	245
Miracles and thaumaturgies	248
The Hour	252
The Soothsayers	253
The mainstream and Taqlid	257
The middle way	262
Our religion	265
Notes	267
Index	269
The Author	277

Publisher's Note

All praise to Allah the Lord of the worlds, and peace and blessings on the most honored of Messengers and the best of creations, Muhammad, a slave of Allah and His Messenger: the trustworthy guide. Peace and blessings also upon his kinsfolk, Companions and all those who followed him in right stead until the day of Judgment.

We feel pleasure at presenting a fresh translation of the fundamentals of Islamic doctrines as formulated by Imam Tahawi and explained by Ibn Abi Al `Izz.

The scholars and the jurists are unanimous that the articles of faith as formulated by Imam Tahawi, may Allah show him mercy, most accurately reflect the mind and understanding of the earliest Muslims. It is free of incorrect interpretations, over exemplification and any distortion of the ideas formulated by Islam. There is also a general agreement that the commentary on the original work as done by Qadi Ibn Abi al `Izz al Adhru`i is an accurate elucidation of what Tahawi meant to express. It strives to be close to the texts of the Qur`an and the *Sunnah*, and, without over stretching the meaning, attempts to project the opinion of the great majority of scholars in matters where differences in opinion prevail.

This version of the Arabic commentary was first published about 75 years ago in Makkah al Mukarramah in 1394 A.H. under the supervision of a team of scholars headed by Sheikh `Abdullah b. Hasan b. Hussayn al Sheikh Muhammad b. `Abdul Wahhab. Subsequently, it was reprinted in Egypt under the supervision of the *Sheikh al hadīth*, Ahmed Muhammad Shakir. A third print was run under the supervision of Sheikh Muhammad Nasiruddin al Albani, may Allah preserve him. Each of the above strove to improve the work, offering suitable suggestions. However, we have chosen to reprint the edition that was revised and improved by Sheikh Ahmed Muhammad Shakir.

The present work is a full text translation of an abridgement done by `Abdul Mun`im Saleh `Ali al-`Izzi and published by the Ministry of Justice and Islamic Affairs and Trusts of the United Arab Emirates in 1401 A.H.

The original author, Al Tahawi, was a scholar of *hadīth* and a jurist. He was born in 239 in Egypt. His mentor was his uncle Isma`il b. Yahya al Muzani who was one of the most learned and a direct pupil of Imam Shafe`i. However, subsequently, Tahawi parted ways with his uncle to adopt the Hanafiyy school of thought, although that did not prevent him from differing with certain opinions of Imam Abu Hanifah himself in preference of opinions of other scholars.

Tahawi also studied under various *hadīth* scholars whose numbers reach a staggering figure of three hundred. Understandably, several scholars of repute have expressed their good opinion of Tahawi. Ibn *Yūnus* said: "Tahawi was a trustworthy, well known, intelligent scholar who did not leave behind him one of his stature." This single opinion should suffice since the opinions of Ibn *Yūnus* are considered to be well deliberated statements of fact, especially when he is talking about scholars of Egyptian origin.

Nonetheless, Dhahabi too has stated in his *"Tarikh al Kabir"* that Al Tahawi was an outstanding, intelligent scholar of repute. Ibn Kathir has said about him in his *"Al Bidayah wa al Nihayah"* that "he was one of the most brilliant and trustworthy scholars of *hadīth*."

As for his writings, their outstanding qualities are, a thorough research, abundance of material, and, an attractive manner of presentation.

One of his works is this *"`Aqidah al Tahāwiyyah."* The textual material, although a short discourse, is compressed with meaning. It follows the methodology of the pious predecessors and is framed in words that can neither be easily misinterpreted nor will soon empty out their meaning to become sterile.

Another of his book is *"Ma`āni al Āthār"*. This is a collection of essays of legal nature where he states a rule and then substantiates it with the help of various evidences. In the course of discussions he also takes up those legal matters over which disagreement prevails among the jurists, presenting various points of view that have been expressed, and then, finally, states his own preference. This work inculcates in the reader a capacity for research and higher learning, raising his intellectual capabilities.

Another of his works is *"Mushkil al Āthār"* in which he presents those traditions of the Prophet, on whom be peace, that seemingly contradict each other. He endeavors, with great success, to show how they could be reconciled. Yet another of his works is *"Mukhtasar fi al Fiqh ʿAla Furūʿ al Hanafiyyah"* which deals with certain derivative principles of Law. These are published works. But there are several others to his credit.

He died in 321 A.H. May Allah be pleased with him.

As for the commentator, *Sādr*uddin ʿAli b. ʿAli b. Muhammad b. ʿAli al ʿIzz al Adhruʿi, he too was a Hanafiyy scholar. He was the Chief Justice of the Dimashq (Damascus) province. Subsequently, he became the Chief Justice of the Egyptian provinces. Some time later he returned to Dimashq once again in the same capacity. Born in 721 A.H. he died in 792. He was one of the students of the famous commentator, Hafiz Ibn Kathir. Ibn Hajr al ʿAsqalani has presented his short biography in the third volume of his *"Al Durar al Kaminah fi Aʿyan al Miʿah al Thaminah."*

We felt however, that this excellent commentary needed some editing and pruning in order to make it more effective, especially from the point of view of the training of the new generations. That would also make it easy for a layman to understand as well as lead to its adoption as a course book in Islamic institutions, in studies conducted in mosques, or in youth circles. Accordingly, quite some material of that nature has been cut off which was in reference to those innovations that seem to have died out with time: for example, those portions that refuted the Muʿtazilah sect. Repetitive statements have also been removed. Likewise, where several evidences were offered in refutation of a certain innovation, they have been cut short to a few. But nothing of the text of al Tahawi has been removed.

Foreword

If we are to draw a list of a hundred books that every knowledgeable Muslim ought to read, the book in your hands could occupy one of the top ten positions. It is a classical work: an all time master piece in logic, level headedness, freedom from passion, prejudice, devious ways, and, because of its subtleties, full of challenge to the intellect. In fact, it would do good to many a philosopher scientists, such as a few neo Darwinists of today, to read the book as an example of dispassionate, deductive reasoning connecting subtle ideas into a logical whole. It would be a pleasure too for any mind that loves to think and can differentiate between speciousness and *finesse*, between a jumble of confused thoughts and a synthesis of facts behind the abstract, to read this book.

There is no effort here to reconcile the irreconcilable or to bombard the reader with a series of thoughts leading up to no concrete sense, or worse, a few acceptable concepts leading up to a plausible theory. It is an explanation of how "a plus b whole square is equal to a square + plus b square, plus 2 multiplied by the sum of a and b." It could be confusing to some, because it does not employ figures, but it is perfect logic and certainly not beyond comprehension. It is the kind of exercise in which one participates in the debate, from either side, and, with the help of the faculties of reason and logic, ends up being on the side of Tahawi and his commentator Ibn Abi al `Izz.

Tahawi`s text, short, to the point, felicitous, full of meaning, yet poetic, also gives us, apart from the creed, an idea of the frame of mind of the earliest believers brought up on a good dosage of the Qur`an. His confident statements challenge the reader to come up with a Qur`anic verse contradicting him. It is amazing too how Tahawi closes all avenues for any kind of wrong interpretation Saddling on his words. His crisp and exact sentences remind us of the Principles of Islamic Law as worked out by the Muslim jurists; but perhaps, no surprise; Tahawi was an excellent man of law also.

It is no less remarkable either that despite a gap of 500 years between them, the two: Tahawi and Ibn abi al `Izz, look at ideas with such coherence. For one to agree with the other, over such wide, varying and complicated issues, with the two thoughts harmonized to such a fine degree, is surely striking. What two other writings, separated by a similar period, will show such harmony? Religion, science, philosophy, literature: can we find another example? But, of course, the binding, coalescing and steering forces are the two principal sources of Islam: the six thousand and odd Qur`anic verses and a hundred thousand and odd Prophetic statements. He who knows the two sources well, knows how Tahawi and al `Izz can in such harmony despite the distance in time. In particular, it is the Qur`an that emerges as the unifying element between the treatise and it commentary. There is not a statement that is not supported by a Qur`anic statement. The Islamic creed turns out to be, in fact, the Qur`an re stated following a particular chain of thought. It can be amazing too to many of those of our times who are otherwise familiar with the Qur`an that these concepts were there in it, all along, but it just did not occur to them that they could look at the Qur`anic texts that way.

That explains also the confidence of the writer and the commentator. They offer us a litmus test: If you found anything in this work refuting any of your ideas, your understanding of the Qur`an and the *Sunnah* was imperfect. Ibn abi al `Izz quietly throws his punch: "Go back to the Qur`an and look for more examples."

On another plane, what other religious text can withstand this kind of test? What religious text really supports the creed held as true by its followers? Trinity is refuted in the *Bible* by no less than Jesus himself: "And one of the scribes came, and having heard them reasoning together, and perceiving that he had answered them well, asked him, Which is the first commandment of all? And Jesus answered him, The first of all commandments is, Hear, O Israel, The Lord our God is one Lord" (Mark, 12: 29). That`s a shattering blow right at the start. And that`s some blow to the rest of the creed also. Stated in 12 short sentences the Christian creed revolves around the personality of Jesus Christ: there is not much about anything else.

The Jewish creed is one line longer. One of the lines states, "Other prophets were obliged to wait for revelations, while Moses was empowered to solicit them." It also states, "This law (as stated in the *Torah*) will not be abrogated, nor will there be any other law of Divine origin. Nothing will be added to or taken away from, it." While the former statement is unacceptable to human reason, as common sense rejects any imposition on God, the latter statement is defeated by the admission of the Biblical scholars that the present day *Torah* is in no way the original revelation. It was entirely re written from memory, after the complete destruction of the original, several centuries after Moses. The Jews themselves have never had enough confidence in the Law to apply it to their lives.

The Encyclopedia of Religion and Ethics has the following to state about Buddhist creed: "The new religion (Buddhism) was *materialistic*, i.e., Buddha denied the soul, or ego; *atheistic*, i.e., there was no place for God in his system of thought; *pessimistic*, i.e., he regarded all existence as intrinsically evil; *egoistic*, i.e., in his scheme of life he taught men to think of themselves and their personal welfare; *nihilistic*, i.e., he regarded Nothing as the supreme reality." It should be obvious that there is no common ground between Islam and Buddhism for a comparison. Indeed, when one places a dozen sentences of Christian, Jewish and Buddhist creeds next to those of Islam, one begins to wonder whether the followers of other religions have ever known God.

Notwithstanding the efforts of Ibn abi al `Izz to simplify Tahawi`s discourses, the work remains difficult for a modern reader. For one thing, surprisingly, today`s man is less logical in his thinking than his predecessors were. This age is in fact the age of twisted logic. Our minds do not seem to be able to digest simple, straight forward logic. What adds to the difficulty is that although today`s minds are full of the same wrong ideas, as held by the misguided sects of the past, they do not recognize them as their own when they see them laid down before them in black and white. One reason perhaps is that those concepts are now differently worded, or, as Ibn abi al `Izz says, given the name of "interpretations" and firmly planted in the mind as unquestionable truths.

The Mu`tazilah, Jahmiyyah, Qadariyyah, and many other sects cited in the work might sound as weird names to the modern reader, well past the age when they first appeared. But as Qurtubi has pointed out, these sects will re appear down the ages under new names. In fact, all the ideas of the past sects are held as true today, by some or most people. The difference is that those weird sects with which the ideas were once associated, have disappeared. Individuals remain. An intelligent reader can use the sect names as pegs to hang the deviant ideas on. It makes classification easy. There is no need now to delve into history to find out who for instance the Qadariyyah were. Whoever holds the opinion stated by al `Izz as theirs, is a Qadari.

Nevertheless, and despite Ibn abi al `Izz`s fine commentary, spread over a vast area, the question concerning free will and pre determination is bound to remain enigmatic for quite a few readers. Not very surprising either. It has been an intriguing question for the best of minds throughout the ages: Muslim and non Muslim alike. The discourses of Tahawi and Ibn abi al `Izz are not so much aimed at solving the mystery as to assure the reader that whatever he thinks could be wrong with regard to the theory. The position, if not explainable, is defendable: so far as the reaches of human reason goes.

We have two elements here: observation and theory. Strangely, what we observe   as ourselves enjoying free will   is proven wrong by our own theory as being predetermined. And support for both: observation as well as theory, comes not only from the religious quarters. Today, it comes from the most unexpected quarters: science.

Today, the scientist are ready to bestow free will to dead matter, but instead, in a quite bizarre manner, withhold it from the living organisms. The particle physicists tell us that matter seems to be free to make its decisions. Depending upon whether it is being observed or not, sub atomic particles behave either as waves or as particles. They also choose the slot they will go through if directed at two, one after another. It appears they have a will of their own. A pair of sub-atomic particles seem to know how the other behaves, even if separated by a wall: when the charge of one of them is changed, the other, on the other side of the partition changes its charge too. Indeed, we are told that energy, another form of matter, is free to come into existence for a brief moment and choose to die. Even the non existent enjoys free will. In a recent article a scientist writes: "Elementary particles, it turned out (with experiments), can spontaneously pop out of nothingness and disappear again, if they do so for a time so short that one cannot measure them directly. Such virtual particles, as they are called, may appear as far fetched as angels sitting on the head of a pin. But there is a difference. The unseen particles produce measurable effects, such as alterations to the energy levels of atoms as well as forces between nearby metal plates. The theory of virtual particles agrees with observations to nine decimal places" (*Cosmological Antigravity*, by Lawrence M. Kraus, Scientific American, Jan. 99).

Note the dig at the concept of angels held by the religious people. All the same, some of the neo Darwinists of today are, in a sense, at the other end of the spectrum. They too accord freedom of will to dead matter, albeit molecules, but at the risk of taking away the freedom of the living, including humankind. They look at living organisms as helpless entities that are mere expressions of their nucleic acid. Bound to their DNA, through a script written in the code, that would require 30 volumes of the *Encyclopedia Britannica* to express, human beings turn out to be clock works ticked by the genes. A man dare not defy the molecules. In this system of thought, if the mind enjoys any free will, it may decide to act according to its choice; but the choice is predetermined by the inviolable command issued by the genes sitting in the nucleus and cut off from the outer world by seven walls. Some biologists have accorded the unknown and the unknown, the undemonstrable and the untestable, the Natural Selection, the power of free will with all living matter subjected to its will.

The question of free will and pre determination is truly mind boggling, and, in the words of John Searle (*Minds, Brains and Science*), "the problem (of free will and determinism) will stay with us."

Or, maybe, the scientists come close to the Islamic concept. The Islamic position has been neatly worded by `Abdul Qadir Jeelani: "Our actions belong to Allah in point of creation (*khalq*), and to His servants in point of acquisition (*kasb*)," *Futūh al Ghayb*, Muhtar Holland. `Ali ibn abi Talib illustrated it in another manner. When asked whether man was free or bound, he asked the questioner to raise his one foot. When he did it, he asked him to raise the other without bringing down the first. When the man said he could not, `Ali told him that those were the limits of freedom and pre determination.

An illustration might help. An industry is set up by a man acting as the top boss. He selected a product, chose a manufacturing system for it, got the machines, tools and equipments fitted on the shop floor, hired the necessary manpower, and designed the flow chart that defines when and where the raw material will arrive, moved on thereonwards undergoing various operations on various machineries, added on to some other components, to finally arrive at the end of the assembly line as the end product, inspected, packed and stored. The man at the top did all the planning and designing, and got not only the industry running but also all the support facilities such as the administration office, accounts, sales, stores, maintenance, and several other departments. Since he designed the whole thing, the man at the top knows, at any given moment, what is happening, where, and, who is doing what.

Let us say he hired an engineer for a well defined job. The engineer is of course obliged to follow the system and keep it running smoothly. He attends to the machines, checks into brake down, reassures himself that the raw material is available on line, and that the right quality and quantity is produced on time by the hundreds of men and machines involved. In doing all that, he is following a pre determined path set by the top boss: the one who drew the operational charts and determined who would do what, when, how, and in what quantity. In actual fact, the engineer does little more than executing the will of the top boss.

Yet, is it possible to say that in the above system the engineer is completely bound and does nothing but follow another`s will? He could as well defy the system and work as he wished. If he does not do that, it is because he realizes that his interests are best served in following the system, rather than his own will. But, that does not turn him into an automat. He is still free, and in fact exercises his free will quite often. For instance, sometimes he slackens or acts in ways that are not in the interest of the industry. Many times he acts differently simply because it suits him that way. That is the reason why the industry has another system in place. It is designed to measure his performance. Depending on the choices the engineer made for himself, his performance chart rates him good or bad: whether his services be retained, or terminated. If he never exercised his will, and, if his choices did not matter, since the actions in the industry were pre determined anyway, surely, the industry would not measure his performance and punish or reward him.

Having admitted that freedom, we still need to remind ourselves of the fact that the engineer in the above example is not free to do every thing that he wishes. He cannot, for instance, change the product. The industry has not been designed but to produce a particular product. He cannot change the sequence of operations. The pre determined machine sequence does not allow that. He can, following the freedom he enjoys, act to choose one way or another, in a few restricted cases only. Thus, he is neither totally free of will, nor bound.

What is true of the engineer in the industry, is true of the human beings in the world. We are bound to a system that has been pre determined. It runs on a pre determined course, unfolding pre determined events, and will terminate at a pre determined time. And there is nothing we can do about it. We can not, for instance, change the speed of the earth`s spin, or its rotation, to change its weather, which largely determines what we do. We can not get the earth out of the solar system. We humans are fully and helplessly bound to the system. The fate of the system is our fate. There is no escape. We might enjoy free will, but it is bound to the system which determines much of what we do in our lives, willy, nilly. Exercising our free will, we ca not change the weather. All we can do is to choose our clothes. However, here again, although we are free to choose summer clothes for winter and winter clothes for summer, but, it does not seem we can really exercise that choice to make independent decisions. We would fall sick if we did that. So, what we wear has been predetermined. In fact, it has been further determined for us by others, so that, say in the West, a man ca not show up without a dinner suit on for a dinner party hosted for dignitaries. Sure, we have been bestowed with a free will. But that does not really seem to mean much. Much of what we do is pre determined.

But, are we fully bound and moving about as automats without a will of our own? Is this world a clock work? Obviously not. Can we not change the landscape of the earth by planting trees? Surely, that should not have been possible if the universe was a clock work. Are we not free to choose the fashion of the clothes we wear? Are we not free to declare war or peace? We are. Yet, are we free to choose neither war nor peace? Rather not. Perforce, we have to choose either of the two. Further, having chosen one of the two, are we free to determine the course of events that follow the moment we chose one of the two: war or peace? Much that follows after our choices, are against our will. We are "forced" to react. In fact, most of the time we are reacting to the pre determined events forced upon us. We choose one of the several options available and possible of action within our limited abilities, natures, idiosyncrasies, potentials, etc., and are accountable for the choices. The question then, of pre determination or free will, rests in between. We are neither fully free, nor fully pre determined. Our failure is the ability to mark the boundaries. But, the obscurity of the dividing line does not absolve us of the responsibility of our choices just like the engineer on the shop floor.

In the example that we cited above, the industry has been pre determined by the man on the top. He has foreknowledge of the events that will take place in it. It is all there in his plans. He knows, for instance, what will come out at the end of the line, when, in what numbers, and of what quality. He picks up a packed box and knows all about its contents. He has the knowledge of the hidden. When he looks through the glass wall separating the workshop from his office chambers, he finds everyone doing just what he had predetermined for each of them. He had programmed it all. Not that he spoke to each of them moving about there on the shop floor, ordering them each, telling them what they should be doing every minute. Rather, he designed the system and can predict how they will behave. Although it is true that none of the men on the manufacturing line has lost his freedom: to work or not to work, to do the right thing or not, etc., yet, the top boss has his will carried out. If the engineer he hired exercised his free will and decided to go away, what will happen? Well, he will probably end up in another manufacturing plant, following someone else`s will, somebody else`s pre determined plan of action: not his own. This is what `Umar ibn al Khattab meant when he decided not to enter a region struck by the plague epidemic. When he decided to leave the stricken place, he was asked, "Are you running away from Allah`s decree?" He replied, "Yes. I`m running away *from* Allah`s decree *towards* Allah`s decree." In short, even though the world and its events are pre determined by Allah, and, in a way, even our own reactions to them, we can still make our choices and reap the consequences of those choices, good or bad, in this world or the next. `Umar could have as well decided to stay.

In the example cited above, let us add another factor. Realizing that his ways will not be followed and full co operation not obtained, unless his employees think the way he believes they should think, the top boss gathers them all together from time to time to explain to them what is happening around, and how it is nothing but for the good of the employees themselves. He constructs his arguments so well that they fail to realize that he is brainwashing them, and putting them on the track that he has laid down for them. Ultimately, they give in and begin to think the way he wants them to think. Thus, to a great extent he also controls the minds and wishes of his employees. Not that they have stopped thinking, or considering the pros and cons of situations and making their own decisions, but, by and large they think the way he decided they should think. It is in the light of this illustration that the Qur`anic verse must be understood which says (76: 30), "*And you do not will, unless Allah wills.*"

The crowning statement of the work in our hands, therefore, rightly comes at the end: "This religion is (the middle way) between two extremes; between anthropomorphism and denial of Attributes; between free will and pre determination; between self assurance and despair."

Before closing, it is appropriate that I should thank brother Muhammad Murshid, presently with WAMY at Dammam who took great pains and helped my out in the preparation of this version.

Syed Iqbal Zaheer
January 2009

Preface

by `Ali b. abi al `Izz

All praise to Allah. We seek His help and forgiveness and seek His refuge from our selves and our evil deeds. He whom Allah guided, no one can misguide. And He whom He did not guide, no one can guide. We testify that there is no deity save Allah, the One, who has no associates. And we testify that our master Muhammad, was His slave and Messenger, peace and blessing on him and on his kinsfolk.

The best of knowledge in Islam is that of its fundamentals. People's dependence, therefore, on these is above any other dependence. For, the life of a heart depends upon knowledge concerning its Lord and the Object of its worship in all its details, including His Names, Attributes and Acts. Now, since it is impossible for a man's mind to acquire this knowledge through its own efforts, in all its possible details, Allah's kindness demanded that Messengers be sent bearing this knowledge, inviting the people to it, giving glad tidings to those who answered the call and warning those who differed with it. Accordingly, the Messengers made this knowledge the central theme of their message upon whose understanding depends a proper appreciation of their mission.

This is followed by two main principles:

Firstly, the way to reach it, viz., the understanding of the *Shari`ah* which deals with sanctions and prohibitions.

Secondly, the knowledge of what is in store for those who take up this path in terms of rewards and blessings; for, the most knowledgeable of Allah are those who i) follow most meticulously the path leading up to Him, and ii) those who know what is in store for them when they have reached their goal. Consequently, we find that Allah Most High called what He sent down on His messenger as the "soul" or the "spirit", for the reason that true life depends on it. He also called it "*Nur*" for the reason that the path of guidance is illuminated by it. He said:

يُلْقِى الرُّوحَ مِنْ اَمْرِهٖ عَلٰى مَنْ يَّشَآءُ مِنْ عِبَادِهٖ

"He casts the Spirit of His bidding upon whomsoever He will of His slaves." (Ghafir, 15)

He also said:

وَكَذٰلِكَ اَوْحَيْنَآ اِلَيْكَ رُوحًا مِّنْ اَمْرِنَا ۚ مَا كُنْتَ تَدْرٖى مَا الْكِتٰبُ وَلَا الْاٖيمَانُ وَلٰكِنْ جَعَلْنٰهُ نُوْرًا نَّهْدٖى بِهٖ مَنْ نَّشَآءُ مِنْ عِبَادِنَا وَاِنَّكَ لَتَهْدٖىٓ اِلٰى صِرَاطٍ مُّسْتَقٖيمٍ

"That is how We have revealed unto you (O Muhammad) the Spirit of Our bidding. You knew not before what was the Book nor what was Faith. But We made it a Light, guiding thereby whosoever We will of Our slaves. And, surely, you lead them to a straight path." (Al Shura, 52)

No doubt that everyone is required to believe, in a general sense, in what the Prophet, peace on him, brought. But the demand on the individuals depends on their specific needs. In fact, there are things that a common man need not be bothered about, such as those that are beyond his comprehension. But the same details might be essential for another. Upon one, for instance, who has heard and understood the texts (Qur`an and *Sunnah*), those finer points become incumbent that are not incumbent upon one ignorant of them. Similarly, what is obligatory upon a jurist to know, or a doctor of the science of *hadīth*, or a ruler, is not so upon one who does not fall in those categories.

It should also be realized that most of those who erred in this field of knowledge, or failed to reach the true meaning, were either those who failed to follow what the Prophet, peace on him, brought, or those who refused to contemplate over what leads to its knowledge. When they abandoned the Book of Allah, they lost the way. Allah said about them:

فَاِمَّا يَأْتِيَنَّكُمْ مِّنّٖى هُدًى فَمَنِ اتَّبَعَ هُدَاىَ فَلَا يَضِلُّ وَلَا يَشْقٰى (١٢٣) وَمَنْ اَعْرَضَ عَنْ ذِكْرٖى فَاِنَّ لَهٗ مَعٖيشَةً ضَنْكًا وَنَحْشُرُهٗ يَوْمَ الْقِيَامَةِ اَعْمٰى (١٢٤) قَالَ رَبِّ لِمَ حَشَرْتَنٖىٓ اَعْمٰى وَقَدْ كُنْتُ بَصٖيرًا (١٢٥) قَالَ كَذٰلِكَ اَتَتْكَ اٰيَاتُنَا فَنَسٖيتَهَا وَكَذٰلِكَ الْيَوْمَ تُنْسٰى (١٢٦)

xvi

"Therefore, whenever guidance comes to you from Me, then whosoever followed the guidance will not go unguided and will not lose his way, nor fall into misery. In contrast, whoever turned his back upon My remembrance, shall have a miserable life. We shall raise him blind on the Day of Judgement. He will say, 'My Lord. Why did You raise me blind, when I was of sight?' He will reply, 'That is how Our signs came to you but you forgot about them. That is how you shall be forgotten today." (Taha, 123 126)

We might also note that Allah Most High declared Himself above what His slaves qualify Him with, save what the Messengers qualified Him with. He said:

سُبْحَٰنَ رَبِّكَ رَبِّ ٱلْعِزَّةِ عَمَّا يَصِفُونَ (١٨٠) وَسَلَٰمٌ عَلَى ٱلْمُرْسَلِينَ (١٨١) وَٱلْحَمْدُ لِلَّهِ رَبِّ ٱلْعَٰلَمِينَ (١٨٢)

"Glorified is Your Lord, the Lord of Honor and Might. (He is free) of what they ascribe (unto Him). And peace be upon the Messengers. And praise be to the Lord of the Worlds." (Al Saffat, 180 182)

Thus we see in the above text that Allah Most High first declared Himself above what the pagans ascribed to Him. Then, after that, He granted peace to the Messengers for not committing the errors the pagans committed in matters concerning His Attributes. Finally, He praised Himself to confirm for Himself those Attributes that deserve praise.

After the Prophet, the tradition (of purity in *Tawhid*) continued through the Companions down to the Followers, the earlier ones passing on the right concepts to the latter ones: all of them treading the same lines as those of the Prophet, peace be upon him. Allah Most High confirmed their right attitude when He said:

قُلْ هَٰذِهِ سَبِيلِي أَدْعُوٓا۟ إِلَى ٱللَّهِ عَلَىٰ بَصِيرَةٍ أَنَا۠ وَمَنِ ٱتَّبَعَنِي

"Tell (them), 'This is my path. I call you to Allah, with a certain knowledge I and my Followers.'" (Yūsuf, 108)

But after them came a people who followed their caprices and broke apart from the main stream. So Allah Most High brought forth those who stood by and expounded the fundamental principles of His religion. The Prophet, peace on him, had predicted this when he said: "A group from my followers will hold fast unto truth. No one opposed to them would be able to do them any harm."

Of those who rose up to defend the concepts of this religion, one was Muhammad b. Salamah al Azadi al Tahawi. He penned down what he knew as the beliefs of the righteous before him, drafting down what Imam Abu Hanifah al Nu`man al Kufi and his two disciples, Imam Abu Yūsuf Ya`qub b. Ibrahim al Himyari al Ansari and Muhammad b. Hassan al Shaybani, may Allah be pleased with them, believed to be the right beliefs of a Muslim.

However, as the years passed by, innovations appeared, and, consequently, greater deviations occurred. That was made possible because those who popularized their deviations did it in the name of interpretations to make them acceptable. For, few there are who can discern the difference between a distortion and an interpretation. Quite often a word is given a meaning that could possibly be deduced from it, but did not happen to be the first meaning that the word would lend and, despite the fact that the context wasn't demanding the meaning that was underscored. This was the root cause of corruptions in faith, for, when they named their distortions interpretations, they were accepted by all those who could not differentiate between the two.

In any case, there are kinds and classes of deviations. Some of them can be classified as outright disbelief. Others are simply corruptions. Yet others are sins and some, mere errors.

Insofar as we are concerned, it is obligatory upon us to follow the messengers and what was revealed unto them by Allah. Allah completed the series with Muhammad (*saws*) and declared His Book the guardian over all other revelations. He declared the Prophet's obedience equal to His own obedience, his disobedience as His own disobedience and swore by Himself that the people would not be believers until they accepted him as the arbiter in all those affairs in which they disagreed among themselves.

The error that the majority of Muslims committed was that they gradually became ignorant of much of what the Prophet had brought, not only in matters concerning faiths and beliefs, but also those that pertain to the rituals of worship, political organization, etc. In their ignorance, they attributed to the Prophet things they had inherited from their forefathers, or removed from his message what originally came with it.

So, because of their ignorance, errors, and excesses, and because of their rebellion against Allah, hypocrisy entered in massive amounts which was the cause of obliteration of much of the knowledge of revelation.

This humble self, although lacking the true knowledge and, at personal level weak of practice in their light, intends, never the less, to become undeserving of criticism by presenting the truth to others and would feel happy over some people putting to good practice what he himself failed at. He intends to take up the task, not as one believing in a part of it and rejecting a part, rather, believing in the whole of it, and endeavors to keep off any of that which is not an integral part of it, whether it be an opinion or a narration of the past, or follow what is not from Allah, be it a matter of faith or practice, as Allah Most High said:

وَلَا تَلْبِسُوا الْحَقَّ بِالْبَاطِلِ وَتَكْتُمُوا الْحَقَّ وَأَنْتُمْ تَعْلَمُونَ

"And do not overlay the truth with falsehood, while ye know." (Al Baqarah, 42)

It was my keen desire to write down a commentary on the *"Fundamentals of Faith"* as composed by Al Tahawi, following the ways of the righteous who went before, weaving on their pattern, mimicking them, child like, that I might be one of those who followed their ways, counted as one of them, and raised in their company in the Hereafter:

فَأُولَٰئِكَ مَعَ الَّذِينَ أَنْعَمَ اللهُ عَلَيْهِمْ مِنَ النَّبِيِّينَ وَالصِّدِّيقِينَ وَالشُّهَدَاءِ وَالصَّالِحِينَ وَحَسُنَ أُولَٰئِكَ رَفِيقًا

"Among those whom Allah favored: the Prophets, the Truthful, the martyrs and the righteous. And a good company are they." (Al Nisa', 69)

The Islamic Creed

بسم الله الرحمن الرحيم

Imam Al Tahawi began his work with the following words:

نقولُ — في توحيدِ اللهِ مُعتقدينَ بتَوْفيقِ اللهِ: أنَّ اللهَ واحدٌ لا شريكَ لهُ

With regard to Allah's Oneness, we say the following, hoping for Allah's good grace: Allah is One, He has no associates.

One must know that Allah's Oneness has always been the first message transmitted by the Messengers. It is the first of the signposts on the way to Truth, and the first check post at which a pilgrim to Allah would be held. Allah Most High said:

لَقَدْ آرْسَلْنَا نُوحًا إلى قَوْمِهِ فَقَالَ يِقَوْمِ اعْبُدُوا اللهَ مَا لَكُمْ مِّنْ إِلهٍ غَيْرُهُ

"Surely, We sent Nūh to his people. He said, `My people! Worship Allah. You have no god besides Him." (Al A`rāf, 59)

Hūd had said:

يِقَوْمِ اعْبُدُوا اللهَ مَا لَكُمْ مِّنْ إِلهٍ غَيْرُهُ

"My People! Worship Allah. You have no god besides Him." (Al A`rāf, 65)

Those were also the words of Saleh and of Shu`ayb, on both be peace. Allah also said:

بَعَثْنَا فِي كُلِّ أُمَّةٍ رَّسُوْلاً أَنِ اعْبُدُوا اللهَ وَاجْتَنِبُوا الطَّاغُوتَ

"We sent a Messenger to every people saying: `Worship Allah and eschew idols." (Al Nahal, 36)

Allah also said:

وَمَآ اَرْسَلْنَا مِنْ قَبْلِكَ مِنْ رَّسُوْلٍ اِلَّا نُوْحِیْۤ اِلَیْهِ اَنَّهٗ لَاۤ اِلٰهَ اِلَّاۤ اَنَا فَاعْبُدُوْنِ

"We did not send a Messenger before you (O Muhammad) but revealed unto him that there is no deity save I. So serve Me." (Al Anbiyā, 25)

The Prophet, upon whom be peace, said: "I have been ordered to fight the people until they testify, 'There is no deity save One Allah and Muhammad is His Messenger.'"

Therefore, it is right to say that the first of the obligations on a man is to testify that there is no deity save One Allah.

Understandably then, the first thing with which a man enters into Islam is *Tawhīd* and it is the last thing required of him before he leaves this world, as said the Prophet, on whom be peace, "Of whosoever the last words were `there is no deity save One Allah,' will enter Paradise." Simply stated, it is the first and the last obligation.

By the use of the term *Tawhīd* above, we mean the first kind of *Tawhīd*, i.e., the *Tawhīd* of Divinity. For, *Tawhīd* is of three kinds:

(i) *Tawhīd* of Attributes: توحيد في الصفات

(ii) *Tawhīd* of Lordship: توحيد الربوبية

This kind tells us that Allah alone is the Creator of all things, and,

(iii) *Tawhīd* of Divinity: توحيد الإلهية

This kind tells us that it is Allah's right that He alone be worshipped, without any associates.

As for the first, those who denied Allah His Attributes incorporated the rejection of Attributes in their version of *Tawhīd*, such as Jaham b. Safwan and his followers. This is obviously a wholesome error. For, a being without Attributes cannot be imagined to have an existence. The mind pre supposes the impossible and gives a free rein to its imagination. This is the worst way of asserting that the universe is without an artificer.

The second, *Tawhīd* of Lordship, is to testify that He is the Creator of all that exists. This *Tawhīd* is of course an uncontested truth. Hence, no sect has, in our knowledge, denied this. It is implanted in the people's souls. In comparison, there is nothing else of the existent in which people believe more passionately. As said the Messengers, as reported by Allah:

قَالَتْ رُسُلُهُمْ أَفِى اللهِ شَكٌّ فَاطِرِ السَّمٰوٰتِ وَالْأَرْضِ

"Their Messengers said, 'Do you doubt (the existence) of Allah the Origina-tor of the heavens and earth?'" (Ibrahīm, 10)

The most famous of those who denied the Creator feigning ignorance, pre-tentiously, was Fir`awn. But in his heart he knew the truth of the matter. Musa, peace on him, said to him:

لَقَدْ عَلِمْتَ مَا أَنْزَلَ هٰؤُلَاءِ إِلَّا رَبُّ السَّمٰوٰتِ وَالْأَرْضِ بَصَآئِرَ

"You know very well that these things were not sent down but by the Lord of the heavens and the earth: as an evidence." (Al Isrā, 102)

And, Allah said about him and his people:

وَجَحَدُوا بِهَا وَاسْتَيْقَنَتْهَآ أَنْفُسُهُمْ ظُلْمًا وَعُلُوًّا

"They disputed what their own selves acknowledged in transgression and rebellion." (Al Namal, 14)

There is no sect in the world therefore which claims two creators of the world equal of power. This is invalidated by what is known as the inductive resistant formula. Or, in simpler words, an "impossibility." To explain: If the world had two creators, then, in case of disagreement between themselves, such as one wishing to leave a thing stationary, while the other wishing to give it a motion, or one wishing to give it life, the other, death, then, either both achieve their objectives, or only one succeeds in doing so, or a third alternative being, none of them succeeds in achieving his objective. The first of this case is an im-possibility, for it would mean bringing together two opposites. The third alterna-tive is also impossibility, for, in such a case both would have failed as creators. Therefore, we are left with the second alternative, viz., one of them succeeds in carrying out his wish, while the other fails. The one who succeeds then, is the creator. The one who failed cannot be a god. Many thinkers believe that this was what intended when Allah Most High said:

لَوْ كَانَ فِيهِمَا آلِهَةٌ إِلَّا اللهُ لَفَسَدَتَا

"If there were in them (the heaven and earth) several deities, surely, they (the heaven and earth) would have run into chaos." (Al Anbiyā, 22)

What led those people understand the verse that way is that they believe that the *Tawhīd* of Lordship in which they believe, is equivalent of the *Tawhīd* of Divinity that the Qur`an described and to which all Messengers invited. But that is not correct. Rather, the *Tawhīd* of Lordship to which the Messengers invited and which the revealed Books called for, is the *Tawhīd* of Divinity that includes *Tawhīd* of Lordship too, which can be defined as worship of none else but Allah alone who has no partners. (That distinction has to be made) because Arab pagans acknowledged *Tawhīd* of Lordship and that the creator of this world was one (without believing in the Oneness of Divinity who alone should be worshipped). Allah Most High told us about them:

وَلَئِنْ سَأَلْتَهُمْ مَّنْ خَلَقَ السَّمٰوٰتِ وَالْأَرْضَ لَيَقُولُنَّ اللهُ

"If you were to ask them, 'Who created the heavens and the earth,' surely they would reply, 'Allah." (Luqmān, 25)

And,

قُلْ لِمَنِ الْأَرْضُ وَمَنْ فِيهَا إِنْ كُنْتُمْ تَعْلَمُونَ (٨٤) سَيَقُولُونَ لِلّٰهِ قُلْ أَفَلَا تَذَكَّرُونَ (٨٥)

"Ask them, 'To whom belong the earth and all those living on it, if you knew?' They will reply, 'To Allah.' Say, 'Will you not then receive admonition?" (Al Mu'minūn, 84-85)

There are many examples of the above kind in the Qur`an.

The pagans then did not believe that the idols had a share in the creation of the world. Rather, they held views similar to the pagans of India, Turkey and other places. They believed that the idols represented pious people. They sought their intercession and attempted to reach Allah through them. This was the reality behind the *Shirk* (Association) of the pagan Arabs, as said Allah, speaking of the people of Nūh:

وَ قَالُوا لَا تَذَرُنَّ اٰلِهَتَكُمْ وَلَا تَذَرُنَّ وَدًّا وَّلَا سُوَاعًا ۙ وَّ لَا يَغُوْثَ وَيَعُوْقَ وَنَسْرًا

"They said (to each other), 'Do not abandon your deities, nor Wudd, nor Suwa`, nor Yaghus, nor Nasr." (Nūh, 23)

It is confirmed by reports in *Sahih Bukhari* as well as in the commentaries on the Qur`an that the names mentioned in the above verse belonged to pious persons of that nation. When the people died, they squatted near their graves. Subsequently, they made images of them. Finally, with the passage of time, they began to worship them.

These people acknowledged that there is a Creator, and admitted that there are no two creators of the world. As for the deities, they took them as intercessors. As Allah said:

وَالَّذِيْنَ اتَّخَذُوْا مِنْ دُوْنِهٖ اَوْلِيَآءَ مَا نَعْبُدُهُمْ اِلَّا لِيُقَرِّبُوْنَآ اِلَى اللهِ زُلْفٰى

"As for those who take for protectors other than Allah, (they say), 'We only serve them in order that they may take us nearer to Allah." (Al Zumar, 3)

And He said,

وَيَعْبُدُوْنَ مِنْ دُوْنِ اللهِ مَا لَا يَضُرُّهُمْ وَلَا يَنْفَعُهُمْ وَيَقُوْلُوْنَ هٰؤُلَآءِ شُفَعَآؤُنَا عِنْدَ اللهِ

"They worship apart from Allah that which can neither harm them nor do them good. They say, `These are our intercessors with God." (Yūnus, 18)

From this we know that the *Tawhīd* that is required of us is *Tawhīd* of Divinity which includes the *Tawhīd* of Lordship. Allah said,

فَاَقِمْ وَجْهَكَ لِلدِّيْنِ حَنِيْفًا ۭ فِطْرَتَ اللهِ الَّتِيْ فَطَرَ النَّاسَ عَلَيْهَا ۭ لَا تَبْدِيْلَ لِخَلْقِ اللهِ ۭ ذٰلِكَ الدِّيْنُ الْقَيِّمُ ۙ وَلٰكِنَّ اَكْثَرَ النَّاسِ لَا يَعْلَمُوْنَ

"Therefore set thy face to the (true) religion declaring it exclusive (to Allah). This is the nature of Allah on which He originated the people. There is no changing in the creation of Allah. That is the true religion, but most people know not." (Al Rūm, 30)

Allah also said,

مُنِيبِينَ إِلَيْهِ وَاتَّقُوهُ وَأَقِيمُوا الصَّلوةَ وَلَا تَكُونُوا مِنَ الْمُشْرِكِينَ (٣١) مِنَ الَّذِينَ فَرَّقُوا دِينَهُمْ وَكَانُوا شِيَعًا ۚ كُلُّ حِزْبٍ بِمَا لَدَيْهِمْ
فَرِحُونَ (٣٢)

"Turn you in repentance to Him, and fear Him. And establish the prayer and be not of the associators; (nor) of those who split up their religion and became sects, with each sect well pleased with what it has." (Al Rūm, 31-32)

The Qur`an is full of verses stressing this kind of *Tawhīd* and similitude that explain it. It conforms the *Tawhīd* of Lordship, stressing that there is no creator save Allah and that it demands that none be worshipped except Allah. Thus, it uses the *Tawhīd* of Lordship as an evidence in favor of *Tawhīd* of Divinity. For, the people acknowledged the former but denied the latter. Allah Most High explained to them that `if you acknowledge that there is no creator save Him, and that it is He who bestows upon the people what is of benefit to them, and removes what is of pain to them, in which acts He has no partners, then, why do you worship others besides Him, declaring gods other than Him?' For instance, He said.

قُلِ الْحَمْدُ لِلَّهِ وَسَلَامٌ عَلَى عِبَادِهِ الَّذِينَ اصْطَفَىٰ ۗ آللَّهُ خَيْرٌ أَمَّا يُشْرِكُونَ (٥٩) أَمَّنْ خَلَقَ السَّمَوَاتِ وَالْأَرْضَ وَأَنْزَلَ لَكُمْ مِّنَ السَّمَاءِ
مَاءً فَأَنْبَتْنَا بِهِ حَدَائِقَ ذَاتَ بَهْجَةٍ مَّا كَانَ لَكُمْ أَنْ تُنْبِتُوا شَجَرَهَا ۗ أَءِلَهٌ مَّعَ اللَّهِ ۚ بَلْ هُمْ قَوْمٌ يَعْدِلُونَ (٦٠)

"Say, `Praise to Allah and peace unto those of His slaves whom He chose. Is Allah better or those they associate Him with? Or, is the One Who created the heavens and the earth and sent down water from the sky then We grew therewith orchards full of beauty and delight it wasn't for you to grow their trees. Is there a god then besides Allah?' Nay, they (the pagans) are, rather, a people, who equate (others with Allah)." (Al Naml, 59-60)

It will be noticed in these passages that after every evidence that Allah offered, He said, "Is there a god besides Allah?" That is, what god besides Allah does these things? This is a rhetorical way of denial. When they acknowledged that none did those things save Allah, then He sealed the argument against them. He wasn't asking them a question, which could be answered in either the positive or negative. Rather, it was another way of making a statement to the effect that there is no god besides Allah although the people associated deities with Allah. Allah said,

6

اِنَّكُمْ لَتَشْهَدُونَ اَنَّ مَعَ اللهِ اٰلِهَةً اُخْرٰى قُل لَّا اَشْهَدُ

"Would you then testify that there are gods besides Allah? Say, (O Muhammad), `I (for one) do not testify (to any such thing)." (Al An`ām, 19)

Now, if *Tawhīd* of Lordship is included in the concept of the *Tawhīd* of Divinity that the Messengers brought, and which the Scriptures came down with, then it is not surprising that its proofs and evidences are aplenty, just as the evidences in favor of Allah being the Creator are aplenty, or the evidences in favor of the Prophet's authenticity. Generally speaking, the more the people in need of a certain kind of knowledge, the more generously spread are its evidences. This is by the mercy of Allah for His creations.

Accordingly, the Qur`an struck  numerous similitude in  favor of this concept. These similitude are rational measures helpful towards the understanding of religion. The Qur`an states the truth and then presents its evidence. What remains after guidance then, save error?

As for the well known basic induction, the Qur`an did not present them for the reasons that they are commonly known. The Qur`an employed them to its own purposes without building up proofs in their favor.

Now, since the people realize that Association in the Lordship of Allah leads to an impossible situation of acknowledging two Creators of equal attributes, some of the pagans adopted the notion that one of the creators created a part of the universe, (while the others created other parts of it). For instance, the Qadariyyah adopted the position that evil was created by other than Allah. Or, as some of the philosophers claim with reference to the heavenly bodies. They declare appearance of things and events that they allege Allah did not bring into being. Thus, they attribute a part of Lordship to others. Most of the Arab pagans too believed in benefits or harms coming off their deities, without Allah creating those benefits or harms.

In view of the wide prevalence of Association in Lordship among the people, the Qur`an refuted it. Allah said:

مَا اتَّخَذَ اللهُ مِنْ وَّلَدٍ وَّمَا كَانَ مَعَهُ مِنْ اِلٰهٍ اِذًا لَّذَهَبَ كُلُّ اِلٰهٍ بِمَا خَلَقَ وَلَعَلَا بَعْضُهُمْ عَلٰى بَعْضٍ

"Allah did not take a son. And there is no other god along with Him. (If

there were to be other gods) then, surely, each god would have separated out with what he created, and some would have lorded over the others." (Al Mu'minūn, 91)

One may look at these words again. They are beautifully precise and to the point. The argument is as follows: It is imperative that the true Lord should also possess the creative power in order to cause benefits to His creation and remove harm from them. Now, had there been with Him another god, sharing in His kingdom, surely, such a second god would have his own creations. But, obviously, he would not be satisfied at being a mere partner. If he could, he would usurp all the power by employing force and drive out the other. If he didn't have power to do so, surely, he would separate out along with all that he created. This is common observation on earth. When there happen to be more than one cla*imān*t to the throne, they separate out their territories, if one of them cannot overcome the other. In like manner, one of the three things would have happened if there were several gods: either they would have separated out, each with his own kingdom, or some of them would have overcome the others, or all of them would have been overpowered by one of them. Then the rest would live under his dominion, who would deal with them the way he deemed fit, with the rest unable to do anything about it. Indeed, the others then would be gods no more. They would be subdued slaves.

The manner of existence of this world, following a single system, is one of the most effective and undeniable arguments that it has one creator, one God and one Lord. The creations have no Lord save Him and no Divinity besides Him. For, if it is impossible to have two Lords of equal power, so too it is impossible to have two Divinities worthy of worship.

Inevitably, the argument that leads us to a single Lord, also leads us to a single Divinity. The verse then agrees with the proof confirming that which is implanted in the heart concerning the existence of a Lord for this universe. It also points to the *Tawhīd* of Divinity.

Something very close to this is stated in the following verse:

لَوْ كَانَ فِيهِمَا آلِهَةٌ إِلَّا اللهُ لَفَسَدَتَا

"If there were other gods, save one Allah, they (the heaven and the earth)

would have run into chaos." (Al Anbiyā, 22)

Some people have thought that this verse is speaking of the impossibility of two Lords. It is not. Rather, it is speaking of the impossibility of two deities. The word "Lord" was not used in it. Further, the verse, "they (i.e., the heavens and the earth) would have run into chaos" would have only been possible after creation. He didn't say "they would not have come into being."

Thus, to emphasize, the concept of the *Tawhīd* of Lordship is inclusive of the *Tawhīd* of Divinity. But not the other way round. For, one who cannot create is inept and an inept cannot be a god. Allah Most High said:

اَيُشْرِكُونَ مَا لَا يَخْلُقُ شَيْئًا وَهُمْ يُخْلَقُونَ

"Do you associate those (with Allah) that cannot create a thing, rather, are (themselves) created?" (Al A`rāf, 191)

Further, the *Tawhīd* to which the Messengers invited and which was the main content of the revealed Books are of two kinds:

i) *Tawhīd* of Acknowledgment and Knowledge, and

ii) *Tawhīd* of Solicitation and Intent.

The first is to acknowledge the Being (and existence) of Allah Most High along with all His Attributes, Acts and Names. In this He is unique. There is none like Him in all these characteristics   as Allah Himself and as His Messengers informed us.

The second, the *Tawhīd* of Solicitation and Intent, has been well defined by the following short chapter of the Qur`an:

قُلْ يَآ اَيُّهَا الْكٰفِرُونَ (١) لَآ اَعْبُدُ مَا تَعْبُدُونَ (٢) وَلَآ اَنْتُمْ عٰبِدُونَ مَآ اَعْبُدُ (٣) وَلَآ اَنَا عَابِدٌ مَّا عَبَدتُّمْ (٤)

"Say, 'O unbelievers. I do not worship what you worship; nor do you worship what I worship; nor am I (ever) going to worship what you worship." (Al Kāfirūn, 1-4)

So also the words of Allah Most High:

The Islamic Creed

قُلْ يَآأَهْلَ الْكِتَبِ تَعَالَوْا إِلَى كَلِمَةٍ سَوَآءٍ بَيْنَنَا وَبَيْنَكُمْ أَلَّا نَعْبُدَ إِلَّا اللهَ وَلَا نُشْرِكَ بِهِ شَيْئًا

"Say, 'O people of the Book! Come to an equitable term between you and us: that we worship none but Allah and associate not aught with Him." (Āl `Imrān, 64)

Most of the chapters of the Qur`an, in fact, all of them, deal with both kinds of *Tawhīd*. For, the Qur`anic revelations contain either information about Allah, His Attributes or His Names. This is the *Tawhīd* of Knowledge and Information (received from Allah by various Prophets); or invitation to worship none but Him who has no associates, and to abandon all else that are worshipped besides Him. This can be termed as the *Tawhīd* of Intent and Demand. (That is, a demand that a man should conscientiously respond to in the positive terms: tr.). Or, thirdly, the Qur`an deals with obligations, prohibitions etc. This is the demand and perfection of *Tawhīd*. Or, fourthly, the Qur`an presents information concerning the people of *Tawhīd* as to what He did with them in this world, how He will honor them in the Hereafter: this is the reward for *Tawhīd*. As for the information concerning the Associaters as to what He did with them in this world, and how He will treat them in the Hereafter: it is the recompense for one who abandoned *Tawhīd*.

Allah Himself testified to this *Tawhīd*, as did the angels and Messengers. Allah said:

شَهِدَ اللهُ أَنَّهُ لَا إِلَهَ إِلَّا هُوَ وَالْمَلَئِكَةُ وَأُولُوا الْعِلْمِ قَآئِمًا بِالْقِسْطِ لَا إِلَهَ إِلَّا هُوَ الْعَزِيزُ الْحَكِيمُ (١٨) إِنَّ الدِّينَ عِنْدَ اللهِ الْإِسْلَامُ

"Allah is witness that there is no god save He, and (so are) the angels and the men of learning, (the One Allah) upholding justice; there is no god save He, the Mighty, the Wise. Verily the (true) religion with Allah is Islam." (Āl `Imrān, 18-19)

This verse establishes the truth of *Tawhīd* and rejects all misguided sects and groups. It comprises the best of testimonies possible, the greatest, the most just, the most truthful, from the Most honored of testifiers because of the importance of the Witness and because of the importance of that which is testified to.

As for the word *"shahida"* of the text, the righteous scholars of the earliest generations (the *Salaf*) have understood it as `a command, a judgment, a

10

notification, a firm statement,' as well as, 'information.' All these meanings can be integrated, for, bearing testimony amounts to making a statement, issuing a command, pronouncing a judgment, etc. The testimony, then, has four levels:

First: the knowledge of a thing and belief in what is being testified as true, and its substantiation.

Second: speaking out the testimony, even if no one else has any knowledge of it. One might even speak out to himself, or write it down.

Third: inform others about what he bore witness to and explain it to them.

Fourth: follow its concomitance and enjoin others the same.

Allah's testimony of *Tawhīd* then carries these four aspects of the meaning: His knowledge, His pronouncement, His informing His creations and, finally, His instruction or command to His creations to accept it.

The objective of this testimony at the four levels, was to rule the affairs by it and to impose it. For Allah to bear testimony to it was the testification of One Who judged by it, commanded it and declared it incumbent upon His creations. He said:

وَقَضَى رَبُّكَ أَلَّا تَعْبُدُوٓا إِلَّآ إِيَّاهُ

"And your Lord has decreed that you worship none but Him." (Al Isrā, 23)

He also said:

لَا تَتَّخِذُوٓا إِلَٰهَيْنِ اثْنَيْنِ

"Do not take two gods." (Al Nahal, 51)

To repeat, when Allah Most High bore the testimony to the effect that there is no God save He, then it was to announce, command, teach and order that apart from Him there is no other god, that the god ship of anyone save Him is null and void, therefore, none is deserving of worship except Him, exactly as Divinity is not for anyone save Him. This demands that He alone be taken as God and none else be taken as gods besides him. This is what a man will understand when he hears these words of confirmation and rejection.

The command contained in Allah's testimony demands acceptance and acknowledgment (by His slaves). Had it been a testimony in the ordinary sense, the people could not have received its knowledge, could not have profited from it and the argument against them would not have been sealed. Rather, the testimony was meant for information of the people, in order that they are clear about what He testified to. Otherwise, the situation would have been similar to someone bearing witness to a thing but keeping the information to himself, without spelling it out. Obviously, no one benefits from it, nor can it be used in an argument against anyone.

Now, since the people would not have profited from the information, had it not been passed on to them, Allah Most High brought home to man this information through three of his faculties: hearing, sight and intellect.

As for the faculty of hearing, man hears the revelations speaking of His Perfect Attributes, His Oneness, etc. Allah said:

هٰذَا بَيَانٌ لِّلنَّاسِ وَهُدًى وَّمَوْعِظَةٌ لِّلْمُتَّقِينَ

"This (Qur`an) is a plain exposition for the people (in general), a Guidance, and an admonition for the God fearing (in particular)." (Āl `Imrān, 138)

Allah also said:

فَاعْلَمُوٓا أَنَّمَا عَلَى رَسُوْلِنَا الْبَلَٰغُ الْمُبِيْنُ

"And be of knowledge that upon Our Messengers (is no more than) deliverance (of the message)." (Al Mā'idah, 92)

He also said:

وَأَنْزَلْنَآ إِلَيْكَ الذِّكْرَ لِتُبَيِّنَ لِلنَّاسِ مَا نُزِّلَ إِلَيْهِمْ

"And We sent down to you (O Muhammad) the Reminder in order that you might make clear to the people what has been sent to them." (Al Nahal, 44)

The *Sunnah* too explains and corroborates what the Qur`an stated. Allah Most High did not leave us in want of the opinion of this or that individual in matters of the principles of religion. Hence you will find those who opposed the Qur`an and *Sunnah*, always in confusion and disarray. Although Allah said:

The Islamic Creed

اَلْيَوْمَ اَكْمَلْتُ لَكُمْ دِينَكُمْ وَاَتْمَمْتُ عَلَيْكُمْ نِعْمَتِى وَرَضِيتُ لَكُمُ الْاِسْلَامَ دِينًا

"This day I have perfected your religion for you, have completed My favor unto you, and have approved for you as religion, Al Islam." (Al Mā'idah, 3)

As for the signs of Allah in His creations, one's perception of them, and a little contemplation over them, leads to the same conclusions as presented in the Qur`anic verses. The intellect assembles them all, (what is heard and what is seen), and testifies the veracity of what is received through the Prophets. Thus, the testimony of hearing, sight and reason agree with each other.

Hence, out of justice, mercy, wisdom, love, and for the reason of leaving no room for rejection, Allah did not send a Prophet, but sent along with him a sign that bore witness to the veracity of what he had brought. Allah said:

لَقَدْ اَرْسَلْنَا رُسُلَنَا بِالْبَيِّنَاتِ وَاَنْزَلْنَا مَعَهُمُ الْكِتَابَ وَالْمِيزَانَ لِيَقُومَ النَّاسُ بِالْقِسْطِ

"Surely, we sent Messengers with manifest signs and sent down with them the Book and a criterion by which the people could establish justice." (Al Hadīd, 25)

Allah also said:

وَاِنْ يُكَذِّبُوكَ فَقَدْ كَذَّبَ الَّذِينَ مِنْ قَبْلِهِمْ جَاءَتْهُمْ رُسُلُهُمْ بِالْبَيِّنَاتِ وَبِالزُّبُرِ وَبِالْكِتَابِ الْمُنِيرِ

"If these people reject you (O Muhammad), then, surely, people earlier to them also rejected (their prophets, those) who brought them clear signs and writs and an illuminating Book." (Al Fātir, 25)

Accordingly, one of the Names of Allah Most High is "Al Mu'min." According to one of the two interpretations it means: one who testifies the truth of that which the truthful spoke   based on the testimony in favor of their truthfulness. It is incumbent upon Him that He should show the people signs in the physical world as well as within their own selves confirming that what they received through revelation is true. Allah said:

سَنُرِيهِمْ اٰيَاتِنَا فِى الْاٰفَاقِ وَفِى اَنْفُسِهِمْ حَتّٰى يَتَبَيَّنَ لَهُمْ اَنَّهُ الْحَقُّ

"We shall soon show them Our signs in the horizons as well as in themselves, until it becomes clear to them that it is the truth." (Fussilat, 53)

The above verse is preceded by:

قُلْ اَرَءَيْتُمْ اِنْ كَانَ مِنْ عِنْدِ اللهِ

"Say, 'do you see, if this were to be from Allah?'" (Fussilat, 52)

Then Allah added,

اَوَلَمْ يَكْفِ بِرَبِّكَ اَنَّهُ عَلَى كُلِّ شَيْءٍ شَهِيدٌ

"Is it not enough that your Lord is witness over all things?" (Fussilat, 53)

Thus, Allah testified to the effect that what the Prophet had brought was true and promised His slaves that He shall show them signs in His creation what would prove it true. Thereafter, He mentioned what outweighs all else: it is the fact of He being witness over all things. Thus, one of His names is *"Shahid"*: One from whose Sight nothing is concealed. Rather, He knows all things, is Observant of them, knowing them in all their details. This is the proof by His Names and Attributes. The first evidence is His own words. As for the evidence with the help of signs in the physical world and those within the self, it is the evidence, which has its basis in His Actions and creations.

وَلاشَيْء مثلُه

Nothing resembles Him.

The main body of Muslims holds the opinion that there is nothing similar to Allah: in His Being, His Attributes, or in His Acts. In common parlance, the word *tashbih* is somewhat ambiguously understood, albeit of right meaning. Sound reason leads to it, viz., what is specific to Allah should not be attributed to His creations, nor is there anything of His creations similar in any way to His Attributes. Thus, the Qur`anic aphorism, *"There is nothing  like unto Him,"* is a rejection of anthropomorphization (*tashbih*), while the words *"and He is the All hearing, the All seeing"* rejects vacuity, (or, the concept that He is devoid of qualities: *ta`attul* in Arabic).

14

Whoever thought of Allah's Qualities as similar to those of His creations is an anthropomorphist (*mushabbih*). And whoever thought of human qualities as similar to those of Allah is a stripper (*mu`attil*). He is similar to the Christians in their disbelief.

However, what happened was that denial of similarity (*tashbih*) was surreptitiously followed by a kind of stripping (or, vacuity: *ta`til* ) which attempts to deny Allah His Names. Those who committed this say, `We will not admit for Him Power, or Knowledge or Life, for humans are also attributed with these qualities.' It follows that Allah cannot be said to be: Powerful, Knowledgeable, or Living because humans are also known to have these qualities. This also applies to His Speech, Hearing, Sight, etc. Although these people agree with the main body of the Muslims, that He is Existing, Knowing, Powerful, Living, etc, while, they should know that it is also said about the humans that they exist, are living, knowing etc. No one would say that this is declaration of similarity with Allah Most High.

This is one of those things that the Qur`an and *Sunnah* lead us to, as well as man's own reasoning. No rational person would oppose it. Allah Most High named Himself with some Names, while He also named some of His creations with some of those same Names. Also, He attributed Himself with certain Attributes, while attributing some of His creations with those same attributes. For instance, He called Himself as Living, Tender, Kind, Knowledgeable, Hearing, Seeing, Mighty, Proud, Overpowering etc., although he used these for His creations too. He said:

يُخْرِجُ الْحَيَّ مِنَ الْمَيِّتِ

"He brings forth the living from the dead." (Al Rūm, 19)

He also said,

بِالْمُؤْمِنِينَ رَءُوفٌ رَّحِيمٌ

"He is, (i.e., Prophet Muhammad) to the believers kind and merciful." (Al Tawbah, 128)

Or,

$$\text{وَبَشَّرُوهُ بِغُلَامٍ عَلِيمٍ}$$

"They gave him the good news of a knowledgeable child." (Al Dhāriyat, 28)

Or,

$$\text{فَجَعَلْنَاهُ سَمِيعًا بَصِيرًا}$$

"Then we made him (i.e., man) hearing, seeing." (Al Insān, 2)

Or,

$$\text{قَالَتِ امْرَأَتُ الْعَزِيزِ}$$

"The wife of `Aziz said." (Yūsuf, 51)

Or,

$$\text{كَذَلِكَ يَطْبَعُ اللهُ عَلَى كُلِّ قَلْبِ مُتَكَبِّرٍ}$$

"That is how Allah seals the heart of every proud person." (Ghāfir, 35)

Further, it is well known that any living being is not similar to another living being, a knowledgeable to another knowledgeable, a mighty to another mighty and so on. Every person endowed with some common sense will acknowledge that.

Therefore, if someone denied an Attribute of Allah that He attributed Himself with, such as Anger, Love, Hatred, etc., on the grounds that it is tantamount to declaring a kind of similarity to Him, or a way of attributing a form to Him, then such a person will be told that 'If you admit for Him qualities such as, intention, speech, hearing and sight, when these are also qualities that His creations enjoy, then, surely, there is nothing strange in admitting for Him the qualities that you deny.'

If he says he will not attribute to Allah any quality, then he will be asked if he does not admit for Him Names such as Living, Knowledgeable, Mighty, etc. Of course he does. But, how could he, following his own principle do that when he knows that these are some of the names of His creations too? The truth is, what applies to names also applies to qualities. The important difference is as stated above: the names and attributes can be used, but they are not the same names and attributes as applicable to Allah, and as applicable to man.

The error lies in not understanding that these qualities when found in humans are not those Perfect Qualities that are possessed by Allah alone. When found in His creations, they are in their incomplete and defective form or expressing only one aspect of the several aspects of the Quality. These Names, therefore, when used for Allah are specific to Him. In contrast, when used for a creation they are specific to that creation. Allah's Existence, or His quality of being the Living, is not shared by any of His creations. Indeed, their presence in a creation of Allah is so specific to that particular creation that no other individual shares them with him exactly in the same sense and magnitude. How then is it imagined that Allah shares qualities with His creations in the same sense and magnitude? Don't you see that when you say: "This is he," then the person pointed out to is one but appearing as two different persons (to two different observers).

This will make it clear that those who committed anthropomorphism took the above meaning, but added to the true concept notions supplied by their own minds, thus going astray. In contrast, those who committed vacuity denied similarity of any kind, but also adding upon the true concept ideas of their own, and led themselves astray. But Allah's Book presented the concept in a manner that does not lack clarity to those who use their reason. Those who denied attributing anything of the humans to Allah did the right thing; but went wrong in denying what is proven to be Allah's attribute. As for those who admitted for him some Qualities, they did the right thing too, but went wrong by committing excesses.

وَلَا شَيْءَ يُعْجِزُهُ

There is nothing that can frustrate Him.

Allah Most High said:

اِنَّ اللهَ عَلَى كُلِّ شَيْءٍ قَدِيْرٌ

"Allah has power over everything." (Al Talāq, 12)

He also said,

وَمَا كَانَ اللهُ لِيُعْجِزَهُ مِنْ شَيْءٍ فِى السَّمٰوٰتِ وَلَا فِى الْأَرْضِ إِنَّهُ كَانَ عَلِيمًا قَدِيرًا

"Allah is not to be frustrated by anything whatsoever in the heavens or in the earth. He is All knowing, All powerful." (Al Fātir, 44)

He also said,

وَسِعَ كُرْسِيُّهُ السَّمٰوٰتِ وَالْأَرْضَ وَلَا يَئُودُهُ حِفْظُهُمَا ۚ وَ هُوَ الْعَلِيُّ الْعَظِيمُ

"His Kursiyy encompasses the heavens and the earth. Guarding them does not tire Him. And He is the Exalted, the Great." (Al Baqarah, 255)

The textual word *ya'uduhū* in the above verse means, they do not tire Him or, alternatively, are not beyond His capacity. This denial of a weakness is to express the full significance of its opposite, i.e., the Power. In the like manner, all that has been recorded in the Book or the *Sunnah* of the denial of a weakness is by way of signifying the perfection of its opposite. Take for example Allah's words:

وَ لَا يَظْلِمُ رَبُّكَ أَحَدًا

"Your Lord does not do injustice to anyone." (Al Kahaf, 49)

The above is to express the perfection of His justice.

Or, His saying:

لَا يَعْزُبُ عَنْهُ مِثْقَالُ ذَرَّةٍ فِى السَّمٰوٰتِ وَلَا فِى الْأَرْضِ

"Not as much as the weight of an atom in the heavens and the earth is hidden from him." (Sabā, 3)

The above is to express the perfection of His knowledge.

Or,

لَا تَأْخُذُهُ سِنَةٌ وَّلَا نَوْمٌ

"Neither slumber nor sleep overtakes Him." (Al Baqarah, 255)

This is to express His Wakefulness and His being in full control of things.

Otherwise, simple negation of qualities does not contribute to praise.

وَلَا إِلَهَ غَيْرُه

There is no deity besides He.

This is the *Tawhīd* that all Prophets invited their peoples to. These words of confirmation and negation are by way of making it specific. For, mere confirmation leaves room for doubt. Hence, after saying, "Your Lord is One God" the following words were added:

وَإِلَهُكُمْ إِلَهٌ وَاحِدٌ

"There is no deity save He." (Al Baqarah, 163)

A simple mind may be deceived by Shaytan: Admitted our Lord is One, but isn't there the possibility that others have their own god beside Him? Therefore, Allah added the words, 'There is no deity save He.'

قَدِيمٌ بِلَا ابْتِدَاء، دَائِمٌ بِلَا انْتِهَاء

The Ancient without a beginning, the Everlasting without an end.

This is expressed in Allah's words:

هُوَ الْأَوَّلُ وَالْآخِرُ

"He is the First and the Last." (Al Hadīd, 3)

And the Prophet (*saws*) said: "O Allah! You are the First with nothing before You and the Last with nothing after You."

Thus, when Tahawi said, "The Ancient without a beginning, the Everlasting without an end," he meant the Names: The First and the Last.

The knowledge of the two is implanted in human nature. For, all that exist have to have their end in One who is non contingent, i.e., a Necessary Being, in order that the chain of cause and effect be broken. One sees, for instance, the coming into being of animals, plants, minerals, or phenomena of heavenly origin such as the coming down of rains, etc. Now, these things and events are not impossibilities. For, the impossible of creation cannot be brought into existence. Nor, are they Necessary Beings. For, a Necessary Being cannot be thought to be non existent at any moment. Whereas, (there was a time when) these things and events were not in existence. Then they came into existence. Thus, the fact that it went into non existence disproves its ability to come into existence. And its coming into existence disproves the impossibility of it being brought into existence by itself. The conclusion is that what is subject to existence and non existence cannot be self creating. Allah said,

اَمْ خُلِقُوا مِنْ غَيْرِ شَىْءٍ اَمْ هُمُ الْخَالِقُونَ

"Or, were they created out of nothing? Or, are they the creators?" (Al Tūr, 35)

In other words, did they come into existence without a creator, or, did they create themselves? Now, it is known that a thing that is contingent cannot bring itself into being. What is possible of existence and is not a self existent nor self annihilating, cannot assume creation by itself. It remains into non existence until it finds a creator. Therefore, all that can exchange its existence, with non existence and the other way round, does not possess the quality of self existence or self annihilation.

If an intelligent man ponders over what the theologians and philosophers have to say in rational terms, he will find that the same has been stated in a more refined, simpler and clearer manner by the Qur`an. Further, in Qur`anic statements there is the rhetoric and an appeal that is missing from their statements. Allah has said:

وَلَا يَأْتُونَكَ بِمَثَلٍ إِلَّا جِئْنَاكَ بِالْحَقِّ وَأَحْسَنَ تَفْسِيرًا

"They bring you not a similitude, but We bring you (one) with truth and better explained." (Al Furqān, 33)

We are not saying, of course, that efforts should not be made at speculative reasoning in order to bring out subtle and hidden points. The hidden and the apparent are, after all, relative terms. There are points that are apparent to some, while inapparent to others. Indeed, there are points that are apparent to a man in a certain state, which were inapparent to him in another state. Further, the usefulness of subtle points cannot be denied. For, some people will accept them with greater willingness, for the sheer reason that they are hidden facts, arguing against what is more obvious and although much more powerful. People feel happier with what they arrive at through research and analysis than with what is obvious to the eye. There isn't any doubt about it that the concept of a Creator and the necessity of His existence, is one of those things firmly implanted in the human psyche, although, for some people, doubts occur, which lead them to speculative thinking.

The theologians have introduced *Al Qadīm* as one of the Names of Allah Most High. But that is an error. It is not one of His names. The Arabs always use the word qadim for something that precedes something else. When they say *qadīm*, they mean "old" just as when they say `*atīq*, they mean something new. It is never used except in the sense of something that is preceded by another and never in the sense of an eternal. For e.g., Allah said:

وَالْقَمَرَ قَدَّرْنَاهُ مَنَازِلَ حَتَّى عَادَ كَالْعُرْجُونِ الْقَدِيمِ

"And the moon We have appointed its course until it returns like an aged palm bough (of old)." (Yasīn, 39)

`*Urjun Al Qadīm* here is that `*urjun* which remains until the new `*urjun* replaces it and which in turn is the bough that carries the dates in the date palm tree.

Allah also said:

وَإِذْ لَمْ يَهْتَدُوا بِهِ فَسَيَقُولُونَ هَذَا إِفْكٌ قَدِيمٌ

"And, if they are not led to this, they would say, `This is an old fib." (Al Ahqāf, 11)

Here *Qadim* is again in the sense of the time that has elapsed.

Therefore, the entry of the term *Al Qadīm* among the names of Allah Most High is incorrect and all scholars of the earliest generations, including Ibn Hazm, have vehemently opposed it. Undoubtedly, if it is used in the sense of someone who preceded others, then, what precedes every creation is better deserving of mention that others. But, Allah's Names, are the Good Names that are specific to Him and are praiseworthy. In contrast, the word Precedent does not indicate precedence over all else. Hence the word "*Al Awwal*" (the First) has been employed. It is more precise than the word "*Al Qadīm*", for the former implies that whatever came, came after Him. *Al Qadīm* does not.

لا يَفْنَى وَلا يَبِيد

He will not perish, nor will He become extinct.

This is to say in other words that He is Everlasting. Allah Most High said:

كُلُّ مَنْ عَلَيْهَا فَانٍ ۞ (٢٦) وَيَبْقَى وَجْهُ رَبِّكَ ذُو الْجَلَلِ وَالْإِكْرَامِ (٢٧)

"All that are on it (i.e., the earth) will perish. It is only the Face of thy Lord that will remain." (Al Rahmān, 26-27)

The two terms "perish" and "extinct" are close in meaning. They have been brought together for emphasis. Also, they help consolidate the meaning expressed in "everlasting, without an end."

وَلا يَكُونُ إِلا مَا يُرِيد

Nothing happens save for what He wills.

This is to reject the Qadariyyah and Mu`tazilah viewpoint. They allege that it was in the Will of Allah that all the people should attain to faith. It was the unbeliever who desired unbelief for himself. Their claim is erroneous and rejected. For it opposes the Qur`an, the *Sunnah* and straightforward reasoning. This of course is the well known problem concerning the Divine Decree. It shall be presently discussed more thoroughly, Allah willing.

The Qadariyyah were so named because of their rejection of *Qadr* (the Divine Decree). The Jabariyyah, who argue by the Divine Decree, are also sometimes referred to as the Qadariyyah although it is the former group to whom the reference goes first.

As for the *Ahl al Sunnah*, they say: Allah Most High, even if He wills sins by His Decree, does not approve of them and does not order them. Rather, He disapproves of them, abhors them and forbids them. This is the standard position of the *Salaf*. They say, 'What Allah wished happened and what He did not wish, did not happen.'

Those of knowledge of the *Ahl al Sunnah* say: 'Will, as it appears in the Book of Allah, is of two kinds. The first: the Decreed, Universal, and Creative Will. The second: the Religious, the Mandatory and the Legal (i.e., what pertains to the Law). The second, the Legal Will, ensures approval and rewards. In contrast, the Universal Will incorporates everything that will ever happen. This can be deduced from the following Qur`anic statement:

فَمَنْ يُرِدِ اللهُ أَنْ يَهْدِيَهُ يَشْرَحْ صَدْرَهُ لِلْإِسْلَامِ وَمَنْ يُرِدْ أَنْ يُضِلَّهُ يَجْعَلْ صَدْرَهُ ضَيِّقًا حَرَجًا كَأَنَّمَا يَصَّعَّدُ فِي السَّمَاءِ

"Whomsoever Allah intends to guide, He opens up his heart for Islam. And whomsoever He intends to lead astray, He closes his heart, constricted, as if he were engaged in sheer ascent toward the heaven." (Al An`ām, 125)

And Allah's statement as uttered by Nuh, on whom be peace:

وَلَا يَنْفَعُكُمْ نُصْحِي إِنْ أَرَدْتُ أَنْ أَنْصَحَ لَكُمْ إِنْ كَانَ اللهُ يُرِيدُ أَنْ يُغْوِيَكُمْ

"Of no profit will be my counsel to you, much as I desire to give you (good) counsel, if Allah wishes to lead you astray." (Hūd, 34)

And Allah's words:

وَلٰكِنَّ اللهَ يَفْعَلُ مَا يُرِيدُ

"Rather, Allah does what He will." (Al Baqarah, 253)

As for His Religious, Mandatory, Legal Will, Allah said about it:

يُرِيدُ اللهُ بِكُمُ الْيُسْرَ وَلَا يُرِيدُ بِكُمُ الْعُسْرَ

"Allah wishes you ease. He does not wish you hardship." (Al Baqarah, 185)

And, His words:

وَاللهُ يُرِيدُ أَنْ يَتُوبَ عَلَيْكُمْ وَيُرِيدُ الَّذِينَ يَتَّبِعُونَ الشَّهَوَاتِ أَنْ تَمِيلُوا مَيْلًا عَظِيمًا ﴿٢٧﴾

"Allah wishes to turn to you (in mercy). Whereas those who follow their carnal desires wish that you swing (toward the sins) whole heartedly." (Al Nisā, 27)

This is the meaning of Allah's Will that the people refer to when they discover someone committing sins. They say about him, "This man does what Allah does not Will." That is to say, he does something that does not please Allah or that which Allah did not command.

Insofar as the Universal Will is concerned, the people express it by saying, "What Allah wished happened, and what He did not wish, did not happen."

The difference stands out clearly when we compare between the wish of a man who wishes to do something, in contrast to someone else wishing that he did it. When a person wishes to do something following his own desire, then this wish is tied up to his own act. But when he wishes someone else do it, then this wish is tied up to someone else's act. The people understand both as in line with logic. Further, a command necessarily demands the second kind of will (or wish) and not the first kind. Now, when Allah Most High orders a thing done by His slaves, then, sometimes He wishes to help the person over what he has been ordered to do; but, at other times He does not wish to help him, even though He might be desirous that the person in question go ahead and do as he has been ordered. To give an example, when Allah Most High ordered Fir`awn and Abu Lahab to believe, He made plain to them what they stood to gain if they did so. But it didn't mean that He wished to assist them too.

Now, as it is possible for one of the creations to order another to do something, without extending a hand of help, it is obviously possible to a greater degree for a Creator to do so, especially in view of His Wisdom. What happened when He ordered someone do a thing and then helped him accomplish it, is that His Will of Creation and Command got tied up to and became a part of the man's action. Thus what He desired of the man was desirable from two angles: that of Creative Will and that of the Mandatory Will.

In contrast, whomsoever He ordered a thing, but did not help him accomplish it, such a one got tied up to, and became part of, His Mandatory Will but not of the Creative Will. That was because of the undesirability of something else that was tied up to its creation, and for the reasons of obtaining its opposite that came into being when the man didn't do as he was commanded. This is following the rule that the creation of one of the two opposites denies the creation of the other. To explain, the creation of a disease in a man which helps inculcate in the man humility, resorting to supplications, repentance, softening of the heart, expiation of the sins and removal of arrogance is opposed to the creation of a healthy state in which the above cannot be achieved. Further, it should be kept in mind that a detailed knowledge of Allah's wisdom in His creations and commandments is beyond the power of the humans.

لا تَبلُغُه الأَوْهَامُ، ولا تُدرِكهُ الأَفْهَام

Neither can conjectures reach Him nor can intellects grasp Him.

Tahawi has paraphrased here the words of Allah:

وَلَا يُحِيطُونَ بِهِ عِلْمًا

"They cannot comprehend Him in knowledge." (Tāhā, 110)

Jawhari has said in his lexicon: "Waham is equivalent of conjecture while faham of knowledge."

What the Sheikh meant to say, Allah show him mercy, is that conjectures cannot fathom Him out nor can knowledge comprehend Him.

It is said that waham is what one anticipates a thing to be. That is, what one expects it to be like. In contrast, understanding is that which the intellect gains and comprehends. But no one can know what in truth Allah is but Himself. We only know Him through His Attributes; such as, He is One, Self sufficient, was not begotten, nor gave birth, etc.

وَلا يُشْبِه الأَنَامُ

Mankind do not resemble Him.

This is to reject the anthropomorphists. Allah Most High said:

لَيْسَ كَمِثْلِهِ شَىْءٌ وَّهُوَ السَّمِيْعُ الْبَصِيْرُ

"There is nothing like unto Him and He is the All hearing, the All seeing."
(Al Shūra, 11)

Never the less, it is not the denial of Attributes that has been intended as some innovatory groups have claimed. Abu Hanifah, Allah be pleased with him, said in his *Al fiqh al Akbar* : "There is none in His creations in His likeness." He also added: "His Attributes are totally different from the attributes of His creation. He knows, but not in the manner we know. He has power, but not in the sense of the power at our disposal, He sees, but not in the manner we see."

Nu`aym b. Hammad, the well trusted Traditionist said: "Whoever declared Allah similar to any of His creation in any manner, committed disbelief. Whoever denied anything that Allah Most High ascribed Himself with, committed disbelief. There is nothing comparable to what Allah Most High or His Messenger described Him with."

However, it should not be imagined that the scholars denied Allah's Attributes when they denied His likeness, or, do not attribute to Him any of what is proven to be His Attribute. All that they mean is that He is not similar to His creation in His Names, Attributes or Acts as Abu Hanifah's statement asserts above. This then, is the meaning of the verse quoted above. For, it will be noticed in the verse above that Allah Most High denied similarity, but affirmed Attributes.

We shall come across in the statements of Tahawi the affirmation of Attributes, as a reminder that denial of similarity does not mean a denial of Allah's Attributes.

To explain: (The essence of) Allah's Knowledge cannot be comprehended with the help of deductive analogy in a manner in which the principal becomes equal to its derivative; nor with the help of a comprehensive analogy in which all the components are treated equal. For, there is nothing similar unto Allah. Therefore, nothing can be used as analogy to describe Him, nor can He be mentioned in any statement that will reduce Him and others to the same status. Therefore, when the philosophers and theologians tried to draw analogies of

Him in their discussions of Divinity, they failed to arrive at a firm faith, rather, ran into contradictions and ended up in confusion.

That said, we might add that the analogy of "precedence" (or "antecedence by default," or "greater deservedness") may be employed, whether it be an analogy with the help of similitude applicable to details, or be it a comprehensive analogy. Allah Himself said (16: 60): *"For Allah is the highest of examples."* To illustrate, whatever perfection is thought to be deserving of a creation in existence, or, that which is possible of existence, having no defect whatsoever, from any angle so long as the perfection in that existent being does not deny its existence itself when absent then, it can be said that *Al Qadīm*, Allah Most High, has precedence over it, that is, is more deserving of that perfection. Further, since every perfection that has no defect from any angle, found in a created being which is sustained by and looked after by another, could only have acquired it from its creator, sustainer and the overseer, (if such is the case, then) the originator is more deserving of that perfection. In contrast, every defect or shortfall in a being which demands the withholding of that perfection, when its denial to any of the created, possible or contingent beings is deemed necessary then, its denial for the Lord is, obviously, more fitting and proper.

حَيُّ لا يَموتُ، قَيُّومٌ لا يَنَام

He is the Living One Who will not die, the Self subsisting by Whom all subsist Who does not sleep.

This is based on a statement of Allah Most High:

اللهُ لَا إِلٰهَ إِلَّا هُوَ الْحَيُّ الْقَيُّومُ لَا تَأْخُذُهُ سِنَةٌ وَّلَا نَوْمٌ

"Allah, there is no deity save Him. The Living One. The Self subsisting by whom all subsist. Neither does slumber overtake Him nor sleep." (Al Baqarah, 255)

Absence of slumber and sleep is a proof of perfection of His qualities of Life and that of Self subsistence by whom all subsist.

The Prophet, on whom be peace and blessing, said, "Allah does not sleep and it does not behoove Him that He should sleep."

When Tahawi denied any similarity in the previous paragraphs, he hinted at where falls the dividing line between Him and His creations and how Allah should be described but not His creation. Such as: He is the Living who does not die. That is, the quality of a Life that is eternal, is for Allah alone not for His creation. For, they die. Or, He is the Self subsisting by Whom all subsist; Who does not sleep. So the denial of slumber and sleep is specific to Him. But not to His creations, since they sleep. This is to imply that rejecting any similarity does not mean denial of Allah's Attributes. Rather, Allah possesses all Qualities to their perfection related to His Perfect Being. Obviously, the One Living with an everlasting life is not similar in any way to one who is living a life that is fleeting. Hence, the life of this world is declared a fleeting life: sports and pastime. Rather:

$$\text{وَإِنَّ الدَّارَ الْآخِرَةَ لَهِيَ الْحَيَوَانُ}$$

"The life of the world to come is the true life." (Al `Ankabūt, 64)

The life of this world is similar to sleep whereas the life of the Hereafter is similar to an awakening. Hence, it cannot be said that the life of the Hereafter is the Perfect life: so far as the creations are concerned. Rather, we say, the Living One whose quality of Life is His Personal Quality, is the One who bestowed the quality of permanence to the life of His creations in the Hereafter. If it is everlasting, it is because Allah Most High gave it that quality, not because that quality is extrinsically its own, as contrasted with the Life of Allah. That applies to the rest of His Qualities. In other words, the Qualities of Allah, are of the kind that are deserving of Him, whereas the qualities of His creation are as deserving of them.

You should also know that these two Names *Al Hayyu and Al Qayyum* have been mentioned in the Qur`an together in three chapters. They are two of the great Names of Allah. Indeed, some say that they  together  are "the Great Name" (*Al Ism al A`zam*). For they combine His various Qualities in a most comprehensive manner. The Quality "*Al Qayyūm*" (the Self subsisting by Whom all subsist), has the connotations of permanence and eternity that is not to be found in the term "*Al Qadīm*." It also points to the fact that He is existent by Himself, meaning, in turn, a non contingent Being (that is, someone who "necessarily exists"). Coupling with this Name that of *Al Hayyu*, attributes to Him all the Qualities of Perfection, while also ensuring their everlasting nature. They also deny Him any defect at any time, since eternity. Hence the verse:

اللهُ لَآ اِلَهَ اِلَّا هُوَ الْحَيُّ الْقَيُّومُ

"Allah, there is no deity save Him, the Living One, the Self subsisting by Whom all subsist." (Al Baqarah, 255)

This verse has been declared by the Prophet, in several authentic reports, as the greatest of verses in the Qur`an.

Thus, on these two Names depend the rest of the good Names, and with them hinge their meaning. We know that the quality of life guarantees the existence of the rest of the qualities of a being: none of them can be absent but because of some weakness in life itself. But, since Allah's Life is the Perfect and the Most Complete, its affirmation is tantamount to the affirmation of every Perfection whose denial would mean imperfection of His quality of Life.

The Quality of being "Self subsisting by whom all subsist" speaks of His self sufficiency and completeness of Power too, for He subsists by Himself; does not depend on anyone, in any manner.

خَالِقٌ بلا حَاجَةٍ، رَازِقٌ بلا مَؤُونة

Creator without the need (to create), Nourisher without the (need of the) means of nourishment.

Allah Most High has said:

وَمَا خَلَقْتُ الْجِنَّ وَالْإِنسَ إِلَّا لِيَعْبُدُونِ (٥٦)مَا أُرِيدُ مِنْهُم مِّن رِّزْقٍ وَمَا أُرِيدُ أَن يُطْعِمُونِ (٥٧) إِنَّ اللهَ هُوَ الرَّزَّاقُ ذُو الْقُوَّةِ الْمَتِينُ(٥٨)

"I have not created mankind and Jinn but that they should worship Me. I don't demand of them nourishment and I don't ask that they feed Me. It is

Allah who is the Provider, the Possessor of Great Strength." (Al Dhāriyat, 56-58)

He also said:

يَاۤ أَيُّهَا النَّاسُ أَنْتُمُ الْفُقَرَآءُ إِلَى اللَّهِ وَاللهُ هُوَ الْغَنِيُّ الْحَمِيدُ

"O People! You are in want before Allah. Allah is Self sufficient, the Praiseworthy." (Fātir, 15)

The Prophet, peace on him, said, narrating the words of his Lord: "O My slaves! Were the first of you and the last of you, the men of you and the Jinn of you, to become as pious as the most pious of you, that will not cause an increase in My kingdom by a bit. O My slaves! Were the first of you and the last of you, the men of you and the Jinn of you, to become as corrupt as the most corrupt of you, that will not cause a decrease in My kingdom by a bit."

مُمِيتٌ بِلا مَخَافَةٍ، بَاعِثٌ بِلا مَشَقَّةٍ

Giver of death without dread and the Quickener without effort.

The above is said because death has its own existence, as opposed to the philosophers and others who believe otherwise. Allah said:

أَلَّذِى خَلَقَ الْمَوْتَ وَالْحَيٰوةَ لِيَبْلُوَكُمْ أَيُّكُمْ أَحْسَنُ عَمَلا

"The One who created death and life in order that He might put you to test (to determine) who is better of deeds." (Al Mulk, 2)

Obviously, the non existent could not have been said to be a created being.

And a *hadīth* says: "Death will be brought in the form of a striped lamb on the day of Judgment and slaughtered between Heaven and Hell."

Although it is a non substantial being, Allah will give it a physical substance on the day of Judgment.

It is also reported about the deeds that they would be weighed in a Scale. Although we know that it is the substantial that carry weight and not the non

30

substantial. Similarly, it has been reported about the chapters *Al Baqarah* and *Āl `Imrān* that they shall be shading those who read and practiced them, like two pieces of cloud or like two hovering birds with wings outspread. Trustworthy reports also say that people's good deeds are raised above to the heaven.

مَا زَالَ بِصِفَاتِه قَد يِماً قبلَ خلقِه، لم يَزْدَدْ بكوِنهم شيئاً لَم يَكُن قبلَهم من صفتِه، وكما كانَ بصفاتِه أَزَلِيًّا كذلك لا يَزال عليها أبديا

He was eternally possessed of His Qualities before His (act of) creation, without any addition caused by them that was not already there (in Him) before their creation. And, as He ever was (in existence) with His Qualities, so He will remain with them forever.

That is to say, Allah Most High has eternally been in existence with His Perfect Qualities: both, the Qualities of His Being, as well as the Qualities of His Acts. It will be wrong to imagine that acquired an Attribute that He did not possess earlier, for His Attributes are the Perfect Attributes: the absence of any of them would mean imperfection. Therefore, it is not allowed to think that He obtained Perfection after He had had an attribute opposite to it.

His Qualities of Choice and the Qualities of Acts are also of the eternal type. Such as: Creating and shaping, quickening and causing death, taking away and bestowing, settling (on the `Arsh), coming, going and descending, getting angry and being pleased and others of this kind that He attributed Himself with, or His Messenger attributed Him with   even if we mortals do not know and understand their reality nor can interpret them satisfactorily. Therefore, we do not take them up for discussion, interpreting with the help of our personal opinions or base desires. Never the less, we know the meaning of the terms used, as said Imam Malik when asked about the how of "being settled" in the verse:

ثُمَّ استَوَى عَلَى الْعَرْشِ

*"Then He assumed Istawā' on the `Arsh,"* (Al A`rāf,54)

he replied, "*Istawā'* is known but its how is obscure." This applies to those Qualities also which change from one time to another, as the Prophet said in a *hadīth*: "Today my Lord was angry in a manner He never was angry at any time in the past and will never be so angry again." For, this kind of appearance (of a Quality) in this guise, is not impossible. It cannot be said that it came into existence, when, earlier, it did not exist. Don't you see that a writer is a writer while he is actually in the act of writing. But he remains a writer even when he is not engaged in writing.

The happening of things to Allah Most High something that the theologians have denied has neither been confirmed by the Book and the *Sunnah*, nor rejected by them. This needs some explanation. If it is said that nothing new happens to the Person of Allah Most High that He acquires from His creations nor an attribute is added that was not part of Him from eternity, then, the denial of the theologians is justified. In contrast, if it is the denial of Attributes of Choice then it is wrong. That is, if it is believed that He does not do what He wishes, that He does not speak out what He wishes, He does not get angry or is not pleased, or cannot be qualified with what He has qualified Himself with us, such as, His *Istawā*, coming or going, etc, then, such a denial is wrong.

The same is true of the "Attribute," whether it is an addition over the Being and Essence or not? By itself the word is ambiguous. So also, the word "detached": it requires clarification. Sometimes what is meant by it is something that is apart from Him. At other times it is used for what can be separated from Him.

Accordingly, the *Sunni* scholars refrain from saying that the Attributes of Allah, or His Word, are detached from, or are not apart from His Being. For, affirmation would mean that it has its separate existence, whereas a denial would be understood as if it is He. Therefore, the word "detached" needs some explanation. It should not be applied without the provision of additional conditions. If it is imagined that there is a Being existent by itself, completely isolated of its Attributes, then such a concept is wrong. In contrast, if it is thought that the Attributes are in addition to the Being which in turn is not understood in the sense in which the attributes are understood, then that is acceptable. But, there is no Being existent devoid of Attributes. Rather, the Being is attributed with the Perfect Attributes as an essential part of it and inseparable of it. The mind of course thinks of the Being and the Attributes as separate entities, but, outside of the mind, there is no existence of the Being without Attributes. That obviously is impossible. If there hadn't been, for example, any attribute but that of existence, then too, it could not be separated from the Being, although the mind thinks of them as two separate entities: the Being and the Attribute. Yet, outside of the mind, the two should not be separated out.

Someone might say: the Attribute is neither the Being itself, nor apart from it. One aspect of this statement is correct, viz., the Attribute is not the Being itself which the mind imagines as a separate entity, rather, it is apart from it. But it is not another Being either. Rather, the Being is   inclusive of the Attributes one and the same and not multiple beings. Accordingly, when you say, "I seek Allah's refuge," you have sought the refuge of a Being who is qualified with the Perfect, proven, Attributes, that cannot be sequestered from Him in any manner. But when you say, "I seek refuge with the Power of Allah," then you have sought refuge with the help of one of the several Attributes of Allah, yet you did not seek the refuge of "other than Allah." This is the meaning derived of the word "Being." For the word "being" is not used independently. It is related to something else. Such as "existent being," or, "powerful being," or, "honored being," and so forth.

In all these kinds of expressions the attribute belongs to the being. From this we understand that a being cannot be imagined apart from its attributes, even if the mind is capable of imagining a being without its attributes. This is because the mind is capable of imagining impossibilities. (But in the real world they go together). The Prophet, on whom be peace, has said: "I seek refuge with Allah, and with His Power, from the evil of what I feel and what I am wary of." He also prayed: "I seek the refuge of the Perfect Words of Allah from the evil He created." Another supplication runs as follows: "O Allah, I seek refuge with Your approval from Your anger, with Your forgiveness from Your punishment, and seek Your refuge from You." But the Prophet never sought the refuge of anyone apart from Allah.

لَيْسَ بَعْدَ خَلْقِ الْخَلْقِ اسْتَفَادَ اسْمُ (الْخَالِقِ) وَلَا بِأَحْدَاثه البَرِيَّة استفاد اسمُ (الباري)

He did not acquire the Name "Creator" after the creation of the creations nor did He acquire the Name "Maker" after giving existence to the beings.

It is apparent from the words of Tahawi that He denies the cycle of contingencies in the past. Presently we shall come across his statements to the effect that he does not deny it for the future when he says, "The Heaven and the Hell are in creation. They will neither perish nor become non existent." This is the opinion of the great majority of scholars. There is no doubt that whoever denied this both for the future as well as the past is wrong, as did, for instance, Jaham and his followers. He has spoken about the destruction of Heaven and Hell. However, this we shall substantiate in detail later, Allah willing.

As for those who have believed in the contingencies without a beginning, or those who said of the contingencies as without an end, the right opinion seems to be to separate and distinguish the two. For Allah Most High has been Living since eternity, and, Action is a necessity of life, therefore, He has ever been doing what He will. That is how He qualified Himself when He said:

ذُو الْعَرْشِ الْمَجِيدُ (١٥) فَعَّالٌ لِّمَا يُرِيدُ (١٦)

"He is the Owner of the magnificent `Arsh. Doer of what He will." (Al Burūj, 15,16)

The verse throws light on several aspects.

First, Allah Most High Acts by His will and desire.

Second, He has always been like that, for He spoke of it as a reason for His praise.

Third, When He wishes a thing, He does it. The *"mā"* of the text (translated as "what") is a generic term applicable to all that He wishes and wills. This is applicable to the will related to His own Acts. As for His will that is related to the acts of His slaves, that is of a different nature. If He desired an act from a slave, but Himself did not wish to aid him in that, then, the act cannot come

34

into existence. But, if He desired an act from a slave, also intending to help him in the execution of that act, then He helps him and brings the act to existence. This is a point that the Qadariyyah and Jabariyyah missed to see and ran into rough waters.

Fourth, His Act and Will are concomitant. When He wishes to do a thing, He accomplishes it. Conversely, whatever He accomplished, He had desired it. In contrast, the creation wish to do what they cannot, and sometimes do what they didn't wish. There is none that does what he will, save Allah.

Fifth, the confirmation of the existence of several desires, in accordance to the acts, and that every act might have a will of its own behind it. This is logical since Allah Most High wishes eternally and does what He will.

Sixth, whatever His will dictates is possible of achievement: whether He desired to "descend" down to the first firmament every night, or wished to "come" on the Day of Judgment, or, wished to show Himself to His slaves, or appear to them as He wished, or wished to talk to them, or laugh, or whatever else that is proven by a report of the Prophet, on whom be peace, is possible of achievement.

Now, to say that the contingents have a beginning, leads to a state of vacuity before it. But Allah Most High has not been a non Doer at anytime to became a Doer at some point in time. Yet, this does not necessarily lead to a world invested with eternity. For, everything that is besides Allah is a created thing and is possible of creation. It is in existence by virtue of Allah's creative activity. Existence is not its intrinsic quality. Dependence and need of another is a necessary quality of everything save Allah Most High. In contrast Allah is the Necessary Self existent Being, Self sufficient unto Himself. Self sufficiency is a necessary Attribute of the Person of Allah Most High.

As for this world, two opinions have prevailed over the question: Is it a created thing from corporeal material, or not? There is also disagreement over the nature of what it was at its beginning. Allah has said:

وَ هُوَ الَّذِىْ خَلَقَ السَّمٰوٰتِ وَالْاَرْضَ فِىْ سِتَّةِ اَيَّامٍ وَّكَانَ عَرْشُهُ عَلَى الْمَآءِ

"It is He who created the heavens and the earth in six phases while His `Arsh was on Water." (Hūd, 7)

Bukhari and others have recorded `Imran b. Hussayn as saying: "The people of Yemen told the Prophet that they had come to gain knowledge of Islam, and to ask about `the beginning of this affair.' He told them: "Allah was, and there was nothing before Him." According to another version: "There wasn't anything along with Him." According to yet another version: "His `Arsh was on Water. He wrote down everything in the Preserved Tablet. And He created the heavens and the earth." The words of another report are: "Then He created the heavens and the earth."

With reference to these reports, two schools of thought are prevalent. One of them believes that the aim of the reports is to establish that Allah was in existence since eternity and had eternally remained so. Then He began creating things and events. That means to say, they and their properties were once non existent. And that Time itself is a created entity and so Allah became a Doer the while He was not a Doer of the possible of creation.

A second school believes that the reports are only telling us about the point in time when the creation of all that can be observed was begun, which He created in six days, and that His `Arsh was then on Water. This is stated at several points in the Qur`an. Further, a rein Muslim narrated by `Abdullah ibn `Amr says: "Allah determined the measures of this world fifty thousand years before He created the heavens and the earth. And His `Arsh was on Water." Thus, the Prophet stated that the measures were pre determined fifty thousand years earlier to creation in six periods, and that His `Arsh was then on Water.

The correctness of this second opinion derives from the words of the people of Yemen who said: "We have come to find out about the beginning of this affair." They were referring to what was created and observable. And by *"al amr"* of the text (translated as affair) the allusion was to "what Allah had created by His command." Answering them, the Prophet told them about the beginning of this observable world, and not about the class and kinds of them. For they hadn't inquired about that. He also informed them about the creation of the heavens and the earth while the `Arsh was on Water. He didn't tell them anything about the creation of the `Arsh, which was created before the creation of the heavens and the earth.

Also, he said: "Allah was, and there was nothing before Him." According to some versions, "nothing along with Him" (ma`a hu). Another version says, "nothing besides Him" (ghayruhu). However, all the reports originate from a single occasion, meaning, one of them quoted the actual words, whereas the others used equivalents. However, the word "before" occurs in other reports. For instance, Muslim has preserved a supplication made by the Prophet reported by Abu Hurayrah: "O Allah, You are the First and there was nothing before You." Whereas the other two words (i.e., ma`a hu and ghayruhu) do not occur individually in any other report. Most of the traditionists, such as Humaydi, Baghwi, Ibn al Athir, used to narrate this *hadīth* with the word "before" (qabl). If this is how we accept it, then the questions about what was before the creations and what not, is not the subject of the *hadīth* of `Imran b. Hussayn.

لَهُ مَعْنَى الرُّبُوِبِيَّة وَلَا مَرْبُوب، ومَعْنَى الْخَالِق وَلا مَخْلُوق

The meaning of Lordship was established (for Him) without (there being) any slaves and that of Creator without (there being) any creations.

What the author means is that Allah Most High was qualified with the Attribute of Lordship before He created anything and He was qualified with the Attribute of creation before the creation was brought into being.

وَكَمَا أَنَّهُ مُحْيِ الْمَوْتَى بَعْدَمَا أَحْيَا، استحق هَذَا الاسمَ قَبْلَ إِحْيَائِهِم، كَذَلِكَ إ استحق اسمَ الْخَالِق قَبْل إِنْشَائِهِم

As He will quicken the dead after He gave them life, He deserved this Name before their life. In the like manner He deserved the name "the Creator" before their creation.

That is, just as Allah Most High deserved to be called the "Quicker of the dead" before anything came to life, He also deserved to be called the Creator before He created anything. This is to reject the Mu`tazilah view and of those who followed them. We have already explained that Allah Most High has ever been doing what He will.

ذَلِكَ بِأَنَّهُ عَلَى كُلِّ شَيْءٍ قَدِير، وَكُلُّ شَيْءٍ إِلَيْهِ فَقَير، وَكُلُّ أَمْرٍ إليه يَسِير، لا يَحْتَاج إِلَى شَيْء (لَيْسَ كَمِثْلِهِ شَئٌ وَهُوَ السَّمِيع البَصِير)

That is because He has power over everything whereas everything is dependent on Him. Every affair is easy for Him. He does not stand in need of anything: "There is nothing like unto Him and He is the All hearing, the All seeing."

The intention by the words above is to emphasize, once again, that His Attributes are eternal. The Mu`tazilah have, however, misinterpreted Allah's words:

وَاللهُ عَلى كُلِّ شَئْءٍ قَدِيرٌ

"Allah has power over everything." (Al Hashr, 6)

They said: Allah is capable of what is within His power. As for the acts of His servants, He has no power over them.

Had this meaning been correct, it would have been said: "He is the Knowledgeable of all that can be known," or, "the Creator of what He created," etc. By alleging the above, they actually sequestered from Him His Quality of Perfect Power over everything.

As for the followers of the prophetic ways, they believe He has power over everything. Thus, everything that is possible is included in the above statement. As for what is impossible by itself, such as, a thing both existent and non existent at the same time, such have no meaning. Their existence cannot be imagined. It cannot be considered as "a thing" by the intelligent.

This is the basis of a complete faith in the Lordship of Allah. No one ever believed that He is the Lord of all things without also believing that He has power over those things. And he will not believe in the completeness and perfectness of His Power, without believing that He has power over everything.

38

The author's words "There is nothing like unto Him" is to reject the anthropomorphists; and, his words, "And He is the All hearing, the All seeing" are to refute those who believe in vacuity. Allah Most High possesses the Attributes to perfection in which He has no one resembling Him. That is, if one of the creations is qualified as the hearing, the seeing, it does not lead to the meaning that his faculty of hearing or sight is similar to that of Allah Most High. Yet, qualifying Him with the Attributes does not lead to suggesting similarities. For each goes with attributes deserving of him. Attributes of the created are of quality deserving of them. And the Attributes of the Creator are of Quality deserving of Him. Allah Most High has declared that the best of similitude are deserving of Him alone. He said:

$$\text{لِلَّذِينَ لَا يُؤْمِنُونَ بِالْآخِرَةِ مَثَلُ السَّوْءِ وَلِلّهِ الْمَثَلُ الْأَعْلَى}$$

"To those who do not believe in the Hereafter, applies an evil similitude, whereas to Allah applies the highest similitude." (Al Nahal, 60)

He also said:

$$\text{وَلَهُ الْمَثَلُ الْأَعْلَى فِى السَّمٰوٰتِ وَالْأَرْضِ}$$

"And for Him is the highest similitude in the heavens and the earth." (Al Rūm, 27)

Thus we see that Allah Most High declared evil similitude for His antagonists the pagans and their deities who are loaded with defects and imperfections and informed that the highest similitude applies to Him alone, Who possesses Attributes that are free of defects and imperfections. Therefore, whoever eliminated perfection from the Attributes of Allah, suggested an evil similitude for Him and denied Him the highest similitude that He declared for Himself. As for the highest similitude itself, it is the Absolute Perfection which are sine quo non of existent beings and established meanings. These, in turn, the more prevalent in any object and to any degree of perfection, are, by default, to be found in a greater degree and perfection in Him than those others.

Now, when it is established that Allah is possessed with Attributes that are the Greatest and the most Perfect, then He alone deserves the highest similitude, in contrast to anyone else. Indeed, it is impossible that two beings should share the highest similitude, for, if they are equal in every sense then one of them cannot be imagined to be higher than the other. And, if they are not equal, then only one of the two can be attributed with the highest similitude. The One who has the highest similitude, cannot have an equal.

He created the creation by His knowledge

He created: That is, He brought them into existence on an original pattern. Sometimes the Arabic word *khalq* is also used in the sense of "to decree." As for the word creation, it is the created that is meant. Finally, the words in His knowledge are to emphasize that He was aware of what He was creating. Allah said:

وَعِنْدَهُ مَفَاتِحُ الْغَيْبِ لَا يَعْلَمُهَا إِلَّا هُوَ وَيَعْلَمُ مَا فِي الْبَرِّ وَالْبَحْرِ وَمَا تَسْقُطُ مِنْ وَرَقَةٍ إِلَّا يَعْلَمُهَا وَلَا حَبَّةٍ فِي ظُلُمَٰتِ الْأَرْضِ وَلَا رَطْبٍ وَّلَا يَابِسٍ إِلَّا فِي كِتَٰبٍ مُّبِينٍ (٥٩) وَهُوَ الَّذِي يَتَوَفَّٰكُمْ بِالَّيْلِ وَ يَعْلَمُ مَا جَرَحْتُمْ بِالنَّهَارِ (٦٠)

"With Him are the keys to the Unseen. No one knows them except He. He knows what is in the land and in the sea. Not a leaf falls but He knows it, not a grain (is there) in the dark (crevices) of the earth, nor a fresh thing or withered, but it is (recorded) in a Clear Book. It is He who takes away your souls by the night and knows what you do by the day." (Al An`ām, 59-60)

Now, to present a logical reason for the above we might say that it would have been impossible for Him to originate things while He was ignorant of them. The act of origination requires a will. The will in turn requires a complete image of that which is to be originated. Obviously, such complete imaging can only be based on knowledge. Thus, origination is a necessary part of the will. In turn, the will requires knowledge. Therefore origination requires knowledge. Further, the created is so well invested with skill and perfection that they require knowledge on the part of the doer. A sand perfect act denies its by one who lacks knowledge. In fact, among the created too there are some that are knowledgeable which is a quality of excellence. This invalidates that the Creator could be without knowledge.

There are two other ways to arrive at the same conclusion.

First, We know that it is a necessary surmise that the creator should be more perfect than the created, and that what is a Necessary Being is more perfect than what is accidental or contingent. Now, suppose we were to think of two beings: one with knowledge and the other without. Then, of the two the first would be more perfect than the other. A corollary of this argument is that if the creator were not to be knowledgeable, the created would be more perfect than Him. That obviously is impossible.

Second, it can be said that all the knowledge that is possible, that is, in the created beings, is from Him. Now, it is impossible to think that the one who gave perfection should be without it Himself. Rather, He is more likely to be invested with it. The highest similitude is for Allah alone. He and His creation are not on par: neither in the symbolic syllogism nor in all comprehensive syllogism. Whatever is found in His creation by way of perfection, is actually becoming of Him, and whatever there is that the created do not deserve to have, is more deserving that He should be without it.

وَقَدَّرَ لَهُمْ أَقْدَارَاً

He decreed for them decrees.

Allah Most High said:

وَخَلَقَ كُلَّ شَيْءٍ فَقَدَّرَهُ تَقْدِيرًا

"He created everything, then He ordained it." (Al Furqān, 2)

And,

إِنَّا كُلَّ شَيْءٍ خَلَقْنَاهُ بِقَدَرٍ

"Verily, We created everything in a just proportion." (Al Qamar, 49)

وَضَرَبَ لَهُم آجَالاً

And appointed for them the terms.

That is, Allah Most High determined for His creations a term, so that when the appointed term arrives, they are not delayed by a moment nor can they advance it in time.

Allah Most High said:

وَمَا كَانَ لِنَفْسٍ أَنْ تَمُوتَ إِلَّا بِإِذْنِ اللهِ كِتَابًا مُّؤَجَّلًا

"It is not for a soul to die save by the will of Allah: a term written down." (Āl `Imrān, 145)

Muslim has a report narrated by Ibn Mas`ud, which says that when Umm Habibah, a wife of the Prophet supplicated: "O Allah. Allow me the living company of my husband Muhammad, my father Abu Sufyan and my brother Mu`awiyyah," the Prophet interjected: "You have asked Allah to over rule the terms that have been determined, the days that are numbered, and the providence that has been distributed. Allah will never bring forward an event from its appointed term, nor will He delay it. Had you asked Allah to relieve you of the chastisement of the Fire and that of the grave, it would have been better."

Therefore, the dead dies because his appointed term has arrived. Allah had known and determined that a particular man was going to die of a disease, another because of murder, yet another due to a fall, and so on of those many reasons. Allah Most High created life and death, and created the means of life and death too.

The Mu`tazilah have maintained that the murdered person's term was cut down. Had he not been killed, he would have lived up to his term. Thus, he had two terms. But this is untrue. For, it does not behoove Allah that He should determine a term that He knows might be cut down. Or, determine two terms for him, in the manner of one ignorant of what is to follow. Rather, he declared just retaliation and blood wit as obligatory upon the murderer for committing what he was forbidden. It is following this line of thought that the *hadīth* of the Prophet has to be understood which says: "Joining the kin increases in (one's) age." That is, treating well and doing good to those related by blood is a cause of increase in the length of life. In other words, Allah had determined that the man should join the kin and live up to the age that was pre determined too. Without that cause viz., joining of the kin he would not have lived up to such and such an age. But, Allah had decreed that cause. Conversely, Allah decreed for another man that he should severe the kin and live up to such and such an age.

If it is asked: Going by the effect of joining the kin on the increase or decrease of one's term, does supplication for the same reasons has the same effect?

The answer is, that is not necessary in the light of the Prophet's words to Umm Habibah, "you have asked Allah to over rule the terms that have been determined" ... to the end of the *hadith*. This means that the terms are pre determined. Supplications to overcome them are not sanctioned. This is in contrast to the escape from chastisement in the Hereafter. For, supplication to that effect has been ordered, and can be profitable in this case. Don't you notice that the supplication for change in one's term, when it guarantees a benefit of the Hereafter has been sanctioned, as in the *hadith* of Nasa'i reported by `Ammar b. Yasir who narrated the Prophet's words of supplication: "O Allah. By Your knowledge of the Unseen, and by Your power over Your creation, let me live until my life proves good for me, and let me die when death is better for me."

The above is corroborated by what Hakim has narrated in his *Sahih*. Thawban reports the Prophet as having said: "The pre determined is not turned back but by supplications, and the term of life is not lengthened but by good deeds. And a man is sometimes denied sustenance because of a sin he committed." The *hadith* (of Umm Habibah) refutes a man's belief that vowing (to spend in the way of Allah if a supplication is granted: *nadhr*) is a cause of removal of a misery or obtaining of a blessing. According to a *hadith* in Bukhari and Muslim, the Prophet dissuaded the people from vowing, saying: "Vow does not cause to bring any good. It only helps to get something out of a miser."

Further, it must be known that supplications can be beneficial and heard by Allah in certain things, but not all. Therefore, Allah does not answer the supplications of those who cross the limits while making a supplication. Imam

Ahmed disapproved that one seek elongation of life, saying: "This is something that Allah is done with." As for Allah's words:

وَمَا يُعَمَّرُ مِنْ مُّعَمَّرٍ وَّلَا يُنْقَصُ مِنْ عُمُرِهِ إِلَّا فِىْ كِتٰبٍ

"Nor a long lived man ages up nor is a decrease made in his age but is in a Book." (Fātir, 11)

It is said about the above verse that the personal pronoun in the word "his term," (i.e., the "hā" of the term `umurihi) is in the same sense as: "I have a Dirham and its half." That is, he has another half of a Dirham. The meaning then would be: "And the age of another aging person is not decreased." It is also said that by the "increase" and "decrease" the allusion is to the writings that the angels possess (and not what is in the Mother of the Books, *Al Lawh al Mahfūz*: tr.).

Allah Most High also said:

لِكُلِّ اَجَلٍ كِتَابٌ (٣٨) يَمْحُوا اللهُ مَا يَشَآءُ وَيُثْبِتُ ۚ وَعِنْدَهُ اُمُّ الْكِتٰبِ (٣٩)

"Each term is written down. Allah blots out or confirms what He will and with Him is the Mother of the Books." (Al Ra`d, 38-39)

It has been explained that the blotting and confirmation are effected in the book that is in the hands of the angels. As for the words: "the Mother of the Books" in the above verse, it is *Al Lawh al Mahfūz* (i.e., the Preserved Tablet).

لَمْ يَخْفَ عَلَيْهِ شَيْءٌ قَبْلَ أَنْ يَخْلُقَهُم وَعَلِمَ مَا هُم عَامِلُون قَبْلَ أَن يَخْلُقَهُمْ

Nothing was hidden from Him before their creation. And He knew what they were going to do, even before He had created them.

Allah knows what was in the past, what is going to be in the future and what's not going to be. And, if it will be, how will it be. Allah said:

وَلَوْ رُدُّوا لَعَادُوا لِمَا نُهُوا عَنْهُ

"And, if they are returned, they would be back to doing what they were forbidden." (Al An`ām, 28)

44

Although He knew that they wouldn't be returned, He informed us that had they been given a new life, they would have gone back to their old ways. He also said:

وَلَوْ عَلِمَ اللهُ فِيهِمْ خَيْرًا لَّأَسْمَعَهُمْ وَلَوْ أَسْمَعَهُمْ لَتَوَلَّوا وَّهُم مُّعْرِضُونَ

"Had Allah known any good in them, He would have made them hear. But, had He made them hear, they would have turned away and shown their backs." (Al Anfāl, 23)

وَأَمَرَهُمْ بِطَاعَتِهِ، وَنَهَاهُم عَن مَعْصِيَتِهِ

He ordered them His obedience and forbid them His disobedience.

After speaking of creation and determination, Tahawi mentioned the commandment and forbiddance to indicate that Allah Most High has created His creations in order that they worship Him. Allah Most High said:

وَمَا خَلَقْتُ الْجِنَّ وَالْإِنسَ إِلَّا لِيَعْبُدُونِ

"I have not created the Jinn and mankind, except that they should worship Me." (Al Dhāriyat, 56)

وَكُلُّ شَيْءٍ يَجْرِي بِتَقْدِيرِهِ، وَمَشِيئَتُهُ تَنْفَذُ، لا مَشِيئَةَ لِلْعِبَادِ، إِلا مَا شَاءَ لَهُمْ، فَمَا شَاءَ لَهُمْ: كَانَ، وَمَا لَمْ يَشَأْ لَمْ يَكُنْ

Everything runs on its determined course by His will. His will is executed and not the will of His slaves, save for what He approves for them. Therefore, what He wished for them came into existence, and what He did not, did not.

This is based on Allah's words:

وَ مَا تَشَاؤُونَ إِلَّا أَن يَّشَاءَ اللهُ ۚ إِنَّ اللهَ كَانَ عَلِيمًا حَكِيمًاۤ

"You cannot will, unless Allah wills. Verily, Allah is Knowing, Wise." (Al Dahar, 30)

He also said,

وَمَا تَشَآءُوْنَ إِلَّا أَنْ يَّشَآءَ اللهُ رَبُّ الْعٰلَمِيْنَ

"You cannot will unless Allah wills the Lord of the worlds." (Al Takwīr, 29)

There are many other verses to the effect that only what Allah wills takes place, and what He doesn't, does not. It is hard to imagine that anything should happen in His kingdom without His approval. Who can be on greater wrong than one who believed that Allah willed belief on the part of an unbeliever, but he willed unbelief for himself, so that, the unbeliever's will prevailed over that of Allah? Surely, Allah is far above all that they allege.

Now, if it is said that the following verse of the Qur`an presents a problem:

سَيَقُوْلُ الَّذِيْنَ اَشْرَكُوْا لَوْ شَآءَ اللهُ مَا اَشْرَكْنَا وَلَآ اٰبَآؤُنَا

"Surely, those who disbelieved will say, `Had Allah willed, neither we nor our forefathers would have committed the sin of Association." (Al An`ām, 148)

and,

وَقَالَ الَّذِيْنَ اَشْرَكُوْا لَوْ شَآءَ اللهُ مَا عَبَدْنَا مِنْ دُوْنِهٖ مِنْ شَيْءٍ

"Those who disbelieved said, `Had Allah willed we would not have worshipped anything besides Him." (Al Nahal, 35)

The above has been answered in several ways, the best of them is as follows. Allah Most High refuted their belief that Allah's Will was equivalent of His approval. They meant to say that had He disapproved of it, or was displeased with it, He would have prevented them from it. Thus, they thought that Allah's Will is a sign of His approval. Allah refuted their claim, informing them that His Will was not the sign of His approval. He also expressed His disapproval of their opposition to the commandments He had sent through His Messengers, and, following His Decree, what he had revealed of the Book. Thus, they placed His general Will as an obstacle to acceptance of what He had ordered. When they spoke of Allah's will, they were not speaking of the Will of His that works through everything, rather, refused to follow His command on a pretext. Their case was similar to that of the corrupt sects and the ignorant people, who, when ordered a thing done, or forbidden, argue by the concept of pre determination.

Once a thief argued with `Umar that he had not stolen but by Divine Decree. `Umar told him that he was not severing his hand but following the Divine Decree.

يَهْدِي مَنْ يَشَاءُ، وَيَعْصِم وَيُعَافِي، فَضْلاً، وَيُضِلُّ مَنْ يَشَاء، وَ يَخْذِلُ وَيَبْتَلِي، عَدْلاً

He guides whom He will: protects and safeguards by His grace. He sends astray whom He will: humiliates and subjects to tribulation following (the rules of) Justice.

This is to refute the Mu`tazilah who say that what is best for the people is binding upon the Lord. Primarily, this is in reference with the question of guidance and misguidance.

The Mu`tazilah speculated that guidance from Allah consists in making manifest the right path. As for misguidance it is a nomenclature for the erroneous humans. They say that Allah's decision to lead a man to error at the time of his creation is an error by itself.

This opinion is based on a wrong assumption, viz., people's action are their own creation.

As for our position, our evidence is in the verse:

إِنَّكَ لَا تَهْدِى مَنْ اَحْبَبْتَ وَلٰكِنَّ اللهَ يَهْدِى مَنْ يَّشَآءُ

"You cannot (O Prophet) guide whom you are pleased with. It is Allah who guides whom He will." (Al Qasas, 56)

If guidance consisted in only showing the way, then Allah should not have denied the Prophet's ability to guide, for, the Prophet showed and made clear the way to one and all: those who approved it as well as those who disapproved of it. Moreover, if guidance from Allah were to simply consist in showing the way, which in any case is found placed in every soul, then, surely, making it conditional to Allah's will wouldn't make much sense.

وَكُلُّهُم يَتَقَلَّبُون فِي مَشِيئَتِهِ بَيْنَ فَضْلِهِ وَعَدْلِهِ

All of them turn about following His Will: moving between His grace and justice.

Allah has said about His creation:

هُوَ الَّذِى خَلَقَكُمْ فَمِنْكُمْ كَافِرٌ وَّمِنْكُمْ مُّؤْمِنٌ

"It is He who created you, then some of you are unbelievers and some of you believers." (Al Taghābun, 2)

Thus, whomsoever He guided, He did it by His grace and so praise to Him for that. And whomsoever He sent astray, it is by His justice, and so He deserves to be praised. We shall expand upon this more presently, for the author did not put together all the relevant material on Divine Decree in one place. He spread it about, and we shall follow his method of presentation.

وَهُوَ مُتَعَال عَنْ الأَضْدَادِ وَالأَنْدَاد

He is exalted above opposites and equals.

Allah has no contender and no one is similar to Him. He said:

وَلَمْ يَكُنْ لَّهُ كُفُوًا أَحَدٌ

"And there is none comparable to Him." (Al Ikhlās, 4)

لا رَادَّ لِقَضَائِهِ، ولا مُعَقِّب لِحُكمِهِ، ولا غَالِبَ لأَمْرِهِ

There is no repeller of His decree, no one can postpone it, nor is there anyone to overcome His command.

To explain: no one can turn back what He decrees, nor can anyone delay or pre pone the execution of His decisions, nor can anyone get better of His command. Rather, He is the sole Lord, the One who overpowers all.

آمنا بِذَلِكَ كُلَّهُ، وَ أَيْقَنَّا أَنَّ كُلاً مِنْ عِنْدِهِ

We believe in all this, and are certain that everything originates from Him (i.e. by His command).

Hereonwards, the author takes up a new topic saying:

وَ أَنَّ مُحَمَّدًا عَبْدُهُ الْمُصْطَفَى، وَنَبِيُّهُ الْمُجْتَبَى، وَرَسُولُهُ الْمُرْتَضَى

And (we believe) that Muhammad is His chosen slave, the elected Prophet and an approved Messenger. And the most eminent of Messengers. The Beloved of the Lord of the Worlds. All claims to Prophethood after him are erroneous and following base desires.

The three terms: 'chosen', 'elected' and 'approved,' are more or less synonyms. The point of note here is that a man's perfection lies in how true a slave he is to Allah Most High. The more true slave a man is, the more perfect and the higher of rank he is. Anyone who believes that the creation can get out of slavery to Allah, howsoever he may achieve that, and attains higher status with Him, is the most ignorant of His creations. Allah said:

وَقَالُوا اتَّخَذَ الرَّحْمَنُ وَلَدًا سُبْحَانَهُ بَلْ عِبَادٌ مُّكْرَمُونَ

"And they say, `The Merciful has taken a son.' Glory is to Him. Rather, they are slaves, honored." (Al Anbiyā, 26)

Further, Allah spoke of the Prophet, Muhammad, as a slave in all those places He wished to honor him. He said:

سُبْحَانَ الَّذِي أَسْرَى بِعَبْدِهِ

"Glorified is He who took His slave in a journey by night." (Al Isrā, 1)

(As against the above) most theologians and polemicists have argued in favor of the greatness of the Prophets and Messengers on the strength of their miracles. No doubt, miracles are strong evidences. But, evidences are not restricted to miracles. For, the most truthful, as well as the greatest liars, claim to be Prophets. But, so far as the discerning minds are considered, this does not cast any doubt on the affair. Rather, the surrounding details speak for themselves. We know that there are several ways by which people can distinguish between a true cla*imān*t and a false one even in ordinary affairs. So, what about claims to Prophethood? Hassan b. Thabit well said:

> *Even if clear signs had not been with him*
> *The evidences would have reached you by report.*

Never did a false prophet rise but his ignorance, lies, corrupt ways, and the devil's hold of him, have been so apparent to anyone endowed with some common sense that he had no difficulty in discovering his falsity. That is because there is no recourse to a Prophet but to order some things and forbid others. Thus, it is in the scheme of things that he should do things that render his truthfulness apparent. On the other hand, an imposter too cannot escape but do some things and inform (about the Unseen) exposing himself in so doing, in ways more than one. An authentic Prophet is just the opposite of him. To be sure, if there were to be two cla*imān*ts to Prophethood, one an imposter and the other a true one, then, the affair cannot terminate but in one's falsehood being exposed and the other's authenticity becoming apparent: even if it might take some time. Truthfulness and virtuosity go hand in hand. And, falsehood and perversion go hand in hand. The Prophet, peace be upon him, said in a report preserved in the *Sahihayn* (Bukhari and Muslim): "Bind yourself to truth. For truth leads to piety, and piety leads to Paradise. A man does not keep uttering and pursuing the truth but is recorded as `a truthful' with Allah. And, beware of lies. For lies lead to impiety and impieties lead to the Fire. A man does not keep lying, and pursuing lies but is written `a liar' with Allah."

Now, when know that a simple thing as the truthfulness of a man, or his falsehood, is apparent from his behavior, then how can a false prophet avoid being detected? No one can fail to distinguish the true prophet from a false one.

Consequently, we notice that when Khadijah, Allah be pleased with her, had known the truthfulness of the Prophet from personal experience, and then heard from him that he had received revelation, and his apprehensions in words:

"I fear for my life," she responded with the words, "Never. By Allah, He will never let you down. For you join the kin, speak the truth, carry (the load of) the feeble, honor the guest, work for the destitute, and lend support to just causes."

Najashi too, when he asked to be read what the Prophet (*saws*) claimed to be receiving, remarked, when he had heard a portion: "By God, this and what Moses had brought have the same lamp as their source."

Warqah b. Nawfal said something close to it when he was told about what the Prophet had experienced. Warqah was no ordinary person. He had converted to Christianity and was learned enough to be able to write the Gospels in Arabic. When Khadijah, Allah be pleased with her, told him about what the Prophet had received, Warqah said: "This is the same Message that came to Moses."

Further, Allah Most High has left survive some of the signs of how He helped His Messengers and how He destroyed those nations that cried lies to them, such as the signs of the Flood, the drowning of Fir`awn and his armies, etc. When Allah narrated the stories of prophets after prophets in the chapter named *Al Shu`arā '*, such as those of Musa, Ibrahīm, Nūh and others, He followed up every episode with the words:

اِنَّ فِى ذٰلِكَ لَاٰيَةً ۭ وَّمَا كَانَ اَكْثَرُهُمْ مُّؤْمِنِيْنَ (٨) وَاِنَّ رَبَّكَ لَهُوَ الْعَزِيْزُ الرَّحِيْمُ (٩)

"In that was a sign. Most of them were not believers. And, surely, your Lord is All powerful, All Merciful." (Al Shu`arā, 8-9)

As for us, we know from reliable traditions of the past detailing the lives of the prophets, of the pious men, as also of their adversaries, to feel assured that they were true. This can be realized in ways more than one:

First, they had forewarned their people of the humiliating chastisement that would descend if they remained obdurate rejecters.

Second, what followed as a consequence when it became apparent that the people were not going to believe, such as, drowning of Fir`awn and the people of Nūh, etc.

Third, anyone who studied the life and works of the Prophets will feel convinced that they bore a high character so that the question of they speaking an untruth was out of the question.

As for our Prophet, his case is so obvious that denying his message is tantamount to denying Allah Most High Himself and alleging tyranny on his part high above that Allah is.

To explain: If someone thought that Muhammad, on whom be peace, was not a Prophet, rather a tyrant ruler, then, what it implies is that he fastened a lie on God, brought before the people something not revealed by Him, then, continued to declare the lawful as unlawful and the unlawful as lawful, declared the old Scriptural Laws null and void, slew the people, and destroyed the true followers of earlier Prophets. Yet, he is led to victories after victories. He alleged that all that was by Allah's command sent down to him. And the Lord God Himself watched him do all that in His Name, annihilating the followers of truth and continuing to lie for no less than twenty three years. Indeed, Allah seem to have helped him achieve all that, let him overcome everyone, prepared the grounds with a couple of supernatural circumstances to lead him to victories. More. He even answered his prayers, destroyed those opposed to him and raised his name over all others. Now, for Allah to let someone commit all that, in His Name, and, instead of uprooting him, help him in his plans, is only possible if Allah Himself is a tyrant, an oppressive Being, and a transgressor. Inevitably, that would lead the people to the belief that this world has no Creator nor a Lord above all. Had there been one, he would have stopped this person from doing all that. Indeed, He would have punished him with an exemplary punishment for the satisfaction of the rest of the world. The `no action' response does not befit even an ordinary king of this world. How then does it fit the King of kings and the Ruler of all rulers?

We do not deny that many liars have been successful in their own days, overcoming several opponents in their ventures. But, firstly, they did not succeed wholly, and secondly, the new situation they helped to create did not last long. In time, Allah's Messengers and their followers did away with all that they had established. This is the *Sunnah* of Allah that has been among the nations of the past. Indeed, even the unbelievers knew that. Allah said:

أَمْ يَقُولُونَ شَاعِرٌ نَتَرَبَّصُ بِهِ رَيْبَ الْمَنُونِ (٣٠) قُلْ تَرَبَّصُوا فَإِنِّي مَعَكُمْ مِّنَ الْمُتَرَبِّصِينَ (٣١)

"They say, `A poet for whom we await the Fate's uncertainty.' Say, `Wait. For I am with you one of those waiting." (Al Tūr, 30-31)

(That is, even the pagans were pretty sure that if the Prophet was phony he would be destroyed and, therefore, the best recourse was to wait for the Divine intervention).

وَ أَنَّهُ خَاتَمُ الْأَنْبِيَاء

And that he is the Last of the Prophets.

This is based on Allah's words:

وَلَٰكِنْ رَسُولَ اللهِ وَخَاتَمَ النَّبِيِّنَ

"Rather, he is Allah's Messenger and the Last of the Prophets." (Al Ahzāb, 40)

The Prophet, on whom be peace, himself said: "My example and that of those prophets who passed before me is like a man who built a house. He made it beautiful and decorated it, but for a brick space left vacant at a corner. People began going around, admiring the structure and remarking: 'Why didn't he place a brick in here too?' Lo! I am that brick. And I am the Last of the Prophets" (Bukhari).

The Prophet, on whom be peace, also said: "I bear five names. I am Muhammad and Ahmed. I am *Māhi*, (the obliterator) through whom Allah will obliterate unbelief. I am *Hāshir* (the gatherer) after whom the people will be gathered. And I am the `*Āqib*, after whom there will be no Prophet" (Bukhari).

وَإِمَام الأَتْقِيَاء

And the leader of the pious.

Leader: in the sense of one who is followed. The Prophet, on whom be peace, was raised in order that he be followed. Allah said:

قُلْ اِنْ كُنْتُمْ تُحِبُّونَ اللهَ فَاتَّبِعُوْنِيْ يُحْبِبْكُمُ اللهُ

*"Tell them: `If you love Allah, follow me. Allah will love you."* (Āl `Imrān, 31)

Thus, whoever followed him is of the pious.

وَسَيِّدُ المُرْسَلِين

And the most eminent of Messengers.

The Prophet said: "I am the most eminent of the children of Adam on the Day of Judgement. I will be the first for whom the grave will split; the first to seek intercession, and the first to be granted it." (Muslim)

If it is said that this report runs counter to the report of the *Sahihayn* which says: "Don't treat me superior to Musa, for everyone will swoon on the Day of Judgement. I will be the first to come to myself. But I will find Musa holding one of the posts of the `Arsh. Now, I don't know if he came to himself before me, or, he was one of those whom Allah spared."

The answer is, there was a good reason why the Prophet said that. What happened was that a Jew said that Musa was the best of mankind. A Muslim could not bear that. He slapped him and said: "Do you say that, even the while the Prophet is amongst us?" The Jew complained to the Prophet. It was then that the Prophet, may Allah send him peace, said these words. The rationale is, when someone is declared superior out of prejudice, fanaticism and on an absolute scale, then it is something that should be disapproved. Indeed, even when *Jihad* is conducted out of prejudice and patronage, then it is disapproved. Otherwise, they enjoyed different ranks. Allah has forbidden pride. He said:

54

تِلْكَ الرُّسُلُ فَضَّلْنَا بَعْضَهُمْ عَلَى بَعْضٍ مِّنْهُمْ مَّنْ كَلَّمَ اللهُ وَرَفَعَ بَعْضَهُمْ دَرَجْتٍ

"Those were Messengers, some of whom We preferred above others (so that) some of them Allah spoke to, and some He raised in their ranks." (Al Baqarah, 253)

Disapproved then, is that declaration of superiority that is based on pride, or with the objective of belittling another.

As for what is reported of the Prophet, who said: "Do not raise me above Yūnus b. Matti," it might be noted that this *hadīth*, in these words has not been reported by any of the authentic books of Tradition. Rather, another has been reported in the authentic collection, in words: "It is not advisable for a Muslim to say `I am better than Yūnus b. Matti.'" Another report says, "Whoever said `I am better than Yūnus b. Matti, lied.'"

The above reports order the Muslims not to imagine themselves superior to Yūnus b. Matti. They do not say that Muhammad cannot be considered better than *Yūnus*. This is because Allah Most High said about Yūnus that a whale swallowed him, and he was in a reproachable state. After that Allah said:

وَ ذَا النُّونِ إِذ ذَّهَبَ مُغَاضِبًا فَظَنَّ اَن لَّن نَّقْدِرَ عَلَيْهِ فَنَادَى فِى الظُّلُمٰتِ اَن لَّا اِلٰهَ اِلَّا اَنْتَ سُبْحٰنَكَ اِنِّى كُنْتُ مِنَ الظّٰلِمِيْنَ

"And (remember) Dhan Nūn (i.e., Yūnus) when he set forth in anger and imagined that We shall not punish him. (But when a whale swallowed him) he cried out in the darknesses: `There is no deity save You. Glory to You. Verily, I have been of the wrongdoers." (Al Anbiyā, 87)

(Influenced by the above verse,) it might occur to some people that they are better than Yūnus and therefore they do not need to seek forgiveness, admitting sins before Allah, and glorifying His name. Whoever thought that way erred. For every slave of Allah is required to say what Yūnus said:

لَّا اِلٰهَ اِلَّا اَنْتَ سُبْحٰنَكَ اِنِّى كُنْتُ مِنَ الظّٰلِمِيْنَ

"There is no deity save You. Glory to you. Verily, I have been of the wrongdoers." (Al Anbiyā, 87)

Those were also the words of other Prophets. First of them was Adam, peace be on him. He said,

رَبَّنَا ظَلَمْنَآ أَنْفُسَنَا وَإِن لَّمْ تَغْفِرْ لَنَا وَتَرْحَمْنَا لَنَكُوْنَنَّ مِنَ الْخَاسِرِيْنَ

"Our Lord! We wronged our souls. If you will not forgive us and show us mercy, most certainly we shall be of the losers." (Al A`rāf, 23)

Similarly, the last Prophet said, as preserved in a trustworthy report: "O Allah! You are the King, there is no deity save You. You are my Lord and I am Your slave. I have wronged myself and admit my sin. Therefore, forgive me all my sins. Surely, none forgives the sins except You."

In a report of *Sahih muslim* the Prophet, on whom be peace, is reported to have said to his Companions: "It has been revealed unto me that you ought to act humbly, so that none of you waxes proud over another."

Thus, Allah Most High forbid that one wax proud over another Muslim. How then can they wax proud over a Prophet?

Now, the Prophet, on whom be peace, informed us that he is the best of Adam's progeny. If he hadn't, we wouldn't have known that, as there was going to be no prophet after him to tell us that. So too, he informed us about the greatness of the Prophets before him: may Allah send peace to all of them. Accordingly, as a report goes, when he spoke of himself being the best of them, he added the words, "And that goes without pride."

Can anyone say then that the one who was taken to Paradise in his night journey, and who is so near unto Allah, occupies the same status as one who fell into the belly of the whale and who was called "blame worthy?"

وَحَبِيب رَبِّ العَالَمِين

The Beloved of the Lord of the Worlds.

The highest status of love has been proven for our Prophet, may Allah send him peace. That highest status is known as *"khullah"* (Friendship). This is proven by a report in which the Prophet said, "Allah took me as a Friend as He took Ibrahim as a Friend." He also said, "Were I to take anyone as my Friend, I would have taken Abu Bakr as my Friend. But, your companion (i.e., himself) is the Friend of the Most Merciful."

Both the above authentic reports refute the opinion of those who hold that Friendship was for Ibrahim and Love for our Prophet. But, they have to know that Allah has declared for other than the Prophets. For instance, a verse says:

$$\text{إِنَّ اللهَ يُحِبُّ التَّوَّابِينَ وَيُحِبُّ الْمُتَطَهِّرِينَ}$$

"Allah loves the repentant, and loves those who seek to purify themselves."
(Al Baqarah, 222)

As for the *hadīth*: "Ibrahim is Allah's friend and I am His beloved, and there is no pride in that," which is transmitted by Tirmidhi, well, this is a weak report because of one of the narrators, Zam`ah b. Saleh.

$$\text{وَكُلُّ دَعْوَى النُّبُوَّة بَعْدَهُ فَغَيٌّ وَهَوَى}$$

All claims to Prophethood after him are erroneous and following base desires.

That is because he is the Last of the Prophets. Anyone who claims prophethood after him is an imposter.

It should not be said, 'How can we reject someone who comes with miracles and other signs of authenticity?' The answer is, no such thing will ever happen. To think that it might happen is to think of the impossibility becoming a possibility. When Allah Most High chose to send him as the Last Messenger, it is impossible to think that someone will make a claim to prophethood and Allah will not expose his deceit.

وَهُوَ المَبْعُوثُ إلى عَامَّة الجِنّ وَكَافَّة الوَرَى، بِالْحَقّ والهُدَى، وبِالنُّور والضِّيَاء

He was sent to every one of the Jinn and mankind: with truth, guidance, a bright Light, and radiance.

As for him being sent to the Jinn, this is proven by the Qur`anic verse:

يَقَوْمَنَا أَجِيبُوا دَاعِى اللهِ وَأمِنُوا بِهِ يَغْفِرْ لَكُمْ مِّن ذُنُوبِكُمْ وَيُجِرْكُم مِّنْ عَذَابٍ اَلِيمٍ

"O our people! Respond to Allah's Caller, and believe in him. He (Allah) will forgive you your sins and save you from a painful chastisement." (Al Ahqāf, 31)

Those who were addressed in the above verse and those who said, `O our people' were the Jinns whom Allah had turned in the direction of the Prophet, on whom be peace, so they could hear the Qur`an. They went back warning their people. *Surah al Jinn* also substantiates this. Apparently, it looks like Musa, peace on him, was sent to the Jinns as well. This draws its support from Allah's statement:

قَالُوا يَقَوْمَنَا إنَّا سَمِعْنَا كِتْبًا أُنزِلَ مِنْ بَعْدِ مُوسى مُصَدِّقًا لِّمَا بَيْنَ يَدَيْهِ يَهْدِىّ إلَى الْحَقّ وَالى طَرِيقٍ مُّسْتَقِيمٍ

"They (i.e., the Jinns said), `O Our people! We have heard a book sent down after Musa confirming that which came before it. It guides to the truth and to a straight path.'" (Al Ahqāf, 30)

As for the statement that the Prophet (*saws*) was sent to the entire mankind, Allah said:

وَمَا أَرْسَلْنَكَ إلَّا كَآفَّةً لِّلنَّاسِ بَشِيرًا وَّنَذِيرًا

"And We have not sent you but unto all mankind: bearer of glad tidings and as a Warner." (Sabā, 28)

Allah also said:

قُلْ يَأَيُّهَا النَّاسُ إنِّى رَسُولُ اللهِ إلَيْكُمْ جَمِيعًا

"Say, `O people. I am a Messenger of Allah unto all of you." (Al A`rāf, 158)

The Prophet, on whom be peace said, "I have been given five things that none of the Prophets before me received: I have been helped with terror from a distance of a month's journey; the earth has been declared clean unto me, therefore, let anyone pray (on plain ground) whenever the prayer time arrives; war spoils have been declared lawful unto me   they weren't lawful to anyone before me; I have been bestowed with the gift of Intercession; and, earlier Prophets were sent specifically to their people, whereas, I have been sent to the entire mankind" (Bukhari and Muslim).

He also said: "None of my own people, nor of the Jews or Christians who heard of me, yet didn't believe in me, but will be in the Fire." (*Muslim*)

Indeed, the fact that the Prophet, peace be upon him, was sent to the mankind in general is one of the basic knowledge of Islam.

As for the claims by the Christian that he was a Prophet for the Arabs alone, that is baseless. For the Prophet, on whom be peace, himself declared that he was sent to the entire mankind. And a Prophet does not lie. He sent his letters of invitation to the emperors of Rome, Persia and rulers of other states such as of Egypt.

وَأَنَّ الْقُرْآن كَلام الله، مِنْهُ بَدَا بِلاكَيْفِيَّةٍ، قَولاً، وَأَنْزَلَهُ عَلَى رَسُولِهِ، وحْيًا، وَصَدَّقَه الْمُؤْمِنُون عَلَى ذَلِكَ، حِقًّا، وَأَيْقَنُوا أَنَّهُ كَلام الله تَعَالَى بِالْحَقِيقَة، لَيْسَ بِمَخْلُوق كَكَلام الْبَرِيَّة، فَمَن سَمِعَهُ فَزَعَمَ أَنَّهُ كَلام الْبَشَر فَقَد كَفَرَ، وَقَد ذَمَّهُ الله وَعَابَهُ وَ أَوْعَدَهُ بِسَقَر، حَيْثُ قَال تَعَالَى: (سَأُصْلِيهِ سَقَر)، فَلَمَّا أَوْعَدَ الله بِسَقَر لِمَن قَال: (إنْ هَذَا إلا قولُ الْبَشَر) عَلِمْنَا وَأَيْقَنَّا أَنَّهُ قَوْل خَالِقِ الْبَشَر، وَلَا يُشْبِه قَولُ الْبَشَر

And that the Qur`an is the Word of Allah. It originated from Him, without (us being able to figure out) the how of it: a Speech. He sent it down upon His Messenger: a Revelation. The believers declared true His avowal and felt assured that it was Allah's Word in truth, and not a created word, in the fashion of the words of the created beings. Therefore, whoever heard it and alleged that they are man's words, disbelieved. Allah has censured him, denounced him, and has promised him Hell fire. He said: "I shall fling him into *Saqar* (Hell fire)." When He promised Hell fire to those who said: "This is nothing but the speech

of a man," we knew and felt assured that this is the Speech of the Creator of mankind; and that the speech of mankind cannot resemble it.

This is an important principle of the religion of Islam and an issue over which many sects of Islam lost their way. Nevertheless, this is the truth, which anyone would conclude who gave a serious thought to the subject, with the evidences of the Qur`an and *Sunnah* in his mind, applying himself with plain logic and a straightforward thinking not affected by doubts, skepticism and fanciful thoughts.

As for the author's words: "It originated from Him, without (us being able to figure out) the how of it: a Speech," is to refute the Mu`tazilah and others who claim that the Qur`an did not originate from Him. They say, ascription to Him is only way of honor, such as: Allah's House, Allah's c, etc. But, their contention is wrong, for, ascription to Allah is of two kinds: those that are of incorporeal nature (related to notions and concepts), and those that are corporeal. No doubt, the ascription to Him of the corporeal beings is by way of honoring them, since they are created, such as "Allah's House." However, ascription of the incorporeal is another thing altogether, such as, Allah's Knowledge, Allah's Power, Allah's Speech, etc. These are His Attributes. It is unthinkable that any of them should be a creation.

The Attribute of Speech is one of the Perfect Attributes. To be without it is a sign of imperfection. Allah said:

وَاتَّخَذَ قَوْمُ مُوسَى مِنْ بَعْدِهِ مِنْ حُلِيِّهِمْ عِجْلاً جَسَدًا لَهُ خُوَارٌ اَلَمْ يَرَوْا اَنَّهُ لَا يُكَلِّمُهُمْ وَلَا يَهْدِيهِمْ سَبِيلاً

"Musa's followers took in his absence a calf (for worship) made out of their jewelry: the body (of a calf) with a lowing. Didn't they notice that it did not talk to them nor could guide them?" (Al A`rāf, 148)

Surely, those who worshipped the calf, despite being unbelievers, knew better than the Mu`tazilah. They did not decry to Musa in reverse objection, "Your Lord also does not speak!?"

Allah Most High also said about the calf:

اَفَلَا يَرَوْنَ اَلَّا يَرْجِعُ اِلَيْهِمْ قَوْلاًوَّلَا يَمْلِكُ لَهُمْ ضَرًّا وَّلَا نَفْعًا

"Did they not notice that it did not return them a word (as answer) and did not have the power to harm them or do them good?" (Tāhā, 89)

It is easy to see that the inability of the calf to respond and speak out was a proof against its divinity.

The most that can be said is that the above leads to anthropomorphism and of suggestion of a form to Him. But when we say that Allah Speaks in a manner that befits Him, the objection is removed. Don't you read the words of Allah?

$$\text{اَلْيَوْمَ نَخْتِمُ عَلَى اَفْوَاهِهِمْ وَتُكَلِّمُنَا اَيْدِيْهِمْ وَتَشْهَدُ اَرْجُلُهُمْ}$$

"Today, We shall seal their mouths. Their hands will speak to Us and their feet will testify." (Yāsin, 65)

We believe that the limbs will speak out, although we do not know how exactly that will happen. So also the words of Allah:

$$\text{وَقَالُوْا لِجُلُوْدِهِمْ لِمَ شَهِدتُّمْ عَلَيْنَا قَالُوْا اَنْطَقَنَا اللهُ}$$

"They will ask their skins, 'Why did you testify against us?' They will reply, 'Allah made us speak out.'" (Fussilat, 21)

The author also hinted at this by using the word: "It originated from Him, without us (being able to figure out) the how of it: a Speech." That is to say, it came of Him, but we cannot explain how the Speech took place. He emphasized his words with the word "a Speech," that should leave no doubt that it was something real and not figurative. It is in the same manner as Allah Most High emphasized His Speech to Musa by saying:

$$\text{وَكَلَّمَ اللهُ مُوْسَى تَكْلِيْمًا}$$

"Allah spoke to Musa, direct." (Al Nisā, 164)

The addition of the word direct (*taklimān*) was to emphasize that it is not the figurative meaning that was intended here.

It is said that one of the Mu`tazilah asked `Amr b. al `Ala, one of the famous seven Reciters, to read in the following manner:

وَكَلَّمَ اللهُ مُوسَى تَكْلِيمًا

that is, with Allah of the text in the accusative, which would give out the meaning, "And Musa spoke to Allah," and not "Allah spoke to Musa." When he said that, Abu `Amr replied, "Assuming that I recite it that way, what will you do with the words of Allah:

وَلَمَّا جَآءَ مُوسَى لِمِيقَاتِنَا وَكَلَّمَهُ رَبُّهُ

"When Musa came up to the place appointed by Us, His Lord spoke to him." *(Al A`rāf, 143)*

That left the Mu`tazilite speechless.

How many times the Qur`an and *Sunnah* have not spoken of Allah's direct speech with the dwellers of Paradise and others? He said:

سَلَمٌ قَوْلاً مِّن رَّبٍّ رَّحِيمٍ

"Peace. A word from their Lord." *(Yāsin, 58)*

He also said:

اِنَّ الَّذِيْنَ يَشْتَرُوْنَ بِعَهْدِ اللهِ وَاَيْمَانِهِمْ ثَمَنًا قَلِيْلًا أُولٰٓئِكَ لَا خَلَاقَ لَهُمْ فِي الْآخِرَةِ وَلَا يُكَلِّمُهُمُ اللهُ وَلَا يَنْظُرُ اِلَيْهِمْ

"Surely, those who sell out Allah's compact and their oaths for a paltry price, they shall have no share in the Hereafter. Allah will not speak to them, nor will He look at them." *(Āl `Imrān, 77)*

Allah disgraced them by denying His kindly speech to them as He said in another place that He will say to them while they are in the Fire:

قَالَ اخْسَئُوا فِيْهَا وَلَا تُكَلِّمُونِ

"He will say, `Be you driven into it (with ignominy) and do not speak to Me." *(Al Mu'minūn, 108)*

Now, if Allah didn't speak to the believers in Him, they and the unbelievers would be on par, nor would there have been any point in saying that He is not going to speak to the unbelievers. Imam Bukhari also understood the reports in the same manner. He composed a whole chapter concerning Allah's Speech to the dwellers of Paradise, narrating several *ahādith* under that head.

The best of blessings for the dwellers of Paradise would be to see Allah's Face and His Speech to them. To deny that is to deny the very essence of the pleasures in Paradise and the most coveted of things for its dwellers.

As for the Mu`tazilah argument with the words, "Allah is the Creator of all things," and that the Qur`an is one of the things included by default, and hence created   this is a strange proposition for them to make. For they themselves believe that people's deeds and acts are their own creation, not created by Allah. How can they exclude this "thing" from the general statement and include the Speech, which is not a thing, rather, an Attribute? Especially so when it is by it (i.e., by His command, which is a Speech), that things are brought into being. Allah said:

وَالشَّمْسَ وَالْقَمَرَ وَالنُّجُومَ مُسَخَّرَاتٍ بِأَمْرِهِ أَلَا لَهُ الْخَلْقُ وَالْأَمْرُ

"The sun, the moon and the stars are subdued by His command. Lo! For Him is the creation, and for Him the command." (Al A`rāf, 54)

We see in the above statement that Allah Most High distinguished the "Creation" from "the command." If the command itself was a created entity, it would require another command to create it, and the next command, another command, and so on. We would run in a circle.

The word "every" however, will depend on the context for its meaning. Don't you see that Allah said?

تُدَمِّرُ كُلَّ شَيْءٍ بِأَمْرِ رَبِّهَا فَأَصْبَحُوا لَا يُرَى إِلَّا مَسَاكِنُهُمْ

"It destroyed everything by the command of its Lord and they ended up (in such a way that) you saw nothing (of them) but their lodges." (Al Ahqāf, 25)

You see in the words above that the word "everything" did not include their lodgings. What was meant is that the wind destroyed all that the winds normally destroy.

In the like manner are Allah's words concerning Bilqis: "She was given everything." That is to say, everything that the rulers require. The kind and nature of 'condition' imposed will depend on the context. In the present context the hoopoe meant that she (Bilqis) was a completely independent queen, possessed of the necessary power. Many other examples can be cited.

The meaning then of, "Allah is the creator of everything," is, "all those things that are creations." That is, all that is 'a being,' save Allah Himself, has been created. This will include the acts of the people. But it does not include Allah Himself. His Attributes are part of His Being, inseparable from Him.

As for their argument with the help of the verse:

إِنَّا جَعَلْنَٰهُ قُرْءَٰنًا عَرَبِيًّا لَّعَلَّكُمْ تَعْقِلُونَ

"We have indeed made it an Arabic Qur`an*,"* *(Al Zukhruf, 3)*

well, it is not a clever argument. For, the word *"ja`ala"* of the text, can be grammatically used in two ways. Either accompanied by a single object, or by two objects. Now, if it is used with a single object, it is possible to derive the meaning of "created." Some examples are:

وَجَعَلَ الظُّلُمَٰتِ وَالنُّورَ

"He created the light." (Al An`ām, 1)

Or,

وَجَعَلْنَا مِنَ الْمَآءِ كُلَّ شَىْءٍ حَىٍّ

"And We created every living thing out of water." (Al Anbiyā', 30)

In contrast, when the word *"ja`ala"* is accompanied by two objects, then, the meaning derived is, "made" and not "created." Allah said:

وَلَا تَنقُضُوا الْأَيْمَٰنَ بَعْدَ تَوْكِيدِهَا وَقَدْ جَعَلْتُمُ اللهَ عَلَيْكُمْ كَفِيلًا

"And do not break the oaths, after confirming them, the while you have made Allah your surety." (Al Nahal, 91)

In the above verse "Allah" and "surety" are the two objects of *"ja`ala"*. Similarly,

الَّذِيْنَ جَعَلُوا الْقُرْآنَ عِضِيْنَ

"Those who made the Qur`an *into shreds." (Al Hijr, 91)*

Once again, there are two objects: "the Qur`an" and "shreds"

The following verse is also in the same style of expression:

اِنَّا جَعَلْنٰهُ قُرْءٰنًا عَرَبِيًّا

"We have made this an Arabic Qur`an *so that you might ponder." (Al Zukhruf, 3)*

In the above verse, "Arabic" and "Qur`an" are two objects.

Now, if it is asked, what do you have to say to the following verse:

اِنَّهٗ لَقَوْلُ رَسُوْلٍ كَرِيْمٍ

"Verily. It is a word of an honored messenger?" (Al Takwīr, 19 & Al Hāqqah, 40)

that is, it can be said, `either of the two Messengers created it: Muhammad or Jibril.' The answer is, the very use of the word "Messenger" tells us that he has been sent and carries the message of someone else. The Qur`an didn't say that it is the word of the angel, or the Prophet (rather, it said, `the word of the Messenger'). This tells us that he was conveying from one who had commissioned him. Moreover, the allusion here by the term "Messenger" is to Jibril. In the other verse (*Al Hāqqah*, 40), the allusion by the term "Messenger" is to Muhammad. This proves that the allusion to them both is to convey the sense of "delivery of message," for, if we accept one of them as the originator then the other is left out.

Also, in the verse that follows the verse quoted above (of *Al Takwīr*), the occurrence of the adjective `trustworthy' lends the meaning that the Messenger does not add or subtract. He merely transmits what is revealed to him. (This also proves that he is not the originator: tr.).

Further, Allah (*swt*) declared a person an unbeliever who said that the Qur`an is the word of a human being. Now, Muhammad was a man. Therefore, whoever said that it is a creation of Muhammad, disbelieved: there being no difference between one who alleged that it is the word of a man, or of a Jinn, or of an angel. Although, the declaration of apostasy would be made against a person only if he happens to make a statement (of faith about it) and did not say so answering a question. (That is, if someone is asked about a verse as to whose words they are , and he gave the wrong answer out of ignorance, then, in that case, he would not be declared a heretic: tr.).

To sum up. The *Ahl al Sunnah*, all of them, the four schools of law included, as well as others of the earlier and the later ones are in agreement that Allah's Word is uncreated. Had people been left to themselves, on their own pristine natures, there would not have occurred any differences between them. But Shaytan whispered to them wrong ideas to create differences among them. Surely, those who divided themselves over the Book are in a far fetched schism.

However, what the statement of Tahawi points out to is that Allah has remained One who speaks, whenever He wishes and howsoever He wishes, and that His words are eternal. Imam Abu Hanifah was also very near this opinion when he wrote in his "*Al fiqh al Akbar*": "The Qur`an which is written down in Scriptures and which is preserved in the hearts, recited by the tongues, and revealed to the Prophet is, when uttered by our mouths, the created word, although the Qur`an by itself is uncreated."

Undoubtedly too, when the Prophets spoke to the people and informed them that Allah had spoken to them, or called them, or whispered to them, or that, 'He said,' etc., they did not mean that these are created qualities, apart from His Being and Essence. Rather, what they meant is that it was Allah Himself who spoke to them, hat He re established the Word, and not without Him and that it was He Himself who spoke (and not someone else on His behalf). Accordingly, we find `A'isha, peace be on her, making the following statement: "I am much more humbler than that Allah should speak about me in a revelation that was to be later recited by the people." Had she any other meaning in mind, she would have then spoken it out, since, this was the most suitable point for it. A delay over such matters, when the need was the most, is disallowed.

66

The Prophet himself, may Allah send peace to him, said: "I seek refuge with the Complete Words of Allah." Can anyone claim that the Prophet sought the refuge of a created thing? The Prophet has made it impossible to extract such a meaning by saying, as in other reports: "(O Allah) I seek refuge in Your Pleasure from Your Anger, and I seek refuge in Your Forgiveness from Your Punishment." All these (words, forgiveness etc.,: tr.) are obviously Allah's Attributes.

The external aspect of Allah's Word is that which is heard from Him or from one who transmitted it from Him. Now, when someone hears it, comprehends it, and preserves it, then, for him, the Word of Allah is that which was heard and which was preserved. Consequently, when the listener repeats it, then it is his recitation. When it is written down, then it is the written word. In all these cases, the Word takes real forms. It cannot be denied as the word of Allah, whereas, as we know, the figurative can be denied. It is not right to say, for instance, that what is written in the scriptures, is not the Word of Allah, or, the reciter did not recite the Word of Allah. Allah Himself said:

وَاِنْ اَحَدٌ مِّنَ الْمُشْرِكِيْنَ اسْتَجَارَكَ فَاَجِرْهُ حَتّٰى يَسْمَعَ كَلٰمَ اللهِ

"And, if one of the pagans seeks asylum with you, grant him asylum until he has heard the Word of Allah." (Al Tawbah, 6)

Of course, he does not hear the Word of Allah from Allah. He hears it from someone who is transmitting it on behalf of Allah. This also refutes the claim of those who say that what is heard can be designated as a 'semantic content originating from Allah,' but it is not 'the Word' of Allah *per se*. That stands refuted because Allah said,

حَتّٰى يَسْمَعَ كَلٰمَ اللهِ

"Until he has heard the Word of Allah." (Al Tawbah, 6)

Note the words. Allah did not say, "Until he has heard what can be designated as a 'semantic content originating from Allah.'"

Those who said that what is written in the book form is a "kind of Allah's Word," or, "a narration from Allah," or like words, and that it does not contain the Words of Allah, opposed the Qur`an, the *Sunnah* and the pious forefathers of this *Ummah*. It is enough to be misguided to believe in that.

Tahawi's words too reject the belief of those who say that it is "a meaning" that cannot be imagined to have been heard from Him; and that what is heard, revealed, recited or written down is a "sort of Allah's Word" not the Word itself. For he said: "It originated from Him." Such are also the statements of the pious predecessors. They said, "It originated from Him and will return unto Him." They had to specifically say the words, "it originated from Him" because the Jahmiyyah an offshoot of the Mu`tazilah used to say that He created the Word in a particular place or position, and then from that point it manifested later. The *Salaf* said, in refutation: "It originated from Him," that is, He is the Speaker. In other words it manifested from Him, and not from any of His creations. As said Allah Most High:

$$\text{تَنْزِيلُ الْكِتَابِ مِنَ اللهِ الْعَزِيزِ الْحَكِيمِ}$$

"Sending down of the Book from Allah the Mighty, the Wise." (Al Zumar, 1)

He also said:

$$\text{وَلَكِنْ حَقَّ الْقَوْلُ مِنِّي}$$

"Rather, a Word from Me will come true." (Al Sajdah, 13)

The meaning of the words of the *Salaf* who said, "To Him it will return," is, it will be removed from the breasts and the Scriptures, so that not a verse will remain in the breasts or in a written form, as reported in several *ahādith*.

His words, "Without (us being able to figure out) the how of it," is to convey the meaning that we do not know the manner of His Speech which was in real words, not figurative. His words, "He sent it down upon His Messenger: a Revelation": That is, He sent it to him through an angel, so that angel Jibril heard it from Allah and the Messenger heard it from Jibril and then recited it to the people. Allah said:

$$\text{نَزَلَ بِهِ الرُّوحُ الْأَمِينُ (١٩٣) عَلَى قَلْبِكَ لِتَكُونَ مِنَ الْمُنْذِرِينَ (١٩٤) بِلِسَانٍ عَرَبِيٍّ مُبِينٍ (١٩٥)}$$

"Jibril brought it down, on your heart so that you might be of the warners in clear Arabic language." (Al Shu`arā, 193-195)

Tahawi's words, "(The believers) declared true His avowal and felt assured that it was Allah's Word in truth, and not a created word, in the fashion of the words of the created beings," are meant to refute the Mu`tazilah and others who said that it is "a meaning established within the Person (of Allah)," which has not been heard form Allah (Himself). Rather, it is the Speech of the Inner Self. That kind of reasoning stands rejected because, if someone spoke to his inner self, without speaking out the words, then he cannot be said to have uttered the words in truth. To say that would be to declare that a dumb spoke, or would be like saying `what is to be found written in the Scriptures is neither the Qur`an nor the Word of Allah, rather, a kind of expression by Allah.' That is, to reduce them to the same status as the signals of a dumb man. Let us say the other man understood the meaning, and wrote it down in words what he thought the dumb person was trying to say. Obviously, what was written down was, at best an expression from the dumb man. Alternatively, what was written down was the understanding of the man (dictated to) of the meaning the other man signaled. This is the example of what the Mu`tazilah say. Although none of them dare say that Allah is dumb, yet, what they say is that what Jibril understood is the meaning that is "established" within Him, without hearing a word from Him or even a voice. Rather, he understood the meaning alone. Then he expressed it in his own words. Thus it works out that it is he who originated the Qur`an and the written scripture we have in the Arabic language.

The words of the following *hadīth* can be quoted to refute him who said that the Qur`an is "a meaning established within the Person (of Allah).," The Prophet said: "Nothing of the words of the people suit this Prayer of ours." (That is, no words of human origin should be introduced into the Prayers. It should be offered in those words alone that have been taught by the Prophet: tr.). Also the Prophet's words: "Allah speaks of His affairs what He will. And, of the things He has said is that you should not utter (your own words) in the Prayers." Hence, the scholars are agreed that if a man spoke out his own words, intentionally, without there being any need of it in the Prayer, then that Prayer is invalid. They are also in unison in saying that what one speaks to oneself, within his heart and mind, of the things of this world, does not invalidate the Prayers. What will invalidate it is speaking out those words by mouth. This tells us that all Muslims agree that what one says to himself, within his self, is not "speech."

Therefore, whoever said that the Word of Allah, is a meaning established in the Person of Allah and that what is recited, compiled in books, or heard from a reciter is an expression from Allah, and that, which in turn is created, alleged that the Qur`an itself is the created word, without realizing the implications of what he is saying. Allah Most High said:

قُل لَّبِنِ اجْتَمَعَتِ الْإِنْسُ وَالْجِنُّ عَلَى اَنْ يَأْتُوا بِمِثْلِ هٰذَا الْقُرْآنِ لَا يَأْتُونَ بِمِثْلِهِ

"Say, `If the Jinn and mankind were to agree upon producing something similar to this Qur'an, *they will not be able to produce anything similar to it." (Al Isrā', 88)*

Do you think that in the above words Allah is speaking of a meaning established in His Person or to what is being recited and heard? Doubtlessly, He is speaking of the recited and the heard, for, what has been spoken of is nothing but what is recited and what is heard and nothing else.

Consider the words, "they will not be able to bring it." Do you think that Allah is saying: 'They will not be able to bring what is in My Person and Self   of what they have not heard and not known?' Additionally, when, as we know that there is no way we can learn what is in Allah's Person.

Tahawi's words, "Whoever heard it and thought that they are man's words, disbelieved," is the standard position and the truth. There is no difference of opinion over the declaration of apostasy in favor of anyone who said that the Qur`an is not the Word of Allah, or whoever alleged that it is the word of Muhammad, or of someone else, either an angel or a human being. As a matter of fact, if one acknowledged that it is the Word of Allah, and then tried to interpret or altered the Word of Allah, then he is one of those who agree   someway or the other, with the one who said:

إِنْ هٰذَآ إِلَّا قَوْلُ الْبَشَرِ

"This is nothing but the words of a man." (Al Muddaththir, 25)

The meaning of Tahawi's words, "And none of the speech of the mankind resembles it," is also to say that it is the most honored Word, at the highest level of rhetoric and the most truthful. Allah Most High said:

وَمَنْ اَصْدَقُ مِنَ اللهِ حَدِيثًا

"And who can be more truthful in speech?" (Al Nisā', 87)

70

And He said:

قُلْ فَأْتُوا بِسُورَةٍ مِّثْلِهِ

"Say, `Bring a chapter similar to it." (Yūnus, 38)

Now, when they—the earlier Arabs—failed, although they were the best of rhetoricians, and most avowed enemies of Islam, in bringing its equal, the authenticity of the Prophet's claim that it is a revelation of Allah stood proven.

As for its miraculous nature, it is both from the point of view of its style as well as its meaning, and not from the point of view of any one of them singly.

و من وَصَفَ اللَّه بمعنى من معاني البَشرِ، فقد كَفَرَ، من أَبْصَرَ هذا اعتَبَرَ، وعن مثلِ قولِ الكفارِ انزجَرْ، وعَلِمَ أنه بصفتِه ليس كالبَشر

Whoever ascribed to Allah a meaning that is employed for the humans committed unsbelief. Therefore, whoever (of the believers) noticed that, might consider (such ascription) thoroughly, and then, treating them like other utterances of the unbelievers, abandon them, as he knows that He does not resemble anyone of the humankind in any Attribute.

When Tahawi stated that the Qur`an is a Speech of Allah, from Whom it originated, he warned in the above passage that none of the Attributes of Allah are like the attributes of the humans so that any thought of similarity should be driven out. In other words, if Allah Most High described Himself as one who Speaks, He cannot be attributed with the sense and meaning that humans attribute to themselves to their talk. For there is nothing like Allah. He is All hearing, All seeing.

والرؤيةُ حقٌّ لأهلِ الجنّةِ، بغيرِ إحاطَةٍ ولا كيفيةٍ، كما نَطَقَ به كتابُ ربِّنا (وُجُوهٌ يَوْمَئِذٍ نَاضِرَةٌ إِلَى رَبِّهَا نَاظِرَةٌ)، وتفسيرُهُ على ما أرادَ اللهُ تعالى و عَلَّمَه، وكلُّ ما جاءَ في ذلك من الحديثِ الصحيح عن رسولِ اللهِ صلى الله عليه وسلم فهو كما قال: ومعناهُ على ما أرَاد، لا نَدخُل في ذَلك مُتَأوِّلين بآرائِنا، وَلا مُتَوهِّمين بأهوائِنا فإنه ما سَلِم في دينه إلا من سَلَّم للهِ عز و جل ولرسوله صلى الله عليه وسلَّمَ، و رد عِلمَ ما اشتَبَه عليه إلى عالِمِه

The Beatific Vision for the dwellers of Paradise is an established fact without (they) encompassing (Him) and without (figuring out) the how of it; as spoke out the Book of our Lord: "Some faces that day shall be bright, looking up at their Lord." The explanation of this should follows what Allah willed and taught. All that has been reported in authentic traditions as the Prophet's statement in this connection, follow the same rule, and have the meaning that he intended. We do not indulge in interpretations following our own judgment or fancies. For no one is safe in his religion but he who submitted himself to Allah and His Messenger and left what he did not understand to one who understood it.

This is Tahawi's refutation of those who rejected the Beatific Vision: that of the believers seeing their Lord when they would have entered Paradise. The Jahmiyyah, the Mu`tazilah and those who followed them have denied this. Their opinion is repudiated by the statements in the Qur`an and *Sunnah*. The Companions, their Followers, the well known Imams (of jurisprudence), the *Ahl al hadīth*, and all those who attribute themselves to the *Ahl al Sunnah wa al Jama`ah* have confirmed the Vision. Tahawi has presented a verse in evidence:

وُجُوهٌ يَوْمَئِذٍ نَّاضِرَةٌ (٢٢) إِلَى رَبِّهَا نَاظِرَةٌ (٢٣)

"Some faces that day shall be bright, looking up at their Lord." (Al Qiyāmah, 22-23)

This verse is one of the clearest of proofs. As for those who are bent upon corruption of the meaning in the name of interpretation, (they failed to realize that) misinterpretation of the texts concerning the Resurrection, Paradise, the Fire, the Reckoning, etc., is much easier than misinterpretation of the verses at hand. Yet, never a person desired to give a wrong interpretation to the texts, but found a way to do it, such as those who misinterpreted this particular text.

This in fact is one of those things that have corrupted religion and the life in general. This is what the Jews and Christians did with the texts of their Scriptures: the *Tawrah* (Torah) and *Injil* (New Testament). We have been warned against following their ways. But those in error refused to submit.

In any case, it might be noticed that the ascription of the sight (of eye) to the face (of the one sighting) and the addition of the article *"ilā"* clearly points to the meaning of the vision by the eye, and, finally, the absence of anything else in the context that would allow for a different meaning, are well placed arguments that Allah intended to assert the vision of His Self, with the eyes that are in one's face. Inarguably, the word *"naẓr"* (sight) is used in several ways, depending on the suffixes and grammatical forms. If it is used in the transitive form that returns to itself, then the meaning is: "wait" or "pause." Such as, in the words of Allah:

انْظُرُونَا نَقْتَبِسْ مِنْ نُورِكُمْ

"Wait for us so that we can borrow of your Light." (Al Hadīd, 13)

On the other hand if it has the article *"fi"* suffixed to it, then it has the meaning of "consideration," or "ponder," etc., as in the words of Allah:

اَوَلَمْ يَنْظُرُوا فِيْ مَلَكُوتِ السَّمٰوٰتِ وَالْأَرْضِ

"Have they not seen in the kingdom of the heavens and the earth?" (Al A`rāf, 185)

In contrast, when it is suffixed with *"ilā"* then, it means to "look up at a thing," to "see it," to "behold it," etc., with one's eyes. Allah said:

اُنْظُرُوا اِلٰى ثَمَرِهٖ اِذَآ اَثْمَرَ وَيَنْعِهٖ

"Behold (then) its fruit when it fructifies and (look at) its ripening." (Al An`ām, 99)

How strongly not then, when the "beholding" is related to the faces with which sighting takes place. Allah also said, elsewhere:

لِلَّذِيْنَ اَحْسَنُوا الْحُسْنٰى وَزِيَادَةٌ

"For those who did well, is the (ultimate) Good and more." (Yūnus, 26)

In the above verse "*husna*" (translated as the "[ultimate] Good"), is Paradise, and with the words "and more" the allusion is to the sighting of Allah Most High, as explained by the Prophet, on whom be peace. A report in Muslim narrated by Suhayb says: "The Prophet, on whom be peace, recited this verse, 'For those who did well, is the (ultimate) Good and more,' and then added, 'When the people of Paradise would have entered Paradise, and the people of Fire, the Fire, a caller will call: "O people of Paradise. Allah has made a promise to you which He wishes to fulfill." They will enquire: 'What is it? Didn't He effect increase in the weight of our balance, brightened our faces, admitted us into Paradise and released us from the Fire?' At that the veil will be removed and they will see Him. And, He wouldn't have given them anything dearer than to be seeing Him. This is the "*ziyādah*" (the more that He spoke of).'"

There are several other reports, differently worded, to the same effect. The Companions also understood it in the same sense. Ibn Jarir al Tabari has reported Abu Bakr, Hudhayfah, Abu Musa al Ash`ari and Ibn `Abbas as holding the same opinion.

Allah also said:

$$\text{كَلَّا إِنَّهُمْ عَن رَّبِّهِمْ يَوْمَئِذٍ لَّمَحْجُوبُونَ}$$

"Nay. That Day they shall be veiled from their Lord." (Al Mutaffifin, 15)

Shafe`i and other Imams have used this verse too as a proof of the Beatific Vision for the dwellers of Paradise. Al Tabari has reported Muzani as narrating the words of Imam Shafe`i: 'If these would be denied the vision because of Allah's anger, it proves that His Friends will see Him.'

As for the Mu`tazilah arguing with the statements of the Qur`an

$$\text{لَن تَرَانِي}$$

"You cannot bear to See Me." (Al A`rāf, 143)

or, the words:

$$\text{لَّا تُدْرِكُهُ الْأَبْصَارُ}$$

"Visions cannot grasp Him." (Al An`ām, 103),

74

The above two verses in fact refute them. The first verse leads us to the Beatific Vision in several ways.

Firstly, it cannot be imagined that Musa, the one who spoke to His Lord directly, an honored Messenger and, during his tenure the most knowledgeable of the people, to be asking Allah what was out of the question. (That is, if it was impossible, Musa, peace on him, would not have made the request in the first place: tr.).

Secondly, Allah Most High did not disapprove of his supplication. In contrast, when Nūh requested the saving of his son, Allah told him (*Hūd*, 46): "*I admonish you not to be of the ignorant.*"

Thirdly, Allah Most High said in response to Musa's request, "You cannot bear to see Me." He didn't say, "I cannot be seen," or, "It is not possible to see Me." The difference between the two kinds of replies should be apparent. What was meant was that Musa, peace on him, could not bear to see Him in this world, because of the weakness inherent in man.

Fourthly, Allah's words:

وَلَكِنِ انْظُرْ إِلَى الْجَبَلِ فَإِنِ اسْتَقَرَّ مَكَانَهُ فَسَوْفَ تَرَانِيْ

"But look at the mountain. If it stays in its place, you will be able to see me."
(Al Aʿrāf, 143)

Allah informed him that if the mountain despite its strength cannot bear the sight of Allah, then how can a human being, much weaker than it, bear to see Him?

Fifthly, Allah's words:

فَلَمَّا تَجَلَّى رَبُّهُ لِلْجَبَلِ جَعَلَهُ دَكًّا

"When His Lord manifested Himself to the mountain, He reduced it to dust."
(Al Aʿrāf, 143)

Now, if it is possible for Allah to manifest Himself to a mountain, which is lifeless, how can it be thought impossible for Allah's Messengers and Friends, (that He should not manifest Himself to them, especially) in a place of Honor (i.e., Paradise)? Rather, Allah simply demonstrated to Musa that if the mountain could not bear to see Him, then, obviously, man is weaker.

Sixthly, Allah spoke to Musa, called out, and whispered to him. Now, if speaking to him directly, without an intermediary, was possible, then seeing should also be possible. Therefore, the Beatific Vision cannot be denied without denying Allah's Speech.

The Mu`tazilah argue with the article "*lun*" of the text (*lun tarani*, in which *lun* [pronounced as "gun"] literally means "never"). But it is incorrect to extend the impossibility of sight to the life of the Hereafter in the light of these words. The presence of the article "*lun*" does not lend the meaning of denial of the sight forever. How then when it is free of the article "*lun?*"

To cite an example, Allah said:

$$وَ لَنْ يَّتَمَنَّوْهُ أَبَدًا$$

"They shall never wish it (i.e., death)." (Al Baqarah, 95)

However, despite the above statement, Allah also told us about them:

$$وَنَادَوْا يٰمٰلِكُ لِيَقْضِ عَلَيْنَا رَبُّكَ$$

"They will cry out (in Hell, unable to bear the punishment), `O Malik. Let your Lord give us death." (Al Zukhruf, 77)

The above shows that the "lun" of the text in discussion is not for eternity. It is for a limited period. If it had been for eternity an exception would not be possible, as in the words of Allah:

$$فَلَنْ أَبْرَحَ الْأَرْضَ حَتّٰى يَأْذَنَ لِيْ أَبِيْ$$

"I shall never depart from (this) land, until my father allows me." (Yūsuf, 80)

The above shows that "*lun*" does not always demand eternity.

In one of his grammatical compositions consisting of a 1000 couplets, Sheikh Jamaluddin b. Malik, may Allah show him mercy, has stated that "*lun*" does not always imply eternity.

As for the second verse (i.e. "Sights cannot perceive Him), it also leads to the deduction, although in a subtle manner, of the possibility of the Beatific Vision. It is as follows.

Allah Most High stated those words in a situation of praise. Now, it is known that praise is for positive Attributes. As for lack of an attribute, it cannot be a proof of one's perfection. Therefore, one cannot be praised for them. Allah may be praised for a negative Attribute only when it guarantees the existence of another attribute such as, He praising Himself over the negation of slumber and sleep. That assures Perfection of Subsistence. Negation of death guarantees perfection of Life. Negation of fatigue and tiresomeness points to perfection of Power. Negation of an associate, a spouse, a son or helper, proves the perfection of His Lordship, Divinity, and Over powering Quality. Negation of Oppression is to speak of the perfection of His Justice, Knowledge, and Self sufficiency. Negation of forgetfulness and unawareness of a thing leads to perfection of His knowledge and all comprehensiveness. Negation of someone similar to Him is to impress the perfection of His Essence and Attributes.

Hence we see that praise is not declared for something (say a bad trait: tr.), lacking in someone   unless it demands the existence of a positive (trait),   for, in such a case, that which is lacking (in a person) shares the one qualified with it, in that non existence. On the other hand, a perfect being is not ascribed with any quality that he shares with the non existent. Therefore, His words: "Sights cannot encompass Him," point to the perfection of His Majesty, that He is greater than anything else, so that He cannot be seen by sights that can encompass Him wholly, for "*idrāk*" of the Arabic is used for encompassing something fully, which is an aspect more than simple sighting. So, Allah Most High can be seen but He cannot be encompassed. As, for example, it is one thing to know, and another to know fully. This is what the Companions and the founders of the schools of thought understood from this verse. Indeed, although the sun is a created thing, it cannot be sighted in a manner that it can be encompassed.

As for the *ahādith* that speak of the Beatific Vision, there are several of them. Abu Hurayrah narrates one of them as preserved in the *Sahihayn*. It says that the Companions asked the Prophet: "O Messenger of Allah. Shall we be able to see our Lord on the Day of Judgement?" The Prophet, may Allah send him peace, replied: "Do you doubt the sighting of the full moon?" They answered: "No, O Messenger of Allah." He asked: "Do you doubt the presence of the sun when there are no clouds?" They replied: "No." He said: "That is how you will see Him."

There is another *hadīth* in the *Sahihayn* narrated by Abu Sa`id al Khudri which is of the same meaning. A version narrated by Jarir b. `Abdullah al Bajali says: "We were seated with the Prophet on the 14th of a night when he looked up at the moon and said, `You will see your Lord as clearly as you see this (moon) without obscuring each other's view.'"

However, looking at the Sun or the moon is not the same as looking at Allah. Rather, it is only the similarity of vision that has been spoken of. The objects have not been equated.

Tahawi's words: "The Beatific Vision for the dwellers of Paradise is an established fact," is to imply that others will not be able to see Him.

To be sure, as they would see Him in Paradise, they would also see Him in the Field of Judgement as proven by reports in the *Sahihayn*. It is also implied in the words of Allah:

تَحِيَّتُهُمْ يَوْمَ يَلْقَوْنَهُ سَلَٰمٌ

"Their greeting on the Day they will meet Him would be `Salam." (Al Ahzāb: 44)

There is consensus of opinion among the scholars of the *Ummah* that nobody can see Him in this life. If they disagreed at all, it was about the Prophet's vision of Him. There are some who denied that the Prophet saw Him with his eyes. Others confirmed it. Qadi `Ayad has discussed the issue in detail in his work *"Al Shifa' "* delineating therein the differences in opinion among the Companions and their followers. He has reported `A'isha as of opinion that the Prophet did not see his Lord with the eyes on his fore head. When Masruq asked her: "Did Muhammad see his Lord?" She replied, "My hair stand on end at what you say." Then she added, "Whoever told you that Muhammad saw his Lord, uttered a lie." Qadi `Ayad states that a number of Companions were of the same opinion. Ibn Mas`ud and Abu Hurayrah have also expressed a similar opinion (the latter at least on one occasion). Qadi `Ayad has also stated that a group of *hadith* scholars (*Muhaddithun*), jurists and dialecticians (*Mutakallimun*) have also rejected the possibility of anyone being able to see Allah in this world. Ibn `Abbas however held the opinion that the Prophet saw Him. `Ata' has said that he saw him with his inner eye.

`Ayad said: "The opinion that he saw Him with his eyes does not have a text in support. The opinion could draw strength from the two verses of the chapter *Al Najm*. The split in opinion is right from the top order. And the possibility of either cannot be denied."

The statement of Qadi `Ayad above sounds as the correct position. For Allah's vision in this world is quite possible. If it had been impossible, Musa (*asws*) wouldn't have requested it. On the other hand there is no report from the Prophet himself that he saw his Lord with the eyes on his head. Indeed, reports suggest that he didn't. One report is in Muslim which is narrated by Abu Dharr. He says, "I asked the Prophet: `Did you see your Lord?' He replied, '(It was all) Light. How could I see Him?'" According to another report he said, "I saw Light."

Muslim has preserved a report of Abu Musa al Ash`ari. He says, "The Prophet stood up amidst us and spoke out five sentences: `Allah does not sleep and it does not behoove Him to sleep. He raises the Scale and lowers it. To Him are raised the deeds of the night before the deeds of the day, and the deeds of the day before the deeds of the night. His veil is Light.'" According to another report he said: "If He were to unveil it, the radiance of His Face would burn up His creations to the extent of His sight." In the light of this the allusion in Abu Dharr's *hadith* seems to be although Allah knows best when he said, `I saw Light (*Nur*):' to the Light which acts as a veil preventing His vision. Therefore, how could he see Him?" That is, `How could I see Him when Light was between me and Him, preventing me from sighting Him?'

This seems to be a clear indication that the Prophet (*saws*) did not see His Lord. Allah knows best.

As for Tahawi's words, 'without (they) encompassing (Him) and without (they figuring out) the how of it,' they are meant to express the Perfection of His Greatness and Splendor. Allah said:

$$\text{وَلَا يُحِيطُونَ بِهِ عِلْمًا}$$

"And they cannot encompass Him in knowledge." (Tāhā, 110)

With regard to Tahawi's words, "No one is safe in his religion, but he who submitted himself to Allah and His Messenger and left what he didn't understand to one who understands," what he meant is, the person surrendered himself to the texts of the Qur`an and *Sunnah* and did not indulge in doubts, cynicism and faulty interpretations imposed on them, or, said for e.g., 'Reason speaks out differently from what the Qur`an and *Sunnah* say, and that the report (i.e., the Qur`an and *Sunnah*) is based in reason, so that, if there is a contradiction between the two, we shall allow preference to reason!'

Firstly, such a situation does not arise. But when something of this nature happens, and the report is authentic, then what appears to be reasonable should be treated as something of doubtful and unknown nature. Greater research would reveal the facts. On the other hand, if it is an unauthentic report, then there is no point in trying to integrate it with reason. True reason and true report will never contradict each other. Therefore, whoever said anything to this effect (i.e., 'whenever there is a contradiction between reason and report, reason will receive preference') will be replied in the following manner: "Whenever there is a contradiction between reason and report, we are obliged to give preference to report." For, (if there is a contradiction), reconciling the two is to try and reconcile the irreconcilable. Further, giving preference to reason is ruled out. It is reason indeed that tells us to hear and obey what we receive as reports from the Prophet, peace be upon him. Now, if we nullify the report, we nullify what reason points to as acceptable. Consequently, if we ignore what reason leads us to, then, it is not proper to hoist it up in the opposition of report (since we have already invalidated reason: tr.). For, whatever is constructed without the help of reason, cannot be used to nullify anything at all. Thus, giving precedence to reason leads us to (in the case of revelation) non precedence of reason (if it seemingly contradicts revelation). Hopefully, the point is clear. To put it differently, it is reason that led us to the acceptance of revelation as a truth. The revelation then, is concordant with reason. Now, if it is allowed that the inference is unacceptable, because of the unreasonableness of the report, then, it means that reason itself does not stand on good ground. If the argument proposed by reason is not dependable at all, then, reason cannot be followed at all, far from giving it preference over report. Thus, precedence of reason over revelation is a kind of admittance of a defect in reason.

Incumbent (upon us then) is a total submission to the Prophet, on whom be peace, and acceptance of everything that he brought. His words are to be acknowledged as true and accepted as such without subjecting them to false ideas in the name of rationalism, or damping it with doubts and cynicism, or giving men's opinion precedence over it. In other words, we consolidate in him surrender and obedience, as we consolidate in the Sender (Allah) our Prayers, supplications, humility, repentance and trust.

Thus, there are two kinds of totality (of surrender) without which a man cannot escape the Fire: it is the total surrender to what Allah has sent and the totality of the obedience to the Prophet, peace be upon him.

Imam Ahmed has preserved the report of Anas b. `Ayad in which Abu Hazim said: "I and my brother were present on an occasion that I wouldn't exchange for red camels. Myself and my brother went up to find some of the senior Companions of the Prophet sitting at the entrance to his quarters. We did not like to split them, so we sat in the (adjacent) enclosure. Someone quoted a verse and they disagreed over its meaning until their voices rose in argument. The Prophet, peace be upon him, emerged (from his adjacent house: tr.) and threw a handful of dust over them, saying: "Take it easy, people. It was in this manner that nations before you were destroyed: through their disagreements with their Prophets and countering one part of the Book with another. The Qur'an has not been revealed with a part contradicting another. Rather, some of its portions confirm others. Therefore, what you understand of it, put it to practice. As for that you do not understand, leave it to the knowledgeable."1

There is no doubt that Allah has declared utterance of any word not based on knowledge as unlawful. Allah Most High said:

قُلْ إِنَّمَا حَرَّمَ رَبِّيَ الْفَوَاحِشَ مَا ظَهَرَ مِنْهَا وَمَا بَطَنَ وَ الْإِثْمَ وَالْبَغْيَ بِغَيْرِ الْحَقِّ وَأَن تُشْرِكُوا بِاللهِ مَا لَمْ يُنَزِّلْ بِهِ سُلْطَانًا وَأَن تَقُولُوا عَلَى اللهِ مَا لَا تَعْلَمُونَ

"Say, `Verily, my Lord has only forbidden indecencies   be they open or concealed   sin, high handedness without justice, that you should associate with Allah that for which He has not sent you down an authority, and that you should fasten upon Allah what you have no knowledge of." (Al A`rāf, 33)

Allah also said:

وَلَا تَقْفُ مَا لَيْسَ لَكَ بِهِ عِلْمٌ

"And pursue not that of which you have no knowledge." (Al Isrā', 36)

Therefore, it is incumbent upon a man that he should treat what Allah has sent through His Messengers and His Books as "the truth" that deserves to be followed. He should acknowledge that it is the truth and that anything else that comes by, as people's opinions, is to be compared with it. If they agree then it is true. If they do not, then it is falsehood. But if the man cannot figure out whether it agrees or disagrees, then, in that case, the opinion could be unclear of meaning and intent, or, its meaning might be clear, but it might be unclear if what the Prophet has brought agrees with it or disagrees with it: in all such situations one should restrain oneself from forming an opinion. He should not speak out, but from a position of knowledge. Knowledge is that which has a good proof in support of it. And the knowledge that is truly beneficial is from the Prophet. At times, a piece of knowledge can originate from other than the Prophet. But they are of worldly nature, such as, for example, that of medicine or mathematics. As for religious knowledge, it is to be taken from the Prophet and none else.

و لا تثبت قَدمَ الإسلام إلا على ظهر التسليمِ و الإستسلامِ

Islam will not be firmly established but on the basis of unreserved submission and complete surrender.

This is a figurative statement. What is meant is, a man's Islam will not be firm if he will not submit himself completely to the two types of revelation: the Qur`an and the *Sunnah* without leveling an objection against them and without confronting them with one's personal opinions either based on reason or on conjectures.

Bukhari has reported Imam Zuhri as saying: "The Message is from Allah. The delivery was by the Messenger and upon us is submission."

فَمن رَامَ عِلمَ ما حُظِرَ عنه عِلْمُه، و لم يَقْنع بالتسليم فَهْمُهُ، حَجَبَهُ مرامهُ عن خَالِص التوحيد، وصافي المعرفةِ، وصحيح الإيمانِ

Whoever attempted the information that his knowledge was barred from, and did not let his intellect submit, the objectives of such a one veiled him from pure monotheism, clear understanding, and a true belief.

This is an explanation of what was stated by Tahawi in the previous sentence. It is to emphasize that one should not speak out without knowledge in matters of the principles of religion. Allah Most High said:

وَمِنَ النَّاسِ مَن يُجَادِلُ فِى اللهِ بِغَيْرِ عِلْمٍ وَيَتَّبِعُ كُلَّ شَيْطَانٍ مَّرِيدٍ

"And, of the people is one who argues without knowledge and follows every rebellious Shaytan." (Al Hajj, 3)

He also said:

وَمَنْ أَضَلُّ مِمَّنِ اتَّبَعَ هَوٰهُ بِغَيْرِ هُدًى مِّنَ اللهِ إِنَّ اللهَ لَا يَهْدِى الْقَوْمَ الظَّلِمِينَ

"And who can be more misguided than he who followed his base desires without a guidance from Allah? Surely, Allah does not guide a transgressing folk." (Al Qasas, 50)

Abu Umamah al Bahiliyy reports the Prophet as having said: "A people did not lose guidance after being on a guidance, but were given to argumentation.' Then he recited, 'They did not strike a similitude for you but out of contention.'" Tirmidhi has recorded this report, grading it as of acceptable status.]

The Islamic Creed

فَيَتَذَبْذَبُ بين الكفر والإيمان، والتصديق والتكذيب، والإقرار و الإنكار، مُوَسْوِساً تَائِهاً، شاكًّا، لا
مؤمناً مصدِّقاً، ولا جاحداً مكذِّباً

**Consequently, he wavers between infidelity and faith, confirmation
and denial, affirmation and rejection, one given to grave doubts, a
cynic, neither a confirmed believer nor an avowed rejecter.**

This is how Tahawi describes him who swerves away from the Book and
the *Sunnah* inclining towards scholasticism (*kalām* : who wishes to reconcile the
Qur`an and *Sunnah* with the personal opinions, and when he runs into contra-
dictions resorts to interpret it giving other opinions preference over the texts,
transforming his situation into that of one who is soaked up in doubts and
errors.

Ibn Rushd, an expert on religious beliefs and philosophical thoughts, said in
his book *Tahāfat al Tahāfat* : "How could anyone who uttered something about
Divinity, be corrected?" Āmidi, the most knowledgeable person of his time,
ended in complete confusion. Al Ghazali just managed to escape. When he in-
dulged in Divinity and scholastic discussion, he landed into chaos. Then, quickly
realizing the error, he abandoned the old path, renewed his faith in the traditions
of the Prophet, and died with Bukhari on his breast.

Similar was the case of Abu `Abdullah Muhammad ibn `Umar Razi. He said:
"I followed the ways of the scholastics, the methods of the philosophers, but
did not find them capable of curing the sick and watering the thirsty. The nearest to the right approach, I found that of the Qur`an. Read then in affirmation,
`The Most Merciful. He assumed *Istawa`* on the `*Arsh*,' and, `Unto Him rises
the good word,' and then read the negation: `There is nothing like Him,' and,
`They do not encompass Him in knowledge.'" Then he added, "Whoever ex-
perimented the way I did, will reach the same conclusions."

We also have the case of Muhammad b. `Abdul Karim al Shahristani. He
said, "I did not find with the philosophers and the scholastics but bewilderment
and regret." He wrote a quartet meaning: "I went around the schools and tarried long in those worlds. I found none but with his chin resting on his palm or
a man broken by despair."

84

We also have before us the case of Abu al Ma`ali al Juwayni. He said: "I dived deep into the vast oceans, abandoning the scholars of Islam and their knowledge and plunged into what they prevented me from, and now, the situation is, if my Lord will not turn to me in kindness, Juwayni is lost. Here I am, dying on the beliefs of my mother and on that of the old men and women of Nisapur."

The medicine that promises certain cure for this kind of sickness is that which has been reported from the Doctor of hearts, on whom be peace and blessings of Allah. He would say, when he stood up for Prayers in the middle of the night:

اللهم ربَّ جبريل وميكائيل وإسرفيل، فاطرَ السماواتِ والأرضِ، عالمَ الغيب والشهادةِ ، أنت تحكُمُ بينَ عبادِكَ فيما كانوا فيه يَخْتَلفون، اهدِني لِما اختُلِفَ فيه من الحقِّ بإذنِك، إنَّك تَهدِي مَن تَشاءُ إلى صِراطٍ مستقيم.

"O Lord of Jibril, Mika'il and Israfil, Originator of the heavens and the earth, Knower of the seen and the unseen, You judge between people in what they differ: guide me by Your leave in what of the truth that was differed over, surely, You guide unto the right course whom You will." (Muslim)

ولا يصحُّ الإيمانُ بالرؤية لأهل دار السلام لمن اعتبرها منهم بِوَهْم، أو تَأَوَّلَها بفهم، إذاكان تأويل الرؤية – وتأويل كل معنى يضاف إلى الربوبية – بترك التأويل، و لزوم التسليم، وعليه دين المسلمين، ومن لم يَتَوَقَّ النفي والتشبيه، زَلَّ و لَم يُصِب التنزية

Faith in Beatific Vision for the dwellers of the World of Peace (Paradise) is incorrect someone is given to skepticism, or tries to interpret it according to his (own) understanding, whereas every interpretation of the Vision   in fact, interpretation of every meaning attributed to the Lordship   is to be refrained from. Rather, the required attitude is total submission. Incumbent upon him is the religion of those who surrendered. One who did not refrain himself from the denial (of the Beatific Vision) or against drawing similarities (with the created beings) deviated (from the true path) and missed to eliminate imperfections (from his concept of Divinity).

Imam Tahawi seems to be referring to the Mu`tazilah and those who follow their philosophy in denying the Beatific Vision. It is also aimed at anyone who strikes a similitude of any kind between Allah and His creations. The Prophet has said: "You shall see your Lord as you see the full moon." His saying, "as you see" leaves no room for an interpretation other than the apparent meaning, viz., sighting with the eye. The similarity here, however, is in sight and not in The Sighted (i.e., Allah, Most High with the moon). The text is very clear about it, lending no ambiguity. But, if such clear texts are subjected to interpretations, then how can one argue with any other text? Do the words here lend the meaning: `You will know your Lord, as you know the moon?'

It might be claimed that the following verse, and several others of the same genre, can be used to arrive at a different interpretation of the term `sight':

اَلَمْ تَرَ كَيْفَ فَعَلَ رَبُّكَ بِأَصْحَبِ الْفِيْلِ

"Have you seen how your Lord dealt with the people of the elephant?" (Al Fīl, 1)

In the above passage, the act of seeing is of the heart and mind (and not of the eyes, since, after all, the Prophet wasn't a witness to the event).

Undoubtedly, the word "seeing" can sometimes be used for sighting with the eye, while on the other hand it can also be used for the vision of the heart. Indeed, it can also be used for a vision in sleep: i.e., for dreams. There are other uses too. The context always tells us about the sense in which it is to be understood. But if the speaker does not make it clear in the context as to in what sense he is employing the term, then the sentence is rendered vague. It will not allow for a clear meaning. However, in this case (when the Prophet said: you will see your Lord as you see the full moon) who can say that the sentence is vague?

Now, if they say: We have been forced to such an argument in view of the fact that sighting Allah is, from the point of reason, out of the question. The answer is, `that is your supposition, with which other men of reason disagree.' There is nothing in reason to declare it impossible. To be sure, if reason was presented with something that has its free existence, but is invisible, then, it would immediately rule that it is impossible!

Tahawi's words: "whoever of them is given to speculation" are meant to convey that 'whoever of them speculated that Allah Most High would be seen in such and such a manner.' That is, he draws a similarity. Then, after such an speculation, if he commits the error of fastening an Attribute upon Allah, then he is of the anthropomorphists. On the other hand, if he denied the vision itself, because of his speculation, then he is one of those who argues against an established fact and holds the concept of a God bereft of Attributes. Accordingly, the right attitude is to shove away speculation itself, not allowing the truth to be swept away along with the untruth. He should not reject the two (the similarity of the vision between the moon and the Lord, and the sighting itself) because of someone who accepts the untruth (of a vision similar to that of the moon). The right course is to reject the untruth and hold on to the truth.

Tahawi has hinted at this meaning by throwing in the parenthetical remark: "One who did not refrain himself from a denial (of the Beatific Vision) or against drawing similarities (with the created beings) deviated (from the true path) and missed to eliminate imperfections (from his concept of Divinity)." The Mu`tazilah allege that they avoid a blemish for Allah by denying that He can be sighted. But, can one remove an imperfection by denying the Quality of Perfection? Obviously, the impossibility of sight is not a Perfect attribute. It is the non existent that cannot be seen. Perfection lies in being visible. The denial (by us) is of a sight that promises a complete comprehension (as one comprehends the moon). The same goes for knowledge. Denial of knowledge is not perfection. Rather, perfection is in confirming knowledge but without complete comprehension (of the nature and quality). Similarly, Allah Most High cannot be fully comprehended by sight, as He cannot be comprehended by knowledge.

Tahawi saying, "one who tries to interpret it according to his understanding" is addressed to one who gave it a meaning that can be interpreted in a way different from what the apparent words would allow, or as understood by anyone who knows Arabic. The word interpretation itself has been given a different meaning by the later generations. Today, it stands for giving a word meaning different from the apparent. This is how the perverters succeeded in distorting the texts. They called their distortions 'interpretations' in order to beautify their distortions and make them acceptable. But Allah has disapproved of those who beautify the false. He said:

وَكَذَلِكَ جَعَلْنَا لِكُلِّ نَبِيٍّ عَدُوًّا شَيَاطِينَ الْإِنْسِ وَالْجِنِّ يُوحِي بَعْضُهُمْ إِلَى بَعْضٍ زُخْرُفَ الْقَوْلِ غُرُورًا

"Thus We have assigned for every Prophet enemies from among the Satans of the Jinn and mankind who inspire one another with ornamental words of deception." (Al An`ām, 112)

The important thing is the meaning and not the words. How often it has not been that a falsehood has been built upon a few beautiful words that relegated the truth to the background?

Obviously, Tahawi does not mean that every interpretation is to be shunned. He means every distorted and innovatory interpretation. (To the earlier generations the word interpretation had a different connotation: tr.). The *ta'wil* as sanctioned by the Qur`an and *Sunnah* is: 'the truth at which the words are focussed.' The interpretation of a piece of news, for instance, should exactly match with the news itself. In the like manner, true interpretation of a word of command is the act that has been commanded. `A'isha (*ra*) used the word in this sense when she said:

i.e., "The Prophet used to say when he bowed down in his Prayer, `Glory be to You O our Lord God and Your praises. O Allah, forgive me,' interpreting the words of the Qur`an." (That is, by practicing what the Qur`an commanded, he gave Allah's words the right interpretation. Or, he gave the words, a tangible form: tr.).

(Allah Most High Himself used the word in the Qur`an in the same sense). He said:

هَلْ يَنْظُرُونَ إِلَّا تَأْوِيلَهُ يَوْمَ يَأْتِي تَأْوِيلُهُ يَقُولُ الَّذِينَ نَسُوهُ مِنْ قَبْلُ قَدْ جَاءَتْ رُسُلُ رَبِّنَا بِالْحَقِّ

"Are they waiting but for its interpretation? (But) the day its fulfillment (ta'wīl) comes, those who had discarded it earlier to oblivion would say, 'Surely, the messengers of our Lord brought the truth." (Al A`rāf, 53)

It is in the above sense that the concepts such as, 'interpretation of the dreams,' or 'interpretation of deeds' are used. Allah Most High said:

هَذَا تَأْوِيلُ رُؤْيَايَ مِنْ قَبْلُ

"This is the interpretation of my dream that I had experienced earlier."
(Yūsuf, 100)

or Allah's words:

وَيُعَلِّمُكَ مِنْ تَأْوِيلِ الْأَحَادِيْثِ

"And He will teach you interpretation of the stories." (Yūsuf, 6)

Who then can deny the interpretation of the above sort? However, what is of the nature of reports received, such as, about Allah, the Day of Judgement, etc., these are matters of which no interpretation can be attempted, that is, in the sense of expressing the reality that is meant. For, if one was given a piece of news, but had no idea of what he was being informed, or had no understanding of it, then he cannot expected to comprehend its reality: i.e., cannot interpret it, with the help of the piece of news alone. The interpretation in question then is with Allah alone. Nevertheless, not knowing the interpretation (i.e., the knowledge of its reality) is not to say that one does not know the meaning of the apparent words that the speaker intended the listener to receive. To be sure, there is not a verse in the Qur`an that Allah did not order us to ponder over. And there is not a verse which does not demand that they be understood, even though their true interpretation (that is the ultimate reality contained in them) is with none but Allah.

The above then is the meaning of the word *ta'wīl* (interpretation) as used in the Qur`an and *Sunnah* or by the Pious Predecessors, whether such *ta'wīl* happened to agree with the apparent words or did not.

But, so far as the later generation of the jurists and scholastics are concerned, the word *ta'wīl* acquired a different connotation for them. It is to turn the word away from the `first possible' (and apparent) meaning towards that which is the `next possible' because of the surrounding circumstances demanding it. This is the *ta'wīl* which has been subject to much contention among the people when applied to the information or commandments received (through revelation). The correct *ta'wīl* then is that which accords well with the rest of the texts of the Book and the *Sunnah*. What disagrees with them, is the distorted interpretation.

To such of those who indulge in this kind of disapproved interpretation it might be said: The door that you have opened by resorting to it has become the gateway for the pagans and the innovators that you have no power now to shut down. When you inflected the text of the Qur`an and *Sunnah* from the apparent meaning, without any evidence, then, by what rule can you allow or disallow similar attempts by others? If you say: We shall give a new meaning to whatever is declared by reason as impossible, and accept it only if that is not the case, then, it will be asked, whose intellect shall be the criterion? A Qarmati alleges that there is definitive proof for the abolition of the clear commandments of the *Shari`ah*. The philosopher believes that there is definitive proof against physical resurrection. Then, we have on hand the Mu`tazilah who believe that there is definitive proof about the impossibility of sighting Allah. If we follow this mode of logic then we run into two dangerous and unavoidable consequences:

First: We do not accord any meaning to anything from the Book and the *Sunnah* before we have conducted a thorough, extensive research to determine if it is possible at all in the light of reason. Further, since every group claims that what they invite the people to is the right meaning, everyone will be left bewildered.

Second: Men's hearts are prone to not being resolute over whatever they believe, such as those things the Prophet informed us about. Added to the above, if it cannot be assured that the apparent is in fact what was intended, while, on the other hand the interpretations offered are uncertain (because of differences between them), then it is tantamount to saying that the Book and the *Sunnah* be abandoned. (That in turn would mean) abandonment of not only the message of guidance they contain, but also the prophecies therein from Allah unto His slaves, whereas, the mission of the Messengers was especially to make prophecies and the Qur`an is itself the Great News (*al naba' al `azim*).

Hence we see that those who resort to interpretations normally quote the Qur`an and *Sunnah* for the reasons of proving contradictions and not by way of working out a concordance. Whatever agrees with what they believe as rational they accept, and whatever does not, they resort to its interpretation. In this manner they opened the door for the freethinkers. May Allah protect us.

90

As for Tahawi saying, "One who did not refrain himself from a denial (of the Beatific Vision) or against drawing similarities (with the created beings) deviated (from the true path) and did not eliminate the anthropomorphic elements," is because both denial as well as anthropomorphism (or, resemblance) are diseases of the heart. The hearts suffer from two kinds of diseases. First, that of doubts and skepticism, and second, that of base desires. Both have been spoken of in the Qur`an. Allah Most High said:

فَلَا تَخْضَعْنَ بِالْقَوْلِ فَيَطْمَعَ الَّذِىْ فِىْ قَلْبِه مَرَضٌ

"Be not too soft of speech lest one in whose heart is sickness is led to desire."
(Al Ahzāb, 32)

That was the disease of base desires. Allah Most High also said:

وَاَمَّا الَّذِيْنَ فِىْ قُلُوْبِهِمْ مَّرَضٌ فَزَادَتْهُمْ رِجْسًا اِلٰى رِجْسِهِمْ

"As for those in whose heart is sickness (of doubt), it added abomination to their abomination." (Al Tawbah, 125)

This is the disease of doubt. It is worse than that of the disease of base desires. For the disease of base desires might find its cure in obtaining the thing desired. But the disease of doubt has no cure, unless Allah were to cure by His mercy.

In matters involving (Allah's) Attributes, the disease is either that of denial or of an anthropomorphic attitude. Of the two, doubts of the nature of denial are worse than the doubts of the nature of anthropomorphism. For the doubts of the nature of denial are rejection and disbelief of what the Prophet brought, whereas anthropomorphism is to commit excesses and cross the bounds.

فإن ربنا جَلَّ وعلا موصوف بصفات الوحدانية، منعوت بِنُعُوت الفردانية، ليس في معناه أحد من البَرِيَّة

For, our Lord, the Exalted, the Supreme, is qualified with the Attributes of Oneness, characterized with the characteristics unique to Him, with none of the creations sharing the same meaning.

By the above statement, the Sheikh meant to eliminate any sense of resemblance of Allah's Attributes (with His creations), as Allah qualified Himself both in the positive as well as in the negative. His words seem to have been extracted from the chapter *Al Ikhlās*. His words "Qualified with the Attributes of Oneness," have been drawn from Allah's words:

$$\text{قُلْ هُوَ اللهُ أَحَدٌ}$$

"Say, Allah is One." (Al Ikhlās, 1)

His words, "characterized with the characteristics unique to Him," have their root in Allah's words:

$$\text{اللهُ الصَّمَدُ , لَمْ يَلِدْ وَلَمْ يُولَدْ}$$

"Allah is eternal, He beget not." (Al Ikhlās, 2 3)

And his words, "with none of His creations sharing the same meaning," are based on:

$$\text{وَلَمْ يَكُنْ لَهُ كُفُوًا أَحَدٌ}$$

"Nor was He begotten. And He has none equal unto Him." (Al Ikhlās, 4)

Furthermore, the interjection at this point by the Sheikh (Tahawi) is to re emphasize what he had stated earlier about conformation of the Attributes and denial of resemblance.

The words *wasf* (Attribute) and *na`t* (Quality) are synonymous. However, (applied to Allah) the former is used for His Person, whereas the latter is used for His Acts. That is how the words Oneness and Uniqueness are used. Some have said, by way of distinction, that Oneness is used for His Person, whereas Uniqueness for His Attributes. In any case, Allah is One in His Person, and Unique in His Attributes.

The Islamic Creed

و تعالى عن الحدود و الغايات، و الأركان و الأعضاء و الأدوات، لا تحويه الجهات الست كسائر المبتدعات

Our Lord is above (the concepts of) limits and confines, parts, limbs and instruments. The six directions cannot contain Him in contrast to the creations.

With reference to the above words we can say that there are three kinds of people.

1) Those who deny, 2) those who confirm, and 3) those who seek details. The last mentioned are the followers of the pious predecessors. They neither reject nor accept until the issue is clear to them. They accept what is clearly stated and reject what has been denied. But among the later generations, these words acquired ambiguity in their usage, as happens to be the case with many of the technical terms. As a result, not everyone seems to be using the words in the same sense. Consequently, there are those who deny both the true as well as the false. They report on behalf of those who accept, things that they didn't utter. There are others of those who confirm but who introduce connotations that are not part of it. In this, they are opposed to the earliest scholars as well as what the Qur`an and the Criteria lead us to since neither the Qur`an nor the *Sunnah* have said anything about their acceptance or rejection. It is not for us to attribute to Allah Most High what He did not attribute to Himself nor did the Prophet: neither in conformity nor in denial. In these matters we are followers and not innovators.

It is required of us to confirm in matters of Attributes what Allah and His Messenger confirmed, and deny, what Allah and His Messenger have denied. Accordingly, only the words that have appeared in the texts might be employed while accepting or denying. As for those words about which there is neither confirmation nor denial, they may be left suspended until it can be determined what the speaker intended. If the meaning were to be correct, it should be acknowledged. It must be observed that the expression of the meaning has to be in the words of the texts themselves, and not in ambiguous terms, unless there were to be a pressing need for it, but, in such a case, it should be provided with the context that would give out the intended meaning clearly; the need itself being of the kind, such as, to give an example, addressing one without whom the meaning wouldn't be complete, if he were not addressed.

The Sheikh, may Allah show him mercy, has intended to refute those of the anthropomorphists who say: Allah has a body, or that He has a torso, or limbs, etc.   Allah is exalted high above what they allege. The meaning that the Sheikh intended by his denial is true. But, after him came people who introduced new connotations both true as well as false. That needs to be explained and is as follows. There was agreement between the pious forefathers that the people do not know Allah's limits, and that they do not place a limit to any of His Attributes.

Abu Da'ud Tayālisi says: "Sufyan Thawri, Sho`ba, Hammad b. Zayd, Hammad b. Salamah, Sharik and Abu `Uwanah would not set limits, would not commit anthropomorphism, and would not strike similarities. They narrated reports without saying 'how.' When inquired, they would speak from the reports alone."

Now, it is known that a limit or a boundary is something that helps separate a thing from another and by which a thing can be distinguished from another. Allah Most High does not dwell in His creation, nor is dependent on His existence upon them. Rather, He subsists by Himself and by Whom all else subsist. Consequently, the word "limit" cannot be used in a way that will contradict the above. For, behind its denial, there is nothing but the denial of the existence of the Lord Himself and the denial of His Reality. As for the limits pertaining to knowledge and the Word, these are limits assigned to Him by the people. This is something that is rejected by the *Ahl al Sunnah* by consensus.

Abu al Qasim al Qushayri has written: "I heard `Abdul Rahman al Sulami, who heard from Abu Mansur b. `Abdullah, who heard from Abu al Hasan al Anbāri, who heard Sahal b. `Abdullah al Tustari say when asked about the Person of Allah, 'Allah's Person is Qualified with Knowledge, one who cannot be encompassed in limits, who cannot be seen in this world. He is present with the truths of faith, without limits, beyond comprehension, and not incarnated (in anyone or anything). The eyes will see Him in the next world. He is apparent in His Kingdom and in His Power, yet has veiled His creation from knowing the essence of His Person, leading them (to Himself) by His signs. Therefore, the hearts recognize Him. And the eyes will see Him. The believers will look at Him with their eyes, but without comprehending Him and without encompassing Him to the full."

As for the words "parts," "limbs" and "instruments," the deniers use them to deny certain of His Qualities that are proven by the irrefutable texts: such as the Hand and the Face.

Abu Hanifah, may Allah be pleased with him, said in his *Al fiqh al Akbar*: "He has Hands, Face and a Self, as He spoke of them in the Qur`an. He possesses them as Attributes, without us questioning the how of them. It should not be said that by the Hands He meant Power or Blessing, for that denies Him an Attribute."

What the Imam said above is proven by irrefutable evidences. Allah Most High said:

مَا مَنَعَكَ أَنْ تَسْجُدَ لِمَا خَلَقْتُ بِيَدَيَّ

"What prevented you from prostrating yourself before one I created with My two Hands?" (Sād, 75)

And He said:

وَالْأَرْضُ جَمِيعًا قَبْضَتُهُ يَوْمَ الْقِيَمَةِ وَالسَّمٰوٰتُ مَطْوِيّٰتٌ بِيَمِينِهِ

"The whole of the earth will be in His grasp on the Day of Judgement, and the heavens rolled up around His right Hand." (Al Zumar, 67)

Allah also said:

كُلُّ شَيْءٍ هَالِكٌ إِلَّا وَجْهَهُ

"Everything will be destroyed, except His Face." (Al Qasas, 88)

And He said:

تَعْلَمُ مَا فِيْ نَفْسِيْ وَلَآ أَعْلَمُ مَا فِيْ نَفْسِكَ

"You know what is within myself, but I do not know what is within Yourself." (Al Mā'idah, 116)

The Prophet said in the well known lengthy 'Intercession *hadīth*:' "When the people will go to Adam requesting his intercession, they will say to him, '(Allah) made you with His Hand and ordered the angels to prostrate themselves to you.'"

Accordingly, that interpretation is erroneous which says that the allusion by the use of the word 'Hand' is to `power.' For Allah used the words:

$$\text{لِمَا خَلَقْتُ بِيَدَىَّ}$$

"When I made Him with my two hands." (Sād, 75)

That is, he used the dual form for the word Hand rendering its translation as power impossible.

Nor is there any force in their argument (that Allah used the word Hand in plural, which will imply Allah has three or more hands) with the verse:

$$\text{اَوَلَمْ يَرَوْا اَنَّا خَلَقْنَا لَهُمْ مِّمَّا عَمِلَتْ اَيْدِينَآ اَنْعَامًا فَهُمْ لَهَا مٰلِكُوْنَ}$$

"Haven't they seen that We have made for them of the things Our Hands have fashioned, cattle that they dominate." (Yasīn, 71)

In the above verse, Allah Most High used the word Hand in plural only in keeping with the plural object that He related thereby.

Nevertheless, by these Attributes, it should not be thought that they are limbs or members of the body, or instruments, or parts of the body. For any part is a part of the whole. But Allah Most High is One, the Eternal, who cannot be divided, Glorified is He. The concept of limbs presupposes divisions. Allah is Exalted above that. Members of the body have the sense of accruing benefit or earning something for themselves. So also, instruments help in certain functions of gaining an advantage or removing a harm. But all these concepts are un befitting of Allah Most High. Accordingly, these have not been mentioned in the list of Attributes of Allah. For the words themselves lend the right meaning, are free from possibilities and unbecoming probabilities. Therefore, it is incumbent that the words be not given new meanings, either in denial or in acceptance, in order that neither an erroneous meaning is attached to them nor a correct meaning is denied. Undeniably, the words that have been used here are open to misuse.

Insofar as the word "direction" is concerned, sometimes it is used for indicating what is existent and sometimes for what is non existent. Now, we know that there is nothing in existence except the Creator and the created. Therefore, if by pointing to a "direction," the allusion is to something that is present apart from Allah, then that thing has to be a created being. As for Allah, He is not bound by anything and cannot be encompassed by His creation   Exalted He is above that. And, if what is meant by pointing to a direction is something that is non existent, over and above the created world, then, nothing exists in that realm except Allah Most High, the One. Now, if it is said that He is in a particular direction, then in this sense, it is alright to say so, the answer would be that the meaning of the words then would be that He is above where His creations end. In other words, He is above all, superseding everything.

Now, the deniers of the term "direction" (when used for Allah)   those who meant to deny the "above all" sense through their denial   say in defense of their statements the following: `All directions are creations of Allah. He existed before the directions existed. Now, if someone says that He is in a certain "direction," then he declares a created being as pre existent. As if, One who was above a direction came to be contained in it.'

This kind of argument leads us to believe that He is not within any part of His creation, whether we call it direction or anything else. This of course is true. But, direction itself does not enjoy an existence of its own. Rather, it is a thing of convention. Nonetheless, there is no doubt about it that directions have no limit, and that what is not found in what is limitless, has no existence.

The Sheikh's words, may Allah show him mercy, "The six directions cannot contain Him in contrast to the creations," is in the sense that none of His creations can encompass Him. Rather, He encompasses everything and is above them. The Sheikh further elaborates this when He adds, later in this work, that Allah is, "overencompassing everything and He is above all." Therefore, if we put together his two statements, that is, "The six directions cannot contain Him in contrast to the creations," and, "overencompassing everything and He is above all," then it can be deduced that the meaning he intended is that He is not contained by anything, nor can anything encompass Him, as it can happen to the created beings, Allah encompasses everything, and that He is above everything.

Invariably, the ignorant suffer various distortions in the meaning; especially when things such as Allah coming down to the earth's firmament every night are spoken of. They imagine that when He descends, as informed by the Prophet, then the `Arsh is above Him, and that, He is then, confined between two heavens. This kind of thinking is contrary to the consensus of opinion of the pious fore fathers, as also contrary to the Book and the *Sunnah*.

Sheikh al Islam Abu `Uthman b. `Abd al Rahman al Sabuni says he heard his teacher Abu Mansur b. Hammad say, after he spoke of the descending down of Allah: "Abu Hanifah was asked about it. He replied, 'Yes, He descends, without (us being able to reckon) the how of it.'"

Some others, unable to reconcile things, because of the lack of a thorough understanding of the Qur`an and *Sunnah* and the statements of the earliest scholars, are left quite puzzled. They resort to denial that Allah is above the `Arsh. They say: "He is neither attached to it nor detached, neither within nor without (the created world)." Thus they describe Him with the Attributes of non existence and what is impossible in itself. They do not describe Him in the manner He described Himself as being High above and over the `Arsh.

والمِعْراج حق، وقد أُسري بالنبي صلى الله عليه و سلم، و عُرج بشخصه في اليقظة إلى السماء، ثم إلى حيث شاء الله من العلا، و أكرمه الله بما شاء، و أوحى إليه ما أوحى: (ما كذب الفؤاد ما رأ) فصلى الله عليه وسلم في الآخرة والأولى

The Night Ascension is true. The Prophet was taken by night and ascended with his physical being, in the state of wakefulness, to the heavens and then higher up to wherever Allah wished. Allah honored him in the way He wished, and revealed to him what He revealed. "The heart did not deny what it saw." Peace and blessing of Allah upon him, both in this world as well as in the next.

The word *mi`rāj* is constructed on the same pattern as *mif`āl*, and renders the meaning of the device with which one can ascend. Functionally, it is similar to a ladder. But no one knows how or what exactly it was. It is ruled by the same principles as others of the Unseen. We believe in it, and do not search for details.

However, there have been differences in opinion over the details of the journey. It has been said for instance that the night journey was with the soul and the body was not missed behind him. Ibn Is haq has reported this as the opinion of `A'isha, Allah be pleased with her. Hasan al Busri is said to be of the same opinion. Nevertheless, the difference between the two sets of words: "the night journey took place in the state of sleep," and: "it was of the spirit, without the body," may be noted. There is a sea of difference between the two. `A'isha and Mu`awiyyah, Allah be pleased with them, did not say it took place in the state of sleep. Rather they said: "His soul was taken on to the journey and the body was not missed behind him." The difference can be explained as follows. What a person sees in a dream are images struck for him as alive. So that he might see that he has been taken up to the heavens, or had been to Makkah and so forth, without his soul going up or journeying. Rather, the angel in charge of dreams illustrates it to him that way. But `A'isha and Mu`awiyyah did not mean to say that the Prophet journeyed in his dream. Instead, what they meant is that his soul was taken on to the journey. It parted from the body to return to it after the travel. Thus the two, (`A'isha and Mu`awiyyah) declared it one of the specialties of the Prophet, for, apart from him, there is none whose soul can journey up to the heavens, except after death.

Some people have conjectured that the Isra' journey took place twice: once when he was awake and once when he was in sleep. It sounds as if those who have said this have tried to reconcile the *hadīth* narrated by Sharik containing the Prophet's statement: "then I woke up" and other *ahādīth* on the subject. Some have said that the journey took place once before revelation started coming to him and a second time after that. Indeed, some have opined that it took place three times: once before revelation, and twice afterward. The fact is, every time these people had a doubt, they added to the number of journeys. This is the work of the weak *hadīth* people. Otherwise what the traditionists have said is that it took place only once, in Makkah, after he was made a Prophet, before the migration by about a year, or a year and a half. This has been mentioned by Ibn `Abd al Barr.

Shamsuddin Ibn Qayyim al Jawziyyah has said: "Strange of those who said that the journey took place several times. Do they imagine that every time he went, fifty Prayers were declared obligatory, so that he went back and forth to his Lord and Musa until it became five?! Then, at that moment Allah remarked: "I have kept my Word and have made it easy for My slaves." But, (if we are to believe in those who claim several journeys to the heavens) in every journey Allah went back to His fifty and then gradually brought it down to five! The truth is, some of the narrators after Sharik committed errors. Accordingly, Imam Muslim narrated several reports and then remarked: 'He (the narrator) changed the order, added or deleted (words).' Surely, Imam Muslim arrived at the right conclusion." (Ibn Qayyim's words end here).

The truth then is that the Prophet was taken through the night journey in the state of wakefulness with his body accompanying him, from the Masjid al Haram unto the Masjid al Aqsa, riding upon *Buraq*.

Bukhari narrated: Hudba b. Khalid reported hearing from Hammam b. Yahya, he from Qatadah, he from Anas b. Malik, he from Malik b. Sa`sa`ah, may Allah be pleased with them, that the Prophet spoke to them about the night in which he was taken on to the journey, saying: "While I was in the *Hateem*" or he said: "in *Hijr*, lying down, when someone appeared and slit open (the breast: tr.)." He (Qatadah) said, 'I heard him say,' "he cut open from here to here;" I (Qatadah) asked Jarud who happened to be by my side, 'What does he mean?' He said, 'From the cavity in the neck down up to his navel.' I also heard him say, 'From the breastbone until the navel.' "He removed my heart. A golden tray filled with faith was produced. My heart was washed and filled up. Then a beast was brought: bigger than a mule, smaller than a horse white." Jarud asked, 'Was that *Buraq*, O Abu Hamzah?' Anas replied, 'Yes.' It placed its foot where the sight ended. I was asked to mount it. Jibril started off with me until we reached the heaven nearest to this world. He asked to be let in. It was inquired: 'Who is it?'

He replied: 'Jibril.'

It was asked: 'Who is with you?'

He replied: 'Muhammad.'

It was asked: 'Has he been invited?'

He replied: 'Yes.'

It was said: 'Welcome to him. The best one ever to be invited has arrived.'

So it was opened. As I entered I came across Adam. Jibril told me: 'This is your father. Greet him.' So I greeted him. He returned the greetings and said: 'Welcome to a righteous son and a righteous Prophet.'"

"Then he ascended," (continues the transmitter), "until he reached the second heaven and sought it to be opened. It was inquired: 'Who is it?'

He replied: 'Jibril.'

It was asked: 'Who is with you?'

He replied: 'Muhammad.'

It was asked: 'Has he been invited?'

He replied: 'Yes.'

It was said: 'Welcome to him. The best one ever to be invited has arrived.'

As I entered, I encountered Yahya and ʿIsa. They were cousins.

Jibril said: 'These are Yahya and ʿIsa. Greet them.' I greeted them and they returned the greetings. They replied: 'Welcome to a righteous brother and a righteous Prophet.'"

"Then he ascended," (continues the transmitter), "until he reached the third heaven and sought it to be opened. It was inquired: 'Who is it?'

He replied: 'Jibril.'

It was asked: 'Who is with you?'

He replied: 'Muhammad.'

It was asked: 'Has he been invited?'

He replied: 'Yes.'

It was said: 'Welcome to him. The best one ever to be invited has arrived.'

As I entered, I met *Yūsuf.*

Jibril said: 'This is *Yūsuf.* Greet him.' I greeted him. He returned the greetings and said: 'Welcome to a righteous brother and a righteous Prophet.'"

"Then he ascended," (continues the transmitter), "until he reached the fourth heaven and sought it to be opened. It was inquired: 'Who is it?'

He replied: 'Jibril.'

It was asked: 'Who is with you?'

He replied: 'Muhammad.'

It was asked: 'Has he been invited?'

He replied: 'Yes.'

It was said: 'Welcome to him. The best one ever to be invited has arrived.'

As I entered, I met Idris.

Jibril said: 'This is Idris. Greet him.' I greeted him. He returned the greetings and said: 'Welcome to a righteous brother and a righteous Prophet.'"

"Then he ascended," (continues the transmitter), "until he reached the fifth heaven and sought it to be opened. It was inquired: 'Who is it?'

He replied: 'Jibril.'

It was asked: 'Who is with you?'

He replied: 'Muhammad.'

It was asked: 'Has he been invited?'

He replied: 'Yes.'

It was said: 'Welcome to him. The best one ever to be invited has arrived.'

As I entered, I came upon Harun.

Jibril said: 'This is Harun. Greet him.' I greeted him. He returned the greetings and said: 'Welcome to a righteous brother and a righteous Prophet.'"

"Then he ascended," (continues the transmitter), "until he reached the sixth heaven and sought it to be opened. It was inquired: 'Who is it?'

He replied: 'Jibril.'

It was inquired: 'Who is with you?'

He replied: 'Muhammad.'

It was asked: 'Has he been invited?'

He replied: 'Yes.'

It was said: 'Welcome to him. The best one ever to be invited has arrived.'

As I entered, I came across Musa.

Jibril said: 'This is Musa. Greet him.' I greeted him. He returned the greetings and said: 'Welcome to a righteous brother and a righteous Prophet.'"

As I left him behind he began to weep. He was asked: 'What makes you cry?' He replied: 'I cry because a young man sent after me will have greater number of his followers entering Paradise than those from my followers.'

"Then he ascended," (continues the transmitter), "until he reached the seventh heaven and sought it to be opened. It was inquired: 'Who is it?'

He replied: 'Jibril.'

It was asked: 'Who is with you?'

He replied: 'Muhammad.'

It was asked: 'Has he been invited?'

He replied: 'Yes.'

It was said: 'Welcome to him. The best one ever to be invited has arrived.'

As I entered, I came upon Ibrahim. Jibril said: 'This is your father. Greet him.' I greeted him. He returned the greetings and said: 'Welcome to a righteous son and a righteous Prophet.'"

Then I was taken up further until I reached the Lote Tree at the farthest end (*the Sidratu al Muntaha*). I found its fruit (as large as) that of Hijr (a place in north of Hijaz); and its leaves as large as the ears of an elephant. He told me: 'This is the Lote Tree at the farthest end.' I found four rivers (springing out from) there. Two rivers in the interior and two at the exterior. I asked: 'What are these Jibril?' He replied: 'The interior ones are the rivers of Paradise, and the exterior ones are Nile and Euphrates.'

Then I was taken up to the *Bayt al Ma`mur*. There I was presented with a cup of wine, a cup of milk and a cup of honey. I chose the one with milk. Jibril remarked: 'That's the natural thing (you did). You and your followers shall tread it.'

Then fifty Prayers a day were made obligatory on me. I returned and came across Musa. He asked: 'What have you been ordered?' I replied: 'I have been ordered fifty Prayers a day.' He said: 'Your nation will not be able to bear fifty Prayers a day. I have, by Allah, tested the people before you and took great pains with the children of Isra'il. Return to your Lord and seek concession for your followers.'

I returned. Allah took off ten of them from me. I returned to Musa. He repeated what he had said earlier. So I returned. Allah took off ten more of them from me. I returned to Musa and he told me what he had told me earlier. So I returned and Allah took off another ten from me. I returned to Musa and he repeated what he had said earlier. So I returned and I was ordered ten Prayers a day. I returned but Musa said the same thing. So I went back and Allah ordered me five Prayers a day. I returned to Musa and he asked: 'What have you been ordered?' I said: 'I have been ordered five Prayers a day.' He said: 'Your nation would not be able to bear five Prayers a day. I have tested the people before you and took great pains with the Children of Isra'il. Return to you Lord and seek concession.'

"The Prophet said," (continues the narrator): "I have made requests to my Lord to the point of being reduced to shame. I would rather be satisfied and submit."

"The Prophet continued," says the narrator, "When I crossed (the heaven) a caller called out: 'I have kept my Word and have granted a decrease to My slaves.'"

Humaydi narrated from Sufyan, he from `Amr, he from `Ikrimah, he from Ibn `Abbas, may Allah be pleased with the two, who said concerning the words of Allah:

$$\text{وَمَا جَعَلْنَا الرُّءْيَا الَّتِي أَرَيْنَاكَ إِلَّا فِتْنَةً لِّلنَّاسِ}$$

"We did not grant the vision that We showed you, but as a trial for men," *(Al Isrā, 60)*

that it refers to the vision that the Prophet's eyes experienced in the night he was taken to the journey to the *Bayt al Maqdis*.

Differences in opinion prevailed between the Companions over whether the Prophet saw Allah with his physical eyes or not? The correct opinion is that he saw Him with his inner vision and not with the physical eyes.

As for Allah's words:

مَا كَذَبَ الْفُؤَادُ مَا رَأَى (١١) أَفَتُمَارُونَهُ عَلَى مَا يَرَى (١٢) وَلَقَدْ رَآهُ نَزْلَةً أُخْرَى (١٣)

"The heart did not falsify what he saw. Will you then dispute what he saw? Indeed, he saw him at a second descent." (Al Najm, 11-13):

Trustworthy reports coming from the Prophet tell us that it is Jibril that has been alluded to by the words above. Twice he (the Prophet) saw him in the form and shape in which he (Jibril) has been created.

As for Allah's words in the chapter al Najm:

ثُمَّ دَنَا فَتَدَلَّى

"Then he came near and hung suspended." (Al Najm, 8),

the words "near" and "suspended" are not related to the night journey. Rather, they are speaking of Jibril who "neared" and who "hung suspended" as said `A'isha and Ibn Mas`ud, may Allah be pleased with them. Allah said:

عَلَّمَهُ شَدِيدُ الْقُوَى (٥) ذُو مِرَّةٍ فَاسْتَوَى (٦) وَهُوَ بِالْأُفُقِ الْأَعْلَى (٧) ثُمَّ دَنَا فَتَدَلَّى (٨)

"He was taught by one mighty in power, very strong, who stood poised, being on the higher horizon. Then he came near and hung suspended." (Al Najm, 5-8)

Each of the personal pronouns in the above verses refers to the 'mighty in power' of the first verse. As for the `coming near and hovering over,' spoken of by the Prophet in the narration about the night journey, there, it is the coming near and hovering over of Allah Most High. As regards the words of the chapter Al Najm that he saw him during the second descent at the Lote Tree of the farthest end, well, that was Jibril. The Prophet saw him twice in his original form: once on earth and a second time near the Lote Tree of the farthest end.

With regard to the journey in the state of wakefulness, the words of the chapter *Al Isrā'* are a strong evidence. Allah Most High said:

سُبْحَانَ الَّذِي أَسْرَى بِعَبْدِهِ لَيْلاً مِّنَ الْمَسْجِدِ الْحَرَامِ إِلَى الْمَسْجِدِ الْأَقْصَا

"Glorified is He Who took His slave for a journey by night from the Sacred Mosque (at Makkah) to the Aqsa Mosque." (Al Isrā', 1)

A "slave," just as any other human being is composed of two elements: the body and the soul. This is common knowledge. The journey then had to be with the combination. Neither is it an impossible feat for the intellect. If it is impossible to think of a human being ascending to the heavens, it is impossible for the angels to descend down from there. Such an assumption will lead to the denial of Prophethood, which is disbelief.

Now, if it is asked, 'What was the wisdom in the night journey and ascension to the heavens?' The answer is although Allah knows best it was to prove the authenticity of the Prophet (*saws*). When the Quraysh asked him to describe the *Bayt al Maqdis*, he was able to do it (although he had never been there). Obviously, if he had traveled to the heavens alone (but not to the mosque), this could not have been achieved, even if he had fully described it. But, they knew what *Bayt al Maqdis* was like, so when he described it, they knew what he was talking about.

Of course, there are several proofs of Allah's Exalted Attributes in this event (of the journey to the heavens)   for those who will ponder.

والحوض– الذي أكرمه الله تعالى به غياثا لأمته – حق

The Pond that Allah has honored the Prophet with, as a means of deliverance of his people, is true.

The reports that speak of the Pond are so numerous as to deny the possibility of agreement of the narrators over a lie. Somewhere around thirty Companions have narrated about it. Our master `Imaduddin ibn Kathir, may Allah shower him with His mercy, has collected them together in his work of history known as *Al Bidayah wa al Nihayah*.

Bukhari preserves one of them, may Allah show him mercy. Anas says, the Prophet said: "My Pond is as large as from Aylah (a port in the Red Sea) to San`a' in Yemen. It is lined up with cups as numerous as the stars."

What can be said in brief in description of the Pond as stated in the traditions is as follows. It is a very large Pond, a halting point for the honored ones. It will have waters of Paradise running into it, connected with the river *Kawthar*.

Its liquid is whiter than milk, cooler than ice, sweeter than honey and more fragrant than *misk*. Its length and width, very large in size, is of equal dimension. Travelling from one of its corner to the other would take a month. Glory to Allah for whom nothing is impossible.

Reports suggest that every Prophet would have his own Pond. The Pond of our Prophet would be the largest, the sweetest and the one visited by the largest number of people. May Allah make us of them by His grace and mercy.

والشفاعة التي ادخرها لهم حق، كما رُوي في الأخبار

The Intercession that he has reserved for them is true, as reported in several narrations.

Intercessions are of several kind: some, over which there is a consensus of opinion among the scholars of the *Ummah* and others over which the Mu`tazilah and others of the innovators have disagreed.

The first kind is the one that is known as the Great Intercession. It is reserved especially for our Prophet apart from all his other brother Prophets, Allah's peace and blessing upon them all. Scores of Companions have narrated about this intercession in reports preserved in the *Sahihayn* as well as other collections.

One of them is as follows. The Prophet said: "I shall proceed to (a place) under the `Arsh and fall in prostration to my Lord, the Mighty the Exalted. Allah will open up my heart and inspire in me the best of words of praise and glorification: those that He didn't inspire anyone with before me. It will be said: 'Muhammad! Raise your head. Ask, you will be given. Intercede, it will be accepted.' I will say, 'O Lord. My people. My people. O Lord. My people. My people. O Lord. My people. My people.' He will say, 'Take into Paradise those of your followers who have no reckoning upon them (because of overwhelming good deeds) through the right hand side door of Paradise.' They would share with the people all other doors except this one." Then the Prophet added: "By Him in whose hand is Muhammad's soul, the width of the door is as much as the distance between Makkah and Hijr (a place in north of Hijaz), or the distance between Makkah and Busra."

The second kind of intercessions is that of the Prophet (*saws*) which he will exercise in favor of those whose good and evil deeds would be equal in magnitude. He will intercede for them so that they enter Paradise. And a third will be in favor of those who would be judged as deserving the Fire but would not enter it.

A fourth kind of intercession marked for the Prophet will help in the raising of ranks in Paradise, above the ranks the people would deserve by their deeds. The Mu`tazilah agree with this kind of intercession but deny all others of other occasions, despite numerous reports on the subject.

A fifth will be in favor of some of those who will be entering Paradise along with those who will enter it without reckoning. One could cite as proof the *hadīth* of `Ukasha b. Muhsin in this connection. The Prophet prayed for him to be included in those seventy thousand that will enter Paradise without reckoning. The *hadīth* is in Bukhari and Muslim.

The sixth kind of intercession will help in the reduction of punishment of those subjected to it because of their deeds. For example, the Prophet's intercession for his uncle Abu Talib for reduction in his punishment. Qurtubi has raised a question and answered it in his book *Al Tadhkirah* while discussing this kind of intercession. If it is asked how it would be possible when Allah has declared that (*Al Muddaththir*, 48): "Intercession of the intercessors will be of no profit to them?" The answer is, the intercession will not help him come out of the Fire, as it would help those of the believers in Allah who would be removed from there and admitted into Paradise.

A seventh kind is the one by which everyone of the believers would be allowed entry into Paradise, as discussed earlier. *Sahih Muslim* records a *hadīth* narrated by Anas, which reports the Prophet as saying: "I am the first of Intercessors in Paradise."

The eighth kind of intercession will be in favor of those of the people of this *Ummah* who would have committed major sins. Those in Fire would be removed and admitted into Paradise by his intercession. Innumerable reports have reached us about this kind of intercession. The Khawarij and the Mu`tazilah seem to have missed its knowledge, for they deny it: some out of ignorance of the authenticity of the reports in question, others out of spite for those who have its knowledge, and because of persistence in innovatory ways.

The angels, Prophets and ordinary believers will also share in this kind of intercession. Our Prophet would exercise it four times.

Of reports speaking of this kind, there is one by Anas b. Malik . He says, the Prophet said: "My intercession will be for those of my *Ummah* who would have committed major sins."

On the basis of ideas about intercession, people can be categorized into three classes. The first category is of the pagans, the Christians and the innovators in Islam who follow their Shuyukh blindly: they believe that such of those they imagine as important persons in the sight of Allah will intercede for them in the manner of intercession in worldly affairs. Mu`tazilah and Khawarij do not believe in the intercession of our Prophet in favor of those who committed major sins. As for the *Ahl al Sunnah wa al Jama`ah*, they believe in the Prophet's intercession for those who committed major sins. They also believe in intercessions by others. However, they add by way of clarification that no one can intercede without Allah's leave, and, further, will have to remain within his limits as proven by authentic reports. For example, one narration says: "The people (on the Day of Judgement) will go to Adam, then to Nūh, then to Ibrahīm, then Musa, then `Isa. `Isa will say, 'Go to Muhammad. He is a slave whose past and future sins are forgiven.' "So," the Prophet continues, "they will come to me. I will go forward until when I see my Lord, I will fall into prostration. I shall praise my Lord in words that He would have inspired in me. At this moment I cannot spell them. He will say, 'Muhammad. Raise your head. Say, you will be heard. Intercede, it will be accepted.' I will say, 'My Lord. My people.' So a limit will be set for me and I will take them to Paradise. Then I will go up again and prostrate myself. Again a limit will be set for me." The Prophet (*saws*) repeated this three times.

As for seeking the Prophet's intercession, or, for that matter, of any other, in this world, in supplications, that requires some explanation. Sometimes the supplicant says: "By the right of so and so (grant me such and such a thing)." He swears upon Allah in the name of one of His creations. This is prohibited for two reasons. First, he swore by other than Allah, which is prohibited. Second, he believes that someone has a right upon Allah. But there is no one who has any right upon Allah except for what He has declared as binding unto Himself. For e.g.,

$$\text{وَكَانَ حَقًّا عَلَيْنَا نَصْرُ الْمُؤْمِنِينَ}$$

"It was a binding upon Us that the believers be helped."(Al Rūm, 47)

A *hadīth* also confirms this. Mu`adh reports: "Once I was the pillion rider of the Prophet. He asked, 'O Mu`adh. Do you know what is Allah's right upon His slaves?' I said, 'Allah and His Messenger know be.' He said, 'It is His right upon them that they worship Him and associate nothing with Him.' Then he asked, 'Do you know what is the right of His slaves upon Him when they have done that?' I said, 'Allah and His Messenger know better.' He said, 'It is their right upon Him that He should not punish them.'"

Thus, these are right imposed by Allah on Himself and which is to come true. This is not because a slave deserves something from His Lord as a right, as for e.g., the rights of some creations over other creations. Allah is the Bestower upon His slaves. If there is any right that the slaves have upon Him, it is by His promise, such as, that He should not punish them. Nevertheless, it does not mean one can swear by the right, nor can one use it as a means of access. Means are for Allah Most High to declare.

This is how that *hadīth* is to be understood which is in *Musnad* of Ahmed. It has been handed down to us by Abu Sa`id al Khudri. It says about the words of those going forth to attend the Prayers: "I ask You by the right of my walking (towards the mosque) and by the right of those who ask You." Thus, this is the right of those who ask, declared a right by Allah upon Himself. It is the right of those who ask that they be answered and of the worshippers that He accept their acts of worship. Someone has put it in a beautiful quartet:

Nothing is there as the slaves' right upon Him
Yet not the littlest of deed is lost with Him
If they are punished, it is by justice, and if bestowed
then by His beneficence, He is the Generous, the All comprehensive.

If it is asked, what is the difference between the statement of the worshipper: "By the right of those who ask You," and in saying, "By the right of Your Prophet?" The answer is, the meaning of the earlier statement is: 'You have promised to answer the prayers of those who ask You. And I am one of those who ask. Therefore, answer my prayer.' In contrast, to say, "By the right of so and so," even if that one had a right upon Allah because of a promise He made to him, would be like saying: 'Answer my prayer, O Allah, because such and such a one is a pious person.' There is a huge difference between the two statements. To be using those words is to exceed one's limits. Allah has, in contrast, commanded us in words:

اُدْعُوا رَبَّكُمْ تَضَرُّعًا وَخُفْيَةً ۚ إِنَّهُ لَا يُحِبُّ الْمُعْتَدِينَ

"Call unto your Lord, humbly and secretly. He does not approve of those who cross the bounds." (Al A`rāf, 55)

The words we are discussing, (i.e., "by the right of so and so"), are those of the innovators. It is not reported of the Prophet that he ever employed them, nor of the Companions, their Followers or the great Imams. This kind of thing can be found on the walls of the forts and edifices that are scrawled by the ignorant and followers of the Sufi orders. What must not be lost sight of is the fact that making supplications is one of the best forms of worship and acts of worship are based upon the Qur`an and *Sunnah*, not upon desire and innovation.

Alternatively, if by the words in question the intention is to swear upon Allah by the right of so and so, then that too is forbidden. Indeed, swearing upon a creation by the right of another creation is not allowed either. What about swearing upon Allah then? The Prophet has said: "Whoever swore by other than Allah, committed the sin of association." Hence Abu Hanifah and two of his closest students have said: "It is undesirable to say: 'I ask You by the right of so and so' or, 'by the right of the Prophets and Messengers', or, 'by the right of the Bayt al Haram or other holy sites of Makkah,' etc." In fact Abu Hanifah and

Hasan al Shaybani have opined that it is undesirable that someone should say in his supplication: "I ask you by the Seat of Honor of Your `Arsh." (Imam) Abu *Yūsuf* allowed it only after he came to know of a report to this effect.

Sometimes a suppliant says: "By the honor in Your sight of so and so." Or, "We seek the means of access (*tawassul*) to You of Your Prophets, Messengers and Friends," meaning, 'Because so and so is honorable in Your sight, You should answer my prayer." These kinds of statements are also unacceptable. If such had been the means of access employed by the Companions during the life of the Prophet, then, surely they would have done so after his death too. Rather, they only sought him as a means of access, so long as he was alive, by requesting him to pray for them, joining up with their *Āmin* to his prayer words, for e.g., when he prayed for rains, or other things. But, after his death, when they had to pray for rain, `Umar said in his supplication: "O Allah. When we were faced up with droughts we sought to use Your Prophet as the means of access (*wasilah*) and You sent us rains. Now, we seek to use the Prophet's uncle as the means of access." What he meant is: 'By his prayers, his intercession and his supplications.' He didn't mean to say: 'We swear upon You by him,' or, 'Ask You by the honor he enjoys in Your sight.' Had that been the intention, then, obviously, the Prophet's honor was greater in the sight of Allah, than that of his uncle.

Some people say in their supplications: "I seek You to answer me by my obedience of Your Prophet," or, "by my love for him and belief in him and the rest of the Prophets and Messengers and my confirmation of them (as authentic Prophets and Messengers)." Employing these kind of means of access is one of the best ways of making supplications.

Using an individual as a "means of access" needs some clarification. Some people, not understanding the import, employ it wrongfully. If it is meant that the person named, act as an intercessor or supplicate on behalf of the suppliant, then, that is possible in the life of that individual. It could be that the suppliant loves him (whose means of access he sought: tr.) and is obedient to him, in which case the intention could be to seek the person's supplication or his intercession. Or, it could be by the suppliant's love of him, or by his obedience of him. Alternatively, it could be that he intended to abjure by an individual, or sought his person as a means of access, then, all these are manners of "the means of access" that the scholars have disallowed.

The same rules apply to asking an act. Sometimes the intention is to ask by it as a means of access, in order that the act becomes a cause for obtaining the thing asked. At other times the intention is to swear by it.

An example is in the *hadīth* of the three who took refuge in a cave. It is a well known tradition recorded in the *Sahihayn*. A rock closed the mouth of the cave. They sought Allah's help by mentioning their good deeds as the means of access (*wasilah*). Each one of them said: "If I did that deed seeking Your Face, then show us a way out of this dilemma. The rock moved aside and they emerged safe and sound. These people supplicated by the means of access of their good deeds. To be sure, to ask by one's good deeds is one of the best ways of supplicating with Allah. He has promised that He will answer the call of those who do good and that He will give them more.

In a word: Intercession with Allah is unlike intercession with the people. No one can intercede with Allah without His permission. He alone makes the decisions. He said:

$$قُلْ إِنَّ الْأَمْرَ كُلَّهُ لِلَّهِ$$

"Say, 'The affair is entirely in Allah's hands." (Āl `Imrān, 154)

He also said:

$$لَيْسَ لَكَ مِنَ الْأَمْرِ شَيْءٌ$$

"You (O Prophet) have no say in the affairs." (Āl `Imrān, 128)

However, even as no one can intercede with Allah, save for him He would allow, He honors the intercessor by accepting their intercession. The Prophet has said: "Intercede, you will be rewarded. And Allah accomplishes by the tongue of His Prophet, what He will." At the same time, a *hadīth* in the *Sahih* books reports the Prophet as having said: "O tribesmen of `Abd Munaf. I have no say in your affairs with Allah. O Safiyyah an aunt of the Messenger I have no say in your affair with Allah. O `Abbas an uncle of the Messenger I have no say in your affair with Allah."

Now if the best of creations and the best of intercessors says to people closest to: "I have no say in your affair with Allah," then what about others?

However, when a suppliant makes a supplication to Allah, and a (living) intercessor intercedes with Him, He hears the call and accepts the intercession. Truly speaking, these things do not have an effect upon Him the way they affect creations dealing with creations. For, it is Allah Himself who granted that one supplicate or another intercede. He is the Creator of the deeds of His creations. He it is who guided a slave to supplicate and then He it is who accepted the supplication. He it is who led the man to a good deed and allowed him to do it rightly. He it is who inspired him to supplicate, and then He it is who answered it. This is based on the principle upon which the *Ahl al Sunnah* are: those who have faith in the Divine Decree. Allah is the Creator of everything.

و الميثاق الذي أخذه الله تعالى من آدم و ذريته: حق

And the compact that Allah took from Adam and his seed is true.

Allah said in the Qur'an:

وَ إِذْ أَخَذَ رَبُّكَ مِنْ بَنِيْ آدَمَ مِنْ ظُهُوْرِهِمْ ذُرِّيَّتَهُمْ وَ أَشْهَدَهُمْ عَلَى أَنْفُسِهِمْ أَلَسْتُ بِرَبِّكُمْ قَالُوْا بَلَى ۛ شَهِدْنَا ۚ أَنْ تَقُوْلُوْا يَوْمَ الْقِيٰمَةِ إِنَّا كُنَّا عَنْ هٰذَا غٰفِلِيْنَ

"When your Lord drew forth from the children of Adam, from their loins, their seed, and made them testify concerning themselves: 'Am I not your Lord?' They replied, 'Yes. We do testify.' That, you might not say on the Day of Judgement: 'We were quite in the dark about it." (Al A`rāf, 172)

By this verse Allah informed us that He brought forth the seeds of the children of Adam from their backs to bear witness that Allah is their Lord, the Master, and that there is no god save He.

Reports of bringing out the children of Adam from his back have also come from the Prophet, with some other details such as their division into those of the right hand side and those of the left hand side. In some of them the testimony is also mentioned to the effect that Allah is their Lord.

و قد علم الله تعالى في الأَزَلِ عدد من يَدْخُل الجنة، وعدد من يَدخلُ النار، جملة واحدة، فلا يزداد في ذلك العدد، ولا ينقصُ منه وكذلك أفعالهم فيما علم منهم أن يفعلوه

Allah has known since eternity the number of those who will enter Paradise and those who will enter the Fire: in one aggregate. There will neither be an increase in this figure nor decrease; so is His knowledge of the deeds that they will commit.

Allah said:

إِنَّ اللهَ بِكُلِّ شَيْءٍ عَلِيمٌ

"Allah has knowledge of everything." (Al Tawbah, 115)

He also said:

وَكَانَ اللهُ بِكُلِّ شَيْءٍ عَلِيمًا

"And Allah is Aware of all things." (Al Fath, 26)

Thus Allah qualified Himself as one who has knowledge of everything: since eternity. His knowledge was not preceded by anything out of ignorance. "And your Lord was not such as to be forgetting."

`Ali said: "We were with a funeral party in Baqee` al Gharqad when the Prophet joined us. He sat down on the ground and we sat down around him. He was carrying a stick in his hand. He (sat there) with his head bent down drawing lines with his stick. Then he said, 'There isn't a soul that breathed but Allah has written for it an abode in Paradise or Hell fire. It is written down if it will be of the wretched ones or of the blessed ones.' At that someone enquired, 'O Messenger of Allah. Should we not then depend on what is written and give up working (for Paradise)?' He replied, 'One who is of the blessed ones will go about working the deeds of the blessed ones. And one who is of the wretched ones will go about committing the acts of the wretched ones.' Then he added, 'Keep working. For unto each has been made easy what he is created for. To the blessed ones, the deeds of the blessed ones shall be made easy. And to the wretched ones, the deeds of the wretched ones shall be made easy.' Then he recited:

فَأَمَّا مَنْ أَعْطَى وَاتَّقَى (٥) وَصَدَّقَ بِالْحُسْنَى (٦) فَسَنُيَسِّرُهُ لِلْيُسْرَى (٧) وَأَمَّا مَنْ بَخِلَ وَاسْتَغْنَى (٨)وَكَذَّبَ بِالْحُسْنَى (٩) فَسَنُيَسِّرُهُ لِلْعُسْرَى (١٠)

"As for him who gave and is god fearing, and testified to the Good, We shall make smooth for him (the path to) the Ease. And, as for him who is miserly and deems himself self sufficient, and cried lies to the Good, We shall surely make smooth for him (the path of) Hardship." (Al Layl, 5-10)

The above *hadith* is in the *Sahihayn.*

وكل ميسر لما خُلق له، والأعمال بالخواتيم: السعيد من سَعِدَ بقضاء الله، والشقي من شَقِيَ بقضاء الله

And everyone has been prepared for that for which he was created. As for the deeds, it is those near the end (of life) that count. Blessed is he who was blessed by the decree of Allah. And wretched is he who was made wretched by the decree of Allah.

Bukhari and Muslim have recorded `Abdullah ibn Mas`ud narrating the Prophet's words   the truthful and the one declared as truthful   as saying: "The structure of each of you is assembled in his mother's womb. It remains as a clot for forty days. Then he becomes like a leach for another forty days. After that for another forty days he acquires the shape of a chewed piece of flesh. Then Allah sends an angel to blow the soul into him. And four things are decreed for him: his provision, age, deeds, and whether he will be a wretched one or a blessed one. These are the things written down for him. By Him besides whom there is no god, one of you keeps performing the deeds of the people of Paradise until he is a foot away from it. But then the written word overtakes him and he begins to perform the deeds of the people of Fire. Consequently, he enters into it. And one of you keeps committing the deeds of the people of Fire until he is just a foot away from it. But then the written word overtakes him and he begins to work the deeds of the people of Paradise. Consequently, he enters into it."

There are several reports on this subject. And no few from the earliest forefathers themselves. Abu `Amr b. `Abd al Barr writes in his book "*Al Tamhid :*" 'Quite a few scholars have collected together the reports on this subject. The dialecticians have discussed it exceedingly. However, the *Ahl al Sunnah* are of one opinion, viz., belief in the reports and restrain from discussions. With Allah is to be sought the protection and guidance to the right attitude.

وأصل القَدَر سِرُّ الله تعالى في خلقه، لم يَطَّلع على ذلك مَلَك مُقَرَّب، ولا نبي مُرسل. والتعمُّق و النظر في ذلك: ذريعة الخُذلان، وسُلَّم الحرمان، ودَرَجة الطغيان، فالحَذَر كل الحذر من ذلك نظَرًا و فِكرًا وَ وَسْوَسَةً، فإن الله تعالى طَوى علمَ القدر عن أنامِه، وفَّاهم عن مَرامه، كما قال تعالى في كتابه: (لا يُسئل عما يفعل وهم يُسئلون) فمن سأل: لِمَ فعل؟ فقَد رد حكم الكتاب، ومن رد حكم الكتاب: كان من الكافرين

The truth about the Divine Decree involving the creation is a Divine secret. Neither an angel close (to Allah) nor a Prophet raised (among a people) has had any knowledge of it. An in depth inquiry and an intellectual exercise over it are a recourse to disappointment, a ladder to loss, and steps leading to rebellion. Therefore, one may remain watchfully on guard against indulgence in it: whether it is by way of ponder, an exercise of the intellect, or a suggestion of doubt. For Allah has concealed the knowledge of the Decree from mankind and has forbidden them to objectivize them. He said in His Book: "He is not questioned for what He does, (but) they shall be questioned." Therefore, whoever asked, 'Why did He do that?' rejected an ordinance of the Book. And whoever rejected an ordinance of the Book became an infidel.

It is the belief of the *Ahl al Sunnah* that everything that happens is by Allah's and by His Decree. The Qadariyyah and the Mu`tazilah have opposed them in this. They allege that Allah wished belief (and faith in Him) from the unbeliever, but it was the unbeliever who wished to be an unbeliever. The unbeliever's will overcame the will of Allah. But this is a most fallacious belief. Further, it is not supported by evidence. Indeed, this opinion is in opposition to the available evidence. Allah said:

وَ لَوْ شِئْنَا لَآتَيْنَا كُلَّ نَفْسٍ هُدٰىهَا وَلٰكِنْ حَقَّ الْقَوْلُ مِنِّى لَأَمْلَأَنَّ جَهَنَّمَ مِنَ الْجِنَّةِ وَالنَّاسِ أَجْمَعِيْنَ

"Had We so willed, We could have awarded to every soul its guidance, but My word will come true that I shall fill Jahannum with the Jinn and mankind all together." (Al Sajdah, 13)

He also said:

فَمَنْ يُّرِدِ اللهُ أَنْ يَّهْدِيَهُ يَشْرَحْ صَدْرَهُ لِلْاِسْلَامِ وَمَنْ يُّرِدْ أَنْ يُّضِلَّهُ يَجْعَلْ صَدْرَهُ ضَيِّقًا حَرَجًا كَأَنَّمَا يَصَّعَّدُ فِى السَّمَآءِ

"Whomsoever Allah intends to guide, He opens up his heart for Islam. And whomsoever He intends to lead astray, He closes his heart, constricted, as if he were engaged in sheer ascent toward the heaven." (Al An`ām, 125)

The clue to the error here is in equating Allah's Will and Desire with His Love and Approval. The Jabariyyah and the Qadariyyah failed to distinguish between the two. And, as it should happen, as they proceeded in their arguments, they disagreed between themselves. The Jabariyyah said: "Everything is by the Will and Decree of Allah. Therefore, (sin) is loved and approved by Allah." To their contrast, the Qadariyyah said: "Sins are neither approved by Allah nor loved by Him. They are neither by His Will nor by His Decree. They are altogether out of the range of His Will and creation."

Allah's Book however, as well as the Prophet's *Sunnah* and a person's incorrupt nature point to the difference between the Will and Approval. As for the Will of Allah, we have already stated evidences from the Book. As for His Approval and Love, here are a few. Allah said:

وَاللهُ لَا يُحِبُّ الْفَسَادَ

"He does not approve of corruption." (Al Baqarah, 205)

and,

وَلَا يَرْضَىٰ لِعِبَادِهِ الْكُفْرَ

"Allah does not approve of disbelief for His slaves." (Al Zumar, 7)

Trustworthy collections report the Prophet as having said: "Allah disapproves of three things for you: (i) 'That was said, this was said (i.e., unauthentic talk), (ii) too much questioning and (iii) wastage of wealth.'" Another *hadīth* in *Musnad*

Ahmed says: "Allah loves it that when He bestows an ease, it be accepted just as He disapproves that sins be sent across to Him."

If it is asked, how can Allah wish a thing but not approve of it? How does He will and how does it come about? How can His will and disapproval be reconciled?

The answer is: This is a question that has divided the people into sects parting away in their ways and ideas. In short, you have to understand that "the desirable" is of two kinds. First, for its own sake, and second, for another's sake. The first kind is desirable and lovable for its own sake and for what good that is obtained because of it. That is "the desirable" of the kind that meets with the ultimate objectives.

As for the desirable for another's sake, sometimes it might not be the objective of the desired nor there might be any benefit in it, for itself, although, it might happen to be a means to something else. Thus it might be an undesirable thing by itself, for itself, but desirable for the sake of the Universal will or the overall plan. Thus, two factors are brought together thereby: His dislike and His will, without any contradiction between them, because of separate objectives. An example is the bitter medicine about which it is established that it is of beneficence. Or, the cutting off of a limb, when it is established that in its severance is the survival of the rest of the body. Or, to give another example, traversing a distance filled with hardships if it is assured that it leads to one's goal and desire. Indeed, a wise man will tolerate the undesirable, even without a full assurance. What about One then, from whom nothing is hidden? Thus, Allah may disapprove of a thing, yet that does not prevent Him desire a thing for the sake of another, and for the reason that in the overall it leads to what is approved by Him.

Let us take some examples. He created Iblis who is the source of corruption in religion, deeds, beliefs and desires, in turn a source of lot of hardship to the people, giving birth to deeds that evoke Allah's anger. Satan strives to achieve what will displease Allah . Yet, and despite that, he is a means to many things that are loved and approved by Allah and which bear their consequences on His creations, whose existence is preferred over their non existence.

One such consequence is that Allah's Power to create the contrasts and contradictions is brought to light. He created this being (i.e. Satan), who is the most abominable of His creation, and, in contrast, created Jibra'il who is the most noble of creations. Glorified is Allah, the creator of this and that. This is also manifested in the creation of the day and the night, the disease and its cure, the beautiful and the ugly: all proofs of His Power and Perfection.

Another is the manifestation of the Attributes of Allah's Subduing and Vanquishing Powers, such as, *Al Qahhār* (the Subduer), *Al Muntaqim* (the Revengeful), the *Shadid al `Iqāb* (the Severe of Chastisement), the *Dhu al Butsh* (the Severe of Seizure), etc. All these Names and Attributes are signs of His Perfection which demand their manifestation in the created world. Had the Jinn and the men been of the same nature as the angels, these Attributes would not have come to light.

Another is the manifestation of those of Allah's Names that are bound with His mercy and forgiveness. Perhaps the Prophet was referring to this when he said: "If you were not to sin, Allah would replace you with a people who would commit sins, seek His forgiveness, so that He may forgive them."

Another wisdom consists in the institution of certain kinds of devotions to Allah which wouldn't have been possible without the creation of Satan. A case in point is *Jihad* that happens to be one of the most approved forms of worship. It wouldn't have been instituted (were not Iblis to be misguiding mankind). Had everyone been a Muslim, these modes of worship and what goes with them would have been non existent. Other examples are love for Allah and hatred for Allah, enjoining the good and forbidding the evil, patience, perseverance, repentance, and many others.

It might be asked: Wasn't the bringing into existence of the above possible without a recourse to these evils? This is an absurd question. It supposes the existence of the effect without a cause, such as to suppose the existence of motion without a mover, and of repentance without there being a reason for repentance.

If it is asked, how does Allah approve of a thing for His slave without aiding him in it? The answer is, His aiding him would mean the loss of something whose loss is dearer to Him than the good deeds that might outflow with His approval. Alternatively, it might be that the good deeds thus obtained might incorporate an evil that is of greater dislike to Allah than that good deed. Allah has hinted at that when He said:

$$\text{وَلَوْ أَرَادُوا الْخُرُوجَ لَأَعَدُّوا لَهُ عُدَّةً وَّلَكِنْ كَرِهَ اللهُ انْبِعَاثَهُمْ فَثَبَّطَهُمْ وَقِيلَ اقْعُدُوا مَعَ الْقَاعِدِيْنَ}$$

"Had they intended to go out (with the Prophet, in Jihad) they would have made preparations thereof. But Allah was averse to their being sent forth, so he made them lag behind and it was said, 'Remain seated with those who sit back." (Al Tawbah, 46)

Allah made it known that He disapproved that they should go out in a campaign in the company of the Prophet. Their going out would have been a virtuous deed. But Allah disapproved of it. Subsequently, He spoke of some of the evil consequences that would have followed had they gone out with the Prophet. He said:

$$\text{لَوْ خَرَجُوا فِيكُمْ مَّا زَادُوكُمْ إِلَّا خَبَالًا}$$

"Had they gone forth with you, they would not have caused anything but disorder." (Al Tawbah, 47)

Then He added:

$$\text{وَلَأَوْضَعُوا خِلَالَكُمْ يَبْغُونَكُمُ الْفِتْنَةَ وَفِيكُمْ سَمَّاعُونَ لَهُمْ وَاللهُ عَلِيمٌ بِالظَّالِمِيْنَ}$$

"They would have hustled to and fro in your midst, sowing sedition between you, while among you are some who would listen to them. And Allah is well aware of the transgressors." (Al Tawbah, 47)

By the above statement, what He meant is that: they would have strived to create dissension. And among you were those who would have responded to them. That would have given birth to greater evil than the good that would have accrued, had they gone out with you. Therefore, wisdom and mercy required that they be restrained from taking up the journey.

Use this example and work out others if you will.

If it is asked: If unbelief is by the Divine Decree, and we have been ordered to be content with the Divine Decree, how then shall we disapprove of unbelief and resent it?

The answer is, firstly, we have not been ordered to be content with 'all' that Allah has decreed. The Book and the *Sunnah* have said no such thing. Rather, of the decreed, there are things to which we are to surrender our wills, while there are others that we are to disapprove and show disdain. A judge can be taken as an example. He cannot be content with the decree of Allah, rather has to show anger (and hand out punishments). In a similar manner, there are those of the decreed of Allah that we show anger to, disapprove of and curse.

Secondly, two elements are involved here. First of them is the Decree of Allah. It is an act associated with Allah's Person. The second is that which was decreed. It is an event that has already occurred and is dissociated from Allah's Person. The first the Divine Decree is entirely good, just and wise. So we approve of it wholly. As for that which has been decreed, of it there are two kinds: one, which we approve, and the other which we do not.

Thirdly, it might be said in answer to the doubt expressed above that the Divine Decree has two aspects. One of them is related to Allah Himself. To this aspect we show approval. The other is related to His creations. Now, this second kind can again be categorized into two. The one with which we can be satisfied, and the other with which we cannot express our satisfaction.

To illustrate, we might take the example of a murder. It has two aspects. Inasmuch as Allah's decree, His Will, command, and His pre determination of the act as the cause of murder is concerned, we show our approval. But, from the point of view of it happening at the hands of the murderer, his determination to carry out the act, and sinning against Allah by the deed, to all these we show our anger and disapproval.

Tahawi's words: "Therefore, whoever asked, 'Why did He do that?' rejected an ordinance of the Book. And whoever rejected an ordinance of the Book became an infidel," express the correct opinion. The foundation of faith in Allah, His Books and His Messengers, rests in surrender to Him and in non questioning of the details of wisdom involved in the commands, forbiddance and in the

Shari`ah laws in general. Accordingly, it can be noticed that Allah did not narrate the case of a single nation, which believed in the Messenger sent to it, yet persisted in knowing the details of wisdom involved in what He commanded or forbade. Had those people done that, they wouldn't have been considered believers at all. Rather, those people submitted themselves and surrendered. What they knew of the wisdom, they knew. What they didn't, they did not use it as a pretext to delay their faith and surrender. Hence, the first few generations of the followers of Prophet Muhammad, the most intelligent of the nations and the most knowledgeable of them never asked their Prophet as to why Allah had ordered a thing or why He had decreed it the way He did. They realized that such an attitude stood in contradiction to faith and submission.

فهذا جُملة ما يَحتاج إليه مَن هو مُنَوَّر قلبُه من أولياء الله تعالى، وهي درجة الراسخين في العلم، لأن العلم علمان: عِلم في الخلق موجود، و علم في الخلق مفقود، فإنكار العلم الموجود: كفر، وادعاء العلم المفقود كفر، ولا يثبت الإيمان إلا بقبول العلم الموجود، وترك طلب العلم المفقود

This in brief is what the Favorites of Allah Most High, the enlightened of heart, need, and this is the rank of the well grounded in knowledge. For, of knowledge there are two kinds. One, existent among the creation, and the other, non existent. Denial of the existent knowledge is infidelity. On the other hand, claiming to have knowledge of the non existent is infidelity too. Faith is not well grounded without acceptance of the existent knowledge and non pursuance of the non existent knowledge.

When Tahawi said "this," he meant all that was stated earlier: of the beliefs and acts concerning those things that pertain to the *Shari`ah.*

His words "this is the rank of the well grounded in knowledge" refer to the knowledge received from the Prophet, peace on him, in brief or in detail, the affirmative or the negative of it.

By the words "the non existent knowledge" he means the knowledge of the Pre destination and the Divine Decree that Allah has concealed from His creation and forbade its pursuance.

By the words "the existent knowledge" he means the knowledge of the religion of Islam, both its principles as well as its details.

We might add for clarity that whoever denied anything of what the Prophet brought is of the infidels and whoever claimed knowledge of the Unseen became an infidel. Allah (*swt*) said:

عَلِمُ الْغَيْبِ فَلَا يُظْهِرُ عَلَى غَيْبِهِ اَحَدًا (٢٦) اِلَّا مَنِ ارْتَضَى مِنْ رَّسُوْلٍ فَاِنَّهُ يَسْلُكُ مِنْ بَيْنِ يَدَيْهِ وَمِنْ خَلْفِهِ رَصَدًا (٢٧) لِّيَعْلَمَ اَنْ قَدْ اَبْلَغُوْا رِسَلَتِ رَبِّهِمْ وَاَحَاطَ بِمَا لَدَيْهِمْ وَاَحْصٰى كُلَّ شَيْءٍ عَدَدًا (٢٨)

"He is the Knower of the Unseen. No one has access to His Unseen. Except for what He will (reveal) to a Messenger, for, He runs guardians before and after him. That He may know that they truly delivered their Lord's messages. And He has encompassed what is in their possession and has taken account of every single thing." (Al Jinn, 26-28)

Thus, the obscurity of Allah's wisdom from us does not mean its non existence, nor our ignorance of it demands its preclusion. Don't you see that ourselves not knowing Allah's wisdom in the creation of scorpions and other such creatures of which we know not but its harm is not enough to deny that Allah is its creator. Nor does it mean that there should be no wisdom hidden from us. Lack of knowledge does not mean non existence of knowledge.

ونؤمن باللوح والقلم، وبجميع ما فيه قد رَقَم

We attest faith in the Tablet and the Pen, and in all that is inscribed in it.

Allah Most High has said:

بَلْ هُوَ قُرْاٰنٌ مَّجِيْدٌ (٢١) فِيْ لَوْحٍ مَّحْفُوْظٍ (٢٢)

"Nay, this is a noble Qur`an, *(written) in a Preserved Tablet." (Al Burūj, 21,22)*

The Tablet mentioned here is the one in which Allah has written down the details of His Decree concerning His creations. The Pen spoken of above is the one which Allah (*swt*) created and with which He got the Decrees written down, as confirmed by a *hadith* in Abu Da'ud. `Ubadah b. Sāmit said: "I heard the Prophet (*saws*) say, 'The first thing Allah (*swt*) created was the Pen. Then He ordered it, "Write." The Pen asked, "O My Lord. What shall I write?" He said, "Write down the Decrees of everything that will come to be until the Day of Judgement.'"

The scholars have disagreed over which of the two was created earlier: the `Arsh or the Pen. Abu al `Alā' Hamdani has discussed the issue and stated that the correct opinion is that it was the `Arsh which was created earlier. This is supported by a *hadith* in trustworthy collections reported by `Abdullah ibn `Amr. He said: "I heard the Prophet (*saws*) say, 'Allah (*swt*) wrote down His Decrees concerning the creations fifty thousand years before He created the heavens and the earth.' He added, `And His `Arsh was then on Water.'" This shows that the Decrees were written down after the creation of the `Arsh, and that the Decrees were the first thing to be written down after creation of the Pen.

Now, the Prophet's words: "The first thing Allah created ... until the end," could be treated either as one sentence, or, as two. If it is treated as one sentence, which seems to be correct, then it would mean, "The first thing He ordered the Pen upon its creation was to write ..." But, if it is treated as two sentences, as in some narrations, then it would mean, "The first thing Allah (*swt*) created was the Pen..." In either case it agrees with the *hadith* of `Abdullah ibn `Amr which says that the `Arsh preceded the Decree and that Decree is simultaneous to the creation of the Pen.

The Pen in question is the first Pen and the most honorable one. More than one commentator of the Qur'an have said that this is the Pen that Allah swore by when He said:

ن وَالْقَلَمِ وَمَا يَسْطُرُونَ

"Nūn. By the Pen and by what they (the angels) scribe." (Al Qalam, 1-2)

The other pen is the pen for revelation. That is, the pen with which the revelations to the Prophets and Messengers are written down. Those who hold these pens are the governors of the cosmos. The rest of the pens serve their pens. The sound of the movement of the pens that our Prophet spoke of in some of his narrations in connection with the night journey and ascension, is of these

126

pens. By these pens are written down the commands of Allah Most High sent to those in charge of the upper and the lower worlds (i.e., the entire universe).

فلو اجتمع الخلق كلهم على شيء كتبه الله تعالى فيه أنه كائن: ليجعلوه غير كائن— لم يقدروا عليه. ولو اجتمعوا كلهم على شئ لم يكتبه الله تعالى فيه، ليجعلوه كائنا— لم يقدروا عليه. جَفَّ القلم بما هو كائن إلى يوم القيامة

If the whole of the creation agreed upon not allowing to come into existence what has been written in it as what will come to exist, they would not be able to do it. Conversely, if they all agreed upon the creation of something that Allah did not write in it, they would not be able to do so. The Pen has dried up over what will be until the Day of Judgment.

This is confirmed by a *hadīth* narrated by Jabir. He reports: "Suraqa ibn Malik b. Ju`tham came up and asked, 'Messenger of Allah. Explain to us our religion as if we were created today. What would be today's act. Would they be what the Pens have dried up with and the course that the decrees have run? Or is the affair tied up to the future?' the Prophet (*saws*) replied, 'Rather, what the Pens have dried up with and the course that the decrees have run.'"

Ibn `Abbas reports: "One day I was the pillion rider of the Prophet. He said, 'My boy. May I not teach you some words? Remember Allah, He will remember you. Remember Allah, and you will find Him ahead of you. When you ask, ask of Allah. When you seek help, seek Allah's help. And know that were the people to agree upon doing you a good, they would not be able to do it, save for what Allah has written for you. And, if they agree upon doing you a harm, they would not be able to do it, save for what Allah has written for you. Pens have been withdrawn and the Books have dried up.' (Tirmidhi recorded it and classified it as quite trustworthy).

Now, once a slave has realized that everything is from Allah, then it is incumbent upon him that he fear none but Him. Allah (*swt*) said:

فَلَا تَخْشَوُا النَّاسَ وَاخْشَوْنِ

"Therefore, do not fear the people. Fear Me." (Al Mā'idah, 44)

Allah Most High also said:

وَمَنْ يُطِعِ اللهَ وَرَسُولَهُ وَيَخْشَ اللهَ وَيَتَّقْهِ فَأُولَٰئِكَ هُمُ الْفَائِزُونَ

"Whoever obeyed Allah and His Messenger, feared Allah and was godfearing, such indeed, they are the successful." (Al Nūr, 52)

Some of the earliest scholars have said: If a person fears Allah, he shall be in need of nothing. For Allah has said:

وَمَنْ يَتَّقِ اللهَ يَجْعَل لَهُ مَخْرَجًا , وَّيَرْزُقْهُ مِنْ حَيْثُ لَا يَحْتَسِبُ

"And whoever feared Allah, He will find a way out for him and will provide him from sources he did not imagine." (Al Talāq, 2,3)

Thus, Allah has assured the believers that He will find for them a way out of situations that prove to be difficult for them, and will provide them from sources they didn't imagine provision could come from. If that does not happen, then it might be assumed that there is something amiss in one's God fearing quality. One might seek Allah's forgiveness and repent to Him.

Allah then followed up with:

وَمَنْ يَّتَوَكَّلْ عَلَى اللهِ فَهُوَ حَسْبُهُ

"And whoever trusts in Allah, then He is sufficient for him." (Al Talāq, 3)

That is to say, Allah is enough for him and shall not leave him dependent on others.

Some people believe that trust in Allah (*tawakkul*) negates striving for a thing, rather, it demands severance of all material means. They say that if things have already been decreed, there is no need to resort to the means. This is untrue. For, of the means, some are obligatory, while others are either desirable, permissible, undesirable, or prohibited. the Prophet (*saws*) was the most excellent in the quality of *tawakkul*, yet would wear coat of arms and go about in the market in search of the means of sustenance. Indeed, the infidels even objected to this. They said:

مَالِ هٰذَا الرَّسُولِ يَأْكُلُ الطَّعَامَ وَيَمْشِيْ فِى الْأَسْوَاقِ

"What's the matter with this Messenger that he eats food and goes about in the market." (Al Furqān, 7)

Accordingly, you will find most of those who think that striving for means contradicts trust in Allah, depend on others for bestowals, either by way of charity or gifts.

و ما أخطأ العبدَ لم يكن ليصيبه، و ما أصابه لم يكن لِيُخطئه

What the slave missed, could not have befallen him and what befell him, could not have missed him.

This has its basis in the preceding discussion, viz., what has been decreed has to happen.

A slave has to know that Allah's knowledge has preceded everything that is ever to happen. He decreed it as firm, irrevocable, without a fault; nor is there any of the creations in the heavens and the earth to reverse it, erase it, change it, or cause a decrease or increase to it.

This is also based on the preceding discussion about Allah's knowledge being precedent to whatever will ever happen, and that He decreed the measure of everything before its creation. the Prophet said: "Allah (*swt*) ordained the decrees fifty thousand years before the creation of the heaven and the earth. His `Arsh was then on Water." This shows that Allah had knowledge of the things that would come into existence, at such and such a point in time, following His all comprehensive wisdom. Accordingly, they came into being in accordance with His knowledge. For, the coming into existence of the creations incorporating the wonderful wisdom that goes with them, cannot be imagined save at the hands of the knowledgeable, whose knowledge preceded their existence. Allah (*swt*) said:

اَلَا يَعْلَمُ مَنْ خَلَقَ وَهُوَ اللَّطِيفُ الْخَبِيرُ

"Should He not know who created, when He is the Subtle, the Aware?" (Al Mulk, 14)

Some at the extreme end of the Mu`tazilah deny that Allah's knowledge preceded since eternity. They said that Allah does not know what deeds are going to issue forth of His slaves, until they have acted. Exalted be Allah, above what they allege.

This is one of the pillars of faith, a fundamental knowledge and the confession of faith in Allah's Oneness and in His Lordship. Allah said in His Book: "He created everything and decreed it in perfect proportion." Allah also said: "And Allah's command was a decree perfectly determined."

Ibn `Abbas is reported to have said: "Divine Decree is the framework of *Tawhīd*. Whoever declared faith in Allah's Oneness but denied the Divine Decree nullified his faith in *Tawhīd*."

This is because faith in the Divine Decree is a component of faith in Allah's all comprehensive knowledge since eternity, and in what of knowledge of the unlimited degree that He manifested including the writing of the decrees of the creations. Quite a few of the polytheists, Sabians, philosophers and others have erred here. They deny the knowledge of the details. This however, is counted as denial of the Divine Decree itself. The Qadariyyah have outright denied Allah's power over everything. They say that He does not create the deeds of the creations. They have considered it beyond Allah's power and creation.

As for the Divine Decree which is beyond doubt proven by the Qur`an, the *Sunnah* and consensus, and over which the Qadariyyah have argued without cause pertains to Allah's ordaining of the decrees of His creation. Most of the statements of the Companions and the great Imams regarding the criticism of the Qadariyyah is aimed at this kind of people.

وَعَلَى العَبْدِ أَنْ يَعْلَمَ أَنَّ الله قَدْ سَبَقَ عِلْمَهُ فِي كُلِّ كَائِنٍ مِنْ خَلْقِهِ، فَقَدَّرَ ذَلِكَ تَقْدِيراً مُحْكَماً مُبْرَماً، لَيْسَ فِيهِ نَاقِضٌ، وَلَا مُعَقِّبٌ وَلَا مُزِيلَ وَلَا مُغَيِّرَ وَلَا نَاقِصَ وَلَا زَائِدَ مِنْ خَلْقِهِ فِي سَمَاوَاتِهِ وَأَرْضِهِ

A slave has to understand that Allah's knowledge has preceded everything that is ever to happen. He decreed it as firm, irrevocable, without a fault; nor is there any of the creations in his heavens or his earth to reverse it, erase it, change it, or cause a decrease or increase to it.

وَذَلِكَ مِنْ عَقْدِ الإِيمَانِ، وَ أُصُولِ المَعْرِفَةِ، والاعْتِرَافِ بِتَوْحِيدِ الله تَعَالَى وَ رُبُوبِيَّتِهِ كَمَا قَالَ تَعَالَى فِي كِتَابِهِ: (وَخَلَقَ كُلَّ شِيءٍ فَقَدَّرَهُ تَقْدِيرًا) وقال تعالى (وكان أمر الله قدرا مقدورا)

This is one of the pillars of faith, a fundamental knowledge and the declaration of faith in Allah's Oneness and His Lordship. Allah said in His Book: "He created everything and decreed it in perfect proportion." He also said, "And Allah's command was a decree perfectly determined."

فويل لمن صار لله تعالى في القدر خصيما، وأحضر للنظر فيه قلبا سقيما، لقد التمس بوهمه في فحص الغيب سرًّا كتيما، وعاد بما قال فيه أفاكا أثيما

Woe unto the man then, whose heart hardened against the Divine Decree. The man tried in his ignorance to look into the very heart of a well guarded secret and overstepped his bounds with utterances concerning (the subject), fastening a lie and sinning thereby.

What you have to realize that the heart undergoes life and death, sickness, and cure; and that these afflictions are more serious of nature than those of the body. Allah Most High said:

أَوَمَنْ كَانَ مَيْتًا فَأَحْيَيْنَاهُ وَجَعَلْنَا لَهُ نُورًا يَمْشِي بِهِ فِي النَّاسِ كَمَنْ مَثَلُهُ فِي الظُّلُمَاتِ لَيْسَ بِخَارِجٍ مِّنْهَا

"Is he who was dead, then We gave him life and set for him a light, whereby he walks amongst men   be equal to one who is in darknesses from which he cannot escape?" (Al An`ām, 122)

That is, the man was dead in the state of unbelief. Allah gave him life by means of faith. The true, pure and living heart then, when it is presented with falsehood and the unclean, turns away from them instinctively, disapproving of them. In contrast, a sick heart cannot distinguish between the good and the bad as `Abdullah ibn Mas`ud said: "Destroyed is the man who hasn't got a heart that cannot distinguish between the virtuous and the deplorable." That is also true of the heart that is sick because of carnal desires overpowering it. Because of its weaknesses, it too falls prey to whatever it encounters, in proportions equal to its weakness.

Of the diseases of the heart, there are two kinds: the disease of the carnal desires and disease of doubts. Of the two, the worse is the disease of doubts. And the worst of doubts is the doubt concerning the Divine Decree. Occasionally, the heart sickens and its state worsens without the man realizing it ever, because of his engrossment in other affairs and because of ignorance of its state of health and the means of its cure. Sometimes, the heart dies altogether without the knowledge of the man. The sign of its death is in the man not feeling any pain over the evils and falsehood. To such a one, his own ignorance does not worry him in the least. Whereas, as we know, when the heart has life in it, it feels pain when it encounters the repugnant and feels *Sād* at its ignorance of the truth. A poetical piece says: "The dead do not feel any pain for injuries done to them."

Of course, sometimes a man feels the sickness of his heart. But the bitter medicine coupled with a prolonged treatment is hard upon him. He prefers the disease of the heart over the bitterness of the medicine. That is because its cure consists in suppressing the carnal desires. But that's hard upon certain souls although there is nothing better than that for them. Sometimes the man begins a course, but gives up too soon because of his want of knowledge and lack of perseverance. His situation is similar to that of a man entering into a fearsome path leading to a place of security. He knows that if he persists he will end up in a secure place. He needs the qualities of persistence and perseverance and belief in the goodness of his mission target. But, when he runs short of patience, he begins to retrace his steps, especially when lack of companionship and being left alone add up to his miseries. He begins to ask: "Where are those people that I had thought I would follow them?" That's what happens to most people and which leads to their destruction. But a persevering person does not worry over the lack of companionship, if he realizes that he is in the footsteps of earlier caravans:

الَّذِيْنَ أَنْعَمَ اللهُ عَلَيْهِمْ مِّنَ النَّبِيّنَ وَالصِّدِّيقِيْنَ وَالشُّهَدَآءِ وَالصُّلِحِيْنَ وَحَسُنَ أُولٰٓئِكَ رَفِيْقًا

"Those whom Allah favored: of the Prophets, the Truthful, the Martyrs and the righteous and a good company they are." (Al Nisā, 69)

How rightly said Abu Muhammad `Abd al Rahman b. Isma`il, popularly known as Abu Shamah, in his book "The Novel and the Innovations" while speaking of the necessity to remain with the *Jama`ah*: "What it truly means is to hold fast unto the truth and follow it, even if those adhering to it be few, and its opponents plenty. For it is truth that the preceding *Jama`ah* held fast unto, at the time of the Prophet (*saws*). We pay no attention to the great numbers after them holding falsehood as true."

Hasan al Busri has said: "The *Sunnah* is by Him besides whom there is no god between the two extremes of negation and indulgence. Therefore, hold fast unto it may Allah show you mercy. The followers of the *Sunnah* have been few in preceding generations too; and they will be few in the people that are left: those who did not opt for the indulgent in their indulgence nor with the innovators in their innovations, rather, stayed on the *Sunnah* until they met their Lord. Be like them."

Another sign of the heart's sickness is its disinclination towards the healthy food in preference of the unhealthy and its disinclination towards the useful cure in preference of the harmful medications. Thus we are led to four things: healthy food, medication that cures, unhealthy food and medication that kills. A healthy heart prefers the healthy and the curing over the unhealthy and the non curing. The sick heart acts exactly in the opposite manner. And the most healthy of foods is faith while the most beneficial of the medicines is the Qur`an. The two provide food as well as medicine. Whoever sought cure in other than the Qur`an and the *Sunnah*, is the most ignorant of the ignorant and the most unguided of the unguided. Allah (*swt*) says:

قُلْ هُوَ لِلَّذِيْنَ اٰمَنُوْا هُدًى وَشِفَآءٌ وَ الَّذِيْنَ لَا يُؤْمِنُوْنَ فِىْ اٰذَانِهِمْ وَقْرٌ وَّهُوَ عَلَيْهِمْ عَمًى أُولٰٓئِكَ يُنَادَوْنَ مِنْ مَّكَانٍ بَعِيْدٍ

"Say, 'It is, (i.e., the Qur`an) a guidance and a cure for the faithful. As for those who do not believe, there is a deafness in their ears and a blind over their eyes. Such, (as if) they are being called from a distant place." (Fussilat, 44)

Allah also said:

وَنُنَزِّلُ مِنَ الْقُرْآنِ مَا هُوَ شِفَآءٌ وَّرَحْمَةٌ لِّلْمُؤْمِنِينَ وَلَا يَزِيدُ الظَّلِمِينَ إِلَّا خَسَارًا

"And We send down of the Qur`an that which is a cure and a mercy for the believers. As for the transgressors, it (the Qur`an) does not cause an increase, but in loss." (Al Isrā', 82)

وَ الْعَرْشُ وَالْكُرْسِيُّ حَقُّ

And the *`Arsh* and the *Kursiyy* are true (facts).

This is evident from the words of Allah in His Book:

ذُو الْعَرْشِ الْمَجِيدُ , فَعَّالٌ لِّمَا يُرِيدُ

"Lord of the Exalted `Arsh, Doer of what He will." (Al Burūj, 15 16)

He also said:

رَفِيعُ الدَّرَجَٰتِ ذُو الْعَرْشِ

"Exalted is He in His Rank, the Lord of the `Arsh." (Ghāfir, 15)

Also:

الرَّحْمَٰنُ عَلَى الْعَرْشِ اسْتَوَىٰ

"The Merciful, assumed Istawā' on the `Arsh." (Tāhā, 5)

Also:

اللهُ لَآ إِلَٰهَ إِلَّا هُوَ رَبُّ الْعَرْشِ الْعَظِيمِ

"Allah. There is no god save He. The Lord of the Supreme `Arsh." (Al Namal, 26)

Bukhari has recorded a *hadīth* of the Prophet (*saws*) according to which the Prophet said: "When you ask Allah for Paradise, ask for *Firdaws*. It is in the middle and the best part of Paradise, above which is the `Arsh of the Merciful."

It is also known that the `Arsh has posts and that the angels carry it. the Prophet (*saws*) said: "Everyone will swoon. I would be the first to recover. I will find Musa up, holding one of the posts of `Arsh. I wouldn't know if he recovered earlier than me, or he was spared in compensation of his swooning at Mount Tur." (Bukhari and Muslim).

Linguistically, `Arsh is used for an elevated seating structure that the kings and emperors use (for their appearance before their audience). Allah used the word in the same sense speaking about Bilqis. He said:

$$وَلَهَا عَرْشٌ عَظِيمٌ$$

"*And she has a magnificent throne.*" (Al Namal, 23)

As regards him who said that the word `Arsh is equivalent of Kingdom he who said that interpolated in the Qur`an. What will he say to the following words of Allah?

$$وَيَحْمِلُ عَرْشَ رَبِّكَ فَوْقَهُمْ يَوْمَئِذٍ ثَمَانِيَةٌ$$

"*That day the `Arsh of your Lord will be borne by eight.*" (Al Hāqqah, 17)

And His words:

$$وَكَانَ عَرْشُهُ عَلَى الْمَاءِ$$

"*Then His `Arsh was on Water.*" (Hūd, 7)

Will he say: That day His Kingdom will be borne by eight? And that His Kingdom was on Water? Or that Musa was holding a post of the many posts of His Kingdom? Will any rational man say that?

As for *Kursiyy*, Allah said:

$$وَسِعَ كُرْسِيُّهُ السَّمَاوَاتِ وَالْأَرْضَ$$

"*His Kursiyy extends over the heavens and the earth.*" (Al Baqarah, 255)

Some scholars have said that *Kursiyy* is nothing but *`Arsh*. But the truth is *Kursiyy* is different from *`Arsh*. This is the opinion of Ibn `Abbas and others.

Ibn Abi Shaybah has stated in his work "The Description of the *`Arsh*," as has also Hakim in his Mustadrak, that a report which meets with the conditions set up by Bukhari and Muslim, although they did not record it, says that Sa`id ibn Jubayr reported Ibn `Abbas as saying, while discussing the words of Allah (2: 255), 'His *Kursiyy* circumscribes the heavens and the earth,': "*Kursiyy* is the place where the Qadamayn rest. As for *`Arsh*, no one knows its extent save Allah."

Some people have attributed the above words to the Prophet himself. But the truth is they are the words of Ibn `Abbas (and not of the Prophet).

Other scholars have said that it is in front of the *`Arsh* functioning like a stepping stool.

وَ هُوَ مُسْتَغْنٍ عَنِ الْعَرْشِ وَمَا دُونَهُ مُحيط بكل شيء وَفَوقَه، وقد أعجزَ عن الإحاطة خلقة

However, Allah is in no need of the *`Arsh* or whatever else. He circumscribes everything and is High above everything. The creation cannot circumscribe Him.

The first part of the statement above has the following words of Allah in evidence:

إنَّ اللَّه لَغَنِيٌّ عَنِ الْعَلَمِينَ

"Verily. Allah is free of needs from all creations." (Al `Ankabūt, 6)

Our Sheikh (Tahawi) added these words after he spoke of the *`Arsh* and the *Kursiyy* in order to lead the minds away from the thought that Allah is in need of them. The *`Arsh* is for His *Istawā* but not because He is any need of it. Rather, it is His wisdom which demands it. Being above a lower thing does not mean at all that the lower circumscribes the upper (as a coin in the pan: tr.), acting as a partition for the one above, with the one above in need of the one lower. Take for example the earth and the heavens. The heavens are above the earth but do

136

not need the earth for holding on to their own. Allah is High Exalted above everything that anything should circumscribe Him. He has the Qualities of being Higher over everything. It is He who holds the lower in its place. The lower is in need of His support. Allah is above the `Arsh, along with those who bear it and by His Power holds them in position. He being in no need of the `Arsh, of the `Arsh being in need of Him, of His being circumscribing the `Arsh, of the `Arsh not being able to circumscribe Him, of His encompassment of the `Arsh, of the `Arsh being unable to encompass Him these are concomitant of His Being Apart from the Creations.

If those who deny the Above ness of Allah, who tend to strip Allah (*swt*) of His Attributes, were to apply their minds to these details, they would surely be rightly guided and would have found that the Revelation confirms with reason and logic. They would have then held an opinion that they could have defended. But, they abandoned proofs and lost a straight path. The final word in these kind of matters are those of Imam Malik who said: "We know (the literal meaning of) *Istawā* (i.e. to settle oneself). But we do not know its How."

With regard to Tahawi's words, "He circumscribes everything and is above everything," we have already offered proofs that the `Arsh is above every creation and that there is nothing of the creation above it.

As for the words that He circumscribes everything, they have their basis in the following words of Allah:

وَلِلّٰهِ مَا فِى السَّمٰوٰتِ وَمَا فِى الْأَرْضِ وَكَانَ اللّٰهُ بِكُلِّ شَىْءٍ مُّحِيطًا

"And to Allah belong all that is in the heavens and the earth, and Allah encompasses everything." (Al Nisā, 126)

None the less, the fact that He circumscribes everything does not mean at all that He surrounds the creation in the manner in which the heaven surrounds the earth: as if the creations are within His Person. High and Exalted Allah is above all that by a great degree. What is meant is: He circumscribes everything by His Greatness, Knowledge and Power. They are like a mustard seed for Him.

As for Him being above His creations, this is clearly proven by several verses of the Qur`an and statements in the *ahādith*. Allah said:

وَهُوَ الْقَاهِرُ فَوْقَ عِبَادِهِ

"He is the Irresistible, above His slaves." (Al An`ām, 18)

He also said:

يَخَافُونَ رَبَّهُم مِّن فَوْقِهِمْ

"They fear their Lord from above them." (Al Nahal, 50)

Abu Hurayrah has narrated the Prophet as having said: "When Allah decreed His creation, He wrote down in a Book, and it is with Him over the `Arsh: 'My mercy shall overcome My anger.' (Bukhari and others have preserved it).

Further, in connection with the incident of Banu Qurayzah, involving Sa`d b. Mu`adh, it is reported that when Sa`d gave his judgement in favor of death for the warriors, and enslavement of the women and children, the Prophet (*saws*) remarked: "You pronounced your over them by the judgement of the King who is above the seven heavens." This is an authentic report that Umawiyy has narrated in his "*Maghāzi*" and has its basis in the collections of Bukhari and Muslim.

Bukhari has also recorded a *hadīth* of Zaynab. She used to proudly say to the other wives of the Prophet (*saws*): "Your folks married you off (here on earth). I was married off by Allah from above the seven heavens."

It is reported that `Umar passed by an old decrepit woman who sought his attention. He stood by quite a while speaking to her. Someone remarked: "O Leader of the faithful. You delayed others because of this old woman!" `Umar replied: "Woe unto you man. Who do you reckon this woman is? This is the woman whose complaint Allah heard from above the seven heavens. This is Khawlah about whom Allah (*swt*) revealed:

قَدْ سَمِعَ اللهُ قَوْلَ الَّتِى تُجَادِلُكَ فِى زَوْجِهَا وَ تَشْتَكِى إِلَى اللهِ

"Allah has heard the words of the one who spoke to you complaining to Allah of her husband." (Al Mujadalah, 1)

(Dārami has preserved the above *hadīth*).

Whoever has a sound understanding of the traditions of the Prophet and of the opinions of the *Salaf* will find ample proofs confirming the concept of "Above-ness." It is said that there are around twenty different kinds of textual proofs to the effect that Allah is above all His creations. Here are most of them.

First, the use of the article *"min"* (from) along with the word "above" which, put together, only give the meaning of being above. Such as in the statement:

يَخَافُونَ رَبَّهُمْ مِّنْ فَوْقِهِمْ

"They fear their Lord from above them." (Al Nahal, 50)

Second, statement carrying the same meaning, even if the article *"min"* is absent such as,

وَهُوَ الْقَاهِرُ فَوْقَ عِبَادِهْ

"And He is the Irresistible, above His slaves." (Al An`ām, 18)

Third, declaration of "ascension" (by His creations) such as,

تَعْرُجُ الْمَلَآئِكَةُ وَ الرُّوحُ إِلَيْهِ

"The angels and the Spirit ascend up to Him." (Al Ma`ārij, 4)

Fourth, the use of the word "rise" such as:

إِلَيْهِ يَصْعَدُ الْكَلِمُ الطَّيِّبُ

"The good word rises up to Him." (Fātir, 10)

Fifth, His raising up of some of His creations to Himself such as,

بَل رَّفَعَهُ اللهُ إِلَيْهِ

"Rather, Allah raised him up to Himself." (Al Nisā', 158)

And His words,

إِنِّي مُتَوَفِّيكَ وَرَافِعُكَ إِلَيَّ

"I will complete your term and will raise you up unto Me." (Āl `Imrān, 55)

Sixth, the declaration of an absolute above ness indicative of all kinds of "above ness," whether it pertains to the Person, rank or honor. As Allah said:

وَ هُوَ الْعَلِيُّ الْعَظِيمُ

"And He is the Most High and the Supreme." (Al Baqarah, 255)

Seventh, the declaration that the Book was sent "down" such as in the verse:

تَنْزِيلُ الْكِتَابِ مِنَ اللهِ الْعَزِيزِ الْعَلِيمِ

"The sending down of the Book is from Allah, the Mighty, the Knowing." (Ghāfir, 2)

And,

تَنْزِيلٌ مِّنَ الرَّحْمَٰنِ الرَّحِيمْ

"The sending down from the Kind, the Merciful." (Fussilat, 2)

And,

قُلْ نَزَّلَهُ رُوحُ الْقُدُسِ مِنْ رَبِّكَ بِالْحَقِّ

"Tell (them), 'The holy Spirit has brought it down from your Lord with truth." (Al Nahal, 102)

Eighth, the declaration that some of the created things are with Him while others are nearer to Him than some others such as:

اِنَّ الَّذِينَ عِنْدَ رَبِّكَ

"Verily, those who are near to your Lord." (Al A`rāf, 206)

Or,

وَلَهُ مَنْ فِي السَّمٰوٰتِ وَالْأَرْضِ وَمَنْ عِنْدَهُ

"And to Him belong whatever is in the heavens and the earth, as well as those who are with Him." (Al Anbiyā, 19)

In the above example, He distinguished between those who belong to Him, generally, and those who are near Him of the angels or slaves.

Ninth, the declaration that He is in the heavens such as:

اَمْ اَمِنْتُمْ مَّنْ فِى السَّمَآءِ اَنْ يُّرْسِلَ عَلَيْكُمْ حَاصِبًا

"Do you feel secure from the One who is in the Heaven that He will not send against you a violent storm?" (Al Mulk, 17)

Tenth, the declaration that He has assumed *"Istawā"* on the `Arsh which, as we know, is over and above all creations.

Eleventh, the implication in the raising of hands towards Allah as in the words of the Prophet (*saws*): "Verily, Allah feels shy that when a slave raises his hands towards Him, He should return them empty."

Twelfth, the declaration that every night He descends to the firmament closest to the world.

Thirteenth, physical signaling towards Him with the pointing of the finger upwards, as done by him who knew his Lord better than anyone else, that is, the Prophet (*saws*), who, when in `Arafah, raised his finger towards the heaven and said: "O Lord, be witness."

Fourteenth, the use of the word "where" such as when the Prophet asked the slave-girl: "Where is Allah?"

Fifteenth, the Prophet's testification of the faith of one who said Allah is in the heaven.

Sixteenth, Allah's information (to us) that Fir`awn wished to ascend up to the heaven in order that he might find the Lord of Musa there. He refused to believe in Musa when he told him that he was sent by One above in the heavens.

يَهَامٰنُ ابْنِ لِى صَرْحًا لَّعَلِّى اَبْلُغُ الْاَسْبَابَ , اَسْبَابَ السَّمٰوٰتِ فَاَطَّلِعَ اِلٰى اِلٰهِ مُوْسٰى وَاِنِّى لَاَظُنُّهُ كَاذِبًا

"Haman. Build for me a lofty structure that I may attain the means   the means of (reaching) the heavens, and that I may look up to the God of Musa: But surely, I think he is a liar." (Al Ghāfir, 36-37)

Seventeenth, the Prophet's narrative that he journeyed several times between Musa and his Lord during his night journey seeking reduction in the number of Prayers. He stated that he rose up to his Lord, came down to Musa several times.

Eighteenth, the textual material conforming the believers' sighting of Allah in Paradise. The material clearly states that they will see Him above themselves. One narration coming down from the Prophet says: "While the people of Paradise will be in their pleasures when they will feel the resplendence of Light. They would raise their heads and lo! It would be the Compeller, Most High who would have appeared above them. He will say, 'People of Paradise! Salam to you.'" (Imam Ahmed in his *Musnad* and others).

Now, since it is not possible to deny the above ness of Allah without denying the beatific vision also, the Jahmiyyah were forced to deny both while the *Ahl al Sunnah* accept both.

The above were some proofs. The truth is, if one wishes to collect all of that which can be presented as proof, they will run into a thousand. Let then, those who deny, sit down and work out a reply to each of them. They might have a hard time doing that.

On the other hand, whoever interpreted the "above ness" as Allah being better than and superior to His creations, such as, for instance, saying, 'the king is above the vizier,' or 'the Dinar is above the Dirham,' etc., attempted a kind of logic which is repugnant to straight thinking. Saying, 'Allah (*swt*) is better than His slaves,' is of the same vein as saying, 'Ice is cool,' or, 'Fire is hot,' or, 'the Prophet is better than the Jews.' This perhaps is not the best way of praising.

Being above everyone in the sense of better than them is automatically achieved with the absolute above ness that we are talking of. Thus, Allah is above everyone in His Irresistibility as well as in His Person. Whoever will accept a part of the meaning, rejecting a part, will damage the concept. Allah (*swt*) is absolutely above everyone in every sense.

If it is said, 'the above ness is in the sense of Allah being well established in the hearts over and above everything else,' it will be replied that this aspect of the meaning is also included. If He wasn't above everything in the absolute sense, He wouldn't have been above everything in the heart either.

Furthermore, the above ness of Allah, as reported by the texts of the Qur`an and *Sunnah*, is also one of those things that is understood instinctively. Muhammad b. Tahir al Maqdisi has reported that once Sheikh Abu Ja`far al Hamdani happened to enter in an assembly held by Abu al Ma`ali al Juwayni, otherwise known as Imam al Haramayn. The Imam denied in his talk the above ness of Allah saying, 'Allah (*swt*) was there when there was no `Arsh. Now He is as He was.' Sheikh Abu Ja`far asked him: 'Tell us, O master, something about this need that we feel in our hearts: no one who knows God and says "O Allah" but feels an upward inclination. He does not turn left or right. How shall we get rid of this?' Abu al Ma`ali slapped himself, came down from his couch saying, with tears in his eyes: 'Hamdani amazed me. He amazed me.' What Hamdani meant was that the above ness of Allah (*swt*) is in our nature, on which Allah created His slaves. They don't need a message from the Messengers towards this effect. They find it already placed in their hearts.

The above has been objected to and said: 'The heaven is simply the direction of supplication, just as the Ka`bah is the direction of Prayers; yet, one annuls this *Qiblah* and turns to another direction when he prostrates himself. He is actually facing the (center) of the earth in that posture.' This objection has been answered in several ways.

First, your saying that the heaven is the direction of supplications is something that none of the earliest scholars has said. Nor has Allah said anything about it in His revelation. If it had been a part of the knowledge of the *Shari`ah*, surely, the pious predecessors and those who followed them would not have remained ignorant of it.

Second, the direction of supplication is the direction of Prayers. the Prophet (*saws*) used to turn towards the *Qiblah* during his supplications.

As for annulment of the *Qiblah* during prostration, it is not for annulment that the prostration has been designed. It is for the expression of humility for the One who is above and not that one feels Him closer to oneself beneath the surface of the earth. Such a thing never occurred to anyone prostrating himself before his Lord.

As for Tahawi saying: "the creation cannot circumscribe Him," he meant that the creation cannot circumscribe Him either in knowledge or by sight.

و نقول: إن الله اتخذ إبراهيم خليلا، و كلم الله موسى تكليما، إيمانا و تصديقا و تسليما

We say in full faith and complete submission that Allah took Ibrahim as a Friend and spoke to Musa directly.'

This is following Allah's words:

وَاتَّخَذَ اللهُ إِبْرِهِيمَ خَلِيلاً

"And Allah took Ibrahim as a Friend." (Al Nisā', 125)

Allah also said:

وَكَلَّمَ اللهُ مُوسْى تَكْلِيمَا

"And Allah spoke to Musa directly." (Al Nisā', 164)

The textual word for what is rendered as "Friend" in the verse quoted above is "*Khalil.*" It has *khullah* in its root denoting a high degree of love.

The Jahmiyyah have denied the existence of love from either side alleging that there can never be love between two that are unequal. They say there is nothing common between the everlasting and the ephemeral for love to take place. They also denied (Allah's) Speech (to Musa). That may be so. But, insofar as we are concerned, we believe in love and speech that is deserving of Allah, just as all other Attributes.

Traditions of the Prophet can also be cited in proof of our statement. It has been recorded in authentic compilations through Abu Saʿid al Khudri that the Prophet (*saws*) said: "Were I to take someone of the people of the earth as a friend, I would have taken Abu Bakr as my friend. But your companion (meaning himself) is a Friend of Allah." According to another report: "Verily, Allah took me as a Friend, just as He took Ibrahim as a Friend."

This is despite the fact that the Prophet admitted that he loved certain people. For instance, he told Mu`adh ibn Jabal: "By Allah, I love you." We also have similar words from him addressing the Helpers. From these we know that "*khullah*" is something different and more specific than love. Further, we also know that the beloved is loved for his own sake, and not because of an esoteric reason, for one dear for the reason of others, comes after those others.

و نؤمن بالملائكة والنبيين، والكتب المنزلة على المرسلين و نشهد أنّهم كانوا على الحق المبين

We also believe in the angels, in the Prophets, in the Books revealed to the Messengers, and confess that they were all on a true path.

These are the articles of faith. Allah said:

أَمَنَ الرَّسُولُ بِمَا أُنزِلَ إِلَيْهِ مِن رَّبِّهِ وَ الْمُؤْمِنُونَ كُلٌّ أَمَنَ بِاللهِ وَمَلَٰئِكَتِهِ وَكُتُبِهِ وَرُسُلِهِ

"The Messenger believed in what was revealed unto him by his Lord and so did the faithful. All of them believed in Allah, His angels, His Books and His Messengers." (Al Baqarah, 285)

Allah also said:

لَيْسَ الْبِرَّ أَن تُوَلُّوا وُجُوهَكُمْ قِبَلَ الْمَشْرِقِ وَ الْمَغْرِبِ وَلَٰكِنَّ الْبِرَّ مَنْ أَمَنَ بِاللهِ وَالْيَوْمِ الْأَخِرِ وَالْمَلَٰئِكَةِ وَالْكِتَٰبِ وَالنَّبِيِّنَ

"Righteousness is not (merely) in that you turn your faces toward the East or the West. Rather, righteousness is to believe in Allah, the Last Day, the angels, the Book and the Messengers." (Al Baqarah, 177)

We can see in the above verses that Allah Most High declared those who believed in all that He mentioned, as believers. In contrast, He declared those who disbelieved in them as the unbelievers. He said:

وَمَن يَكْفُرْ بِاللهِ وَمَلَٰئِكَتِهِ وَكُتُبِهِ وَرُسُلِهِ وَالْيَوْمِ الْأَخِرِ فَقَدْ ضَلَّ ضَلَٰلًا بَعِيدًا

"Whoever disbelieved in Allah, His angels, His Books, His Messengers, and the Last Day, surely fell into an utmost error." (Al Nisā', 136)

The Islamic Creed

In the well known report called as the *hadīth* of Jibril, as recorded in Bukhari and Muslim, the Prophet (*saws*), when he was asked what "*imān*" was, replied,: "That you believe in Allah, His angels, His Books, His Messengers, the Last Day and in the Divine Decree, the good of it and the evil of it."

This is the reason why the last two verses of chapter *Al Baqarah* are considered of extreme importance as compared to any other. Abu Mas`ud `Uqbah b. `Amr has narrated the Prophet (*saws*) as having said: "The last two verses of *Surah Al Baqarah* should suffice anyone who recited them in a night."

The Book and the *Sunnah* have further defined the kinds of angels. They also tell us that they serve various functions related to the humans. Some of them are carriers of mercy. Others of chastisement. Yet some others bear the `*Arsh*. There are others who do nothing but glorify Allah and sing His praise, and so forth.

The word "*malak*" lends the connotation of someone who has been delegated to carry out a command. They have no will of their own. Rather, all command is Allah's, the One, the Irresistible. They merely carry out His orders. Allah (*swt*) said:

$$ لَا يَسْبِقُونَهُ بِالْقَوْلِ وَهُم بِأَمْرِهِ يَعْمَلُونَ $$

"They do not speak before He speaks, and they act by His command." (Al Anbiyā', 27)

Also, they are the honored creations. Some of them circumambulate the `*Arsh*. Others glorify Allah. None there is among them but has a position and a rank marked for him. He does not commit an error in executing a command: neither exceeding his limits, nor falling short. The most honored ones are with Allah. As He said:

$$ لَا يَسْتَكْبِرُونَ عَنْ عِبَادَتِهِ وَلَا يَسْتَحْسِرُونَ ۝ يُسَبِّحُونَ اللَّيْلَ وَالنَّهَارَ لَا يَفْتُرُونَ $$

"They are not too proud to serve Him nor do they get weary. They celebrate His praises morning and night without intermission." (Al Anbiyā', 19 20)

Three of them are well known: Jibril, Mika'il and Israfil. They are agents of life. Jibril is commissioned to deliver the Revelations in which is the life of the

146

hearts and souls. Mika'il is commissioned with rain which is the harbinger of physical life of the animals, plants etc. And Israfil has been commissioned to blow the *Sūr* (Trumpet) which will effect the resurrection of life after death. They are no more then than Allah's ambassadors between Him and His creations carrying out His commands.

The Qur`an is replete with the mention of angels, their kinds and ranks. Sometimes, Allah mentions one of them in the Qur`an in conjunction with His own Name, their sending of peace with His own sending of peace, appends their names in places of honor, speaks of them as going round the `*Arsh* and that they bear it. The Qur`an also attributes to them honor, nearness, highness in ranks, purity, power and sincerity. Allah (*swt*) said:

هُوَ الَّذِى يُصَلِّى عَلَيْكُمْ وَمَلَآئِكَتُهُ لِيُخْرِجَكُمْ مِّنَ الظُّلُمٰتِ إِلَى النُّورِ

"He it is who sends peace to you (O believers) and His angels so that He might bring you out of darknesses into Light." (Al Ahzāb, 43)

And,

اَلَّذِيْنَ يَحْمِلُوْنَ الْعَرْشَ وَمَنْ حَوْلَهُ يُسَبِّحُوْنَ بِحَمْدِ رَبِّهِمْ وَيُؤْمِنُوْنَ بِهِ وَيَسْتَغْفِرُوْنَ لِلَّذِيْنَ اٰمَنُوْا

"Those who bear the `Arsh and those around it sing glory of their Lord and celebrate praises of their Lord. They believe in Him, and seek forgiveness for the faithful." (Al Ghāfir, 7)

Allah also said:

وَتَرَى الْمَلٰئِكَةَ حَآفِّيْنَ مِنْ حَوْلِ الْعَرْشِ يُسَبِّحُوْنَ بِحَمْدِ رَبِّهِمْ

"And you will see the angels circling the `Arsh, singing glories and praises of their Lord." (Al Zumar, 75)

He also said:

فَاِنِ اسْتَكْبَرُوْا فَالَّذِيْنَ عِنْدَ رَبِّكَ يُسَبِّحُوْنَ لَهُ بِالَّيْلِ وَالنَّهَارِ وَهُمْ لَا يَسْـَٔمُوْنَ

"Yet if they (the unbelievers) wax proud, then those who are near your Lord, sing His glory day and night and they do not feel weary." (Fussilat, 38)

Or He said about them:

كِرَامًا كَاتِبِيْنَ

"The honored scribes." (Al Infitār, 11)

He also said:

يَّشْهَدُهُ الْمُقَرَّبُوْنَ

"To which bear witness those who are nearest (to Allah)." (Al Mutaffifin, 21)

Prophetic traditions refer to them quite often. Hence, belief in angels is considered one of the six articles of faith.

As for the Prophets and Messengers we are required to believe in those that Allah has named in His Book, and to believe that Allah sent Prophets and Messengers other than them. No one knows their names or number save Allah. We are required to believe in them in general terms, for the texts did not reveal their number. Allah (*swt*) said:

وَلَقَدْ أَرْسَلْنَا رُسُلاً مِّن قَبْلِكَ مِنْهُم مَّن قَصَصْنَا عَلَيْكَ وَمِنْهُم مَّن لَّمْ نَقْصُصْ عَلَيْكَ

"We sent Messengers before you (O Prophet). Of them there are some about whom We spoke to you, while about others We did not speak to you." (Al Ghāfir, 78)

It is also for us to believe that they delivered the whole of the message they were entrusted with in accordance with what Allah ordered them. We are to believe that they delivered the message in such a manner as to make it clear, not leaving it inadequately explained to anyone concerned.

As for those of firm resolution among the Messengers (*ulu al `azm*), there are various opinions. The one nearest to being correct is what Baghwi and others have reported of Ibn `Abbas and Qatadah to the effect that they were five: Nuh, Ibrahim, Musa, `Isa and Muhammad Allah's peace and blessing on them all. It is said that it is of these that the following verse is speaking of:

وَإِذْ أَخَذْنَا مِنَ النَّبِيِّنَ مِيثَاقَهُمْ وَمِنكَ وَمِن نُّوحٍ وَّإِبْرَاهِيمَ وَمُوسَى وَعِيْسَى ابْنِ مَرْيَمَ

"And when We took from the Prophets their Covenant, as also from you and from Nuh, Ibrahim, Musa and `Isa the son of Maryam." (Al Ahzāb, 7)

And also the words of Allah:

شَرَعَ لَكُمْ مِّنَ الدِّينِ مَا وَصّى بِهِ نُوحًا وَّالَّذِيَ أَوْحَيْنَآ إِلَيْكَ وَمَا وَصَّيْنَا بِهِ إِبْرٰهِيمَ وَمُوسٰى وَعِيسٰى أَنْ أَقِيمُوا الدِّينَ وَ لَا تَتَفَرَّقُوا فِيْهِ كَبُرَ عَلَى الْمُشْرِكِينَ مَا تَدْعُوْهُمْ إِلَيْهِ

"He has appointed for you the same religion as He enjoined on Nuh and that which We revealed unto you (O Muhammad) and that which We enjoined on Ibrahim, Musa, and `Isa: that you shall establish the religion and will not differ therein. (Yet) what you call unto is heavy upon the pagans." (Al Shurā, 13)

With regard to Muhammad, we are required to believe in him and what he brought as the Message both in general terms as well as in specificities.

With regard to the belief in the revealed Books, we believe in what Allah named of them in the Qur`an, such as the *Tawrah*, the *Zabur*, the *Injil*. As for others we believe in general terms that Allah (*swt*) revealed other Books than these, of which no one knows the names or numbers except Allah.

With regard to the belief in the Qur`an, we are required to confess in it as well as follow it. This happens to be something more than what we are required to do with regard to other revealed books. Our faith has to be that the Books revealed to the Messengers came to them from Allah, and that they are the truth, the guidance, the light, the explanation and the healing. Allah (*swt*) said:

قُولُوآ امَنَّا بِاللهِ وَمَآ أَنْزِلَ إِلَيْنَا وَمَآ أَنْزِلَ إِلَى إِبْرٰهِمَ وَإِسْمٰعِيلَ وَإِسْحٰقَ وَيَعْقُوبَ وَ الْأَسْبَاطِ وَمَآ أُوْتِيَ مُوسٰى وَعِيسٰى وَمَآ أُوْتِيَ النَّبِيُّونَ مِنْ رَّبِّهِمْ لَا نُفَرِّقُ بَيْنَ أَحَدٍ مِّنْهُمْ وَنَحْنُ لَهُ مُسْلِمُونَ

"Say, 'We believe in Allah, in what has been sent down unto us, in what was sent unto Ibrahim, Isma`il, Is haq, Ya`qub, and the tribes, and what was given to Musa, `Isa, and what other Prophets were given by their Lord. We do not distinguish between them and we have surrendered ourselves unto Him." (Al Baqarah, 136)

ونُسَمِّي أهلَ قِبلتنا مسلمين مؤمنين، ما داموا بما جاء به النبي صلى الله عليه و سلم معترفين، و له بكل ما قاله وأخبر مصدقين

We refer to those who face our *Qiblah* as "Muslims" and "believers," so long as they confess in what the Prophet brought and acknowledge (as true) all that he informed (us) about. And his words are all those that he uttered and reported by the trustworthy.

The Prophet (*saws*) has said: "Whoever prayed like we pray, faced our *Qiblah*, and ate our slaughtered, is a Muslim. He shall have what we have and upon him shall be what will be upon us."

The Sheikh also meant to say that the two terms "Islam" and "*imān*" are synonymous and that a Muslim does not go out of the fold of Islam because of a sin he committed so long as he does not declare it legal (while its illegality is well known). Further, by employing the terms "face our *Qiblah*" he meant to include those of the sinners who declare their faith in Islam and face our *Qiblah*, but follow their carnal desires   so long as they do not deny any of what the Prophet (*saws*) brought.

ولا نخوض في الله، ولا نُماري في دين الله

We do not indulge in (discussions about the nature of) Allah, and do not obstinately dispute in the religion of Allah.

The Sheikh intends to say that we withhold ourselves from discussing about Allah Most High, the way the theologians and dialecticians discuss Him. He condemned their knowledge. They speak about Allah without knowledge and without authority delegated to them.

Abu Hanifah has said: "It does not behoove anyone to say anything about the Person of Allah. All that he can do is to attribute to Him what He attributed to Himself."

As for his words: "we do not obstinately dispute in the religion of Allah," what he meant is that we do not dispute with the people of truth and righteousness planting doubts raised by those who follow their base desires. For, that is another way of inviting people to untruth, the tongue rolling about the truth and spread of corruption among the people.

ولا نجادل في القرآن، ونشهد أنه كلام رب العالمين، نزل به الروح الأمين، فعلمه سيد المرسلين محمدًا صلى الله عليه وسلم، وهو كلام الله تعالى، لا يساويه شيء من كلام المخلوقين، ولا نقول بخلقه، ولا نخالف جماعة المسلمين

We do not dispute with the Qur`an, rather, testify that it is the Word of the Lord of the worlds, brought down by the trustworthy Spirit. He taught it to the best of the Messengers, Muhammad, on whom be peace. (We also testify that) it is the Speech of Allah, which cannot be equaled by any of the speech of the created. We do not say it was created, nor do we disagree (over the issue) with the great majority of the believers.

By the words "trustworthy Spirit" the allusion is to Jibril, so called because he brought down to the human Messengers revelations that gave life to the hearts. He is the truest of the trustworthy, Allah's peace on him. Allah said:

نَزَلَ بِهِ الرُّوحُ الْأَمِينُ (١٩٣) عَلَى قَلْبِكَ لِتَكُونَ مِنَ الْمُنْذِرِينَ (١٩٤) بِلِسَانٍ عَرَبِيٍّ مُّبِينٍ (١٩٥)

"The trustworthy Spirit brought it down, on your heart (O Muhammad) so that you might be a Warner in a clear Arabic language." (Al Shu`arā', 193 195)

Allah also said:

إِنَّهُ لَقَوْلُ رَسُولٍ كَرِيمٍ (١٩) ذِى قُوَّةٍ عِنْدَ ذِى الْعَرْشِ مَكِينٍ (٢٠) مُطَاعٍ ثَمَّ أَمِينٍ (٢١)

"This is the Word of a most honored Messenger. Endowed with power, held in honor with the Lord of the `Arsh; with authority, moreover, faithful to his trust." (Al Takwīr, 19-21)

These are the qualities of Jibril. However, when Allah said:

اِنَّهُ لَقَوْلُ رَسُوْلٍ كَرِيْمٍ ، وَمَا هُوَ بِقَوْلِ شَاعِرٍ

"Truly, it is the Word of the honored Messenger. It is not the word of a poet."
(Al Hāqqah, 40-41)

the allusion by the word "Messenger is to Muhammad."

Tahawi says, "We do not say it was created nor do we disagree with the great majority of believers" because the earliest scholars were unanimous over the issue that the Qur`an is the uncreated Word of Allah.

ولا نكفر أحدا من أهل القبلة بذنب، ما لم يستحله ولا نقول لا يضر مع الإيمان ذنب لمن عمله

We do not declare anyone of those who face the *Qiblah* an apostate for a sin that he commits, so long as he does not declare it lawful nor do we say that no sin will harm a man so long as he is faithful.

By saying "those who face the *Qiblah*" the author alluded to those he talked of when he said: "And we name those who face the *Qiblah* as Muslims."

The author seems to be refuting the Khawarij who believed in the apostasy of a person for the commitment of a sin.

You must know, O reader may Allah show mercy to you and us that the question of declaring someone an apostate or not declaring apostate is of great consequence. Many divisions have taken place over the issue and plenty of capricious opinions have been forwarded over it, with conflicting evidences and proofs presented for or against it.

So far as the question of declaring or not declaring the people apostates is concerned we mean concerning those who make questionable statements and hold objectionable beliefs the people are divided into those who are at two extremes and those in the middle exactly as they are divided over the issue of declaring or not declaring apostate those who commit major sins.

One group says: We shall not declare anyone apostate who faces the *Qiblah*. Thus, they are strongly opposed to declaration of apostasy despite the knowl-

152

edge that among the people of the *Qiblah* are hypocrites among whom are some who are worse unbelievers than the Jews and Christians. Further, there is no difference of opinion among the Muslims that if a man denies the well known obligations and the well known forbidden things, he will be asked to repent, and, if he doesn't, he will be declared an infidel and condemned to death.

Hence, the great Imams do not agree with the statement: 'We do not treat anyone apostate for any sin that he commits.' Rather, it should be said: We do not declare him an apostate for every sin that he commits. (That is, there are some sins that will throw one out of the bounds of Islam). In keeping with this perhaps and Allah knows best we find the author adding the conditional words: "so long as he does not declare it lawful." He also seems to be throwing the hint that by the "sin" he meant the sins of deeds and not those of the realm of faiths and beliefs.

Further, his words, "no harm will come to a man so long as he is a believer" are meant to refute the Murji'ah who say that sins will cause no harm to a person so long as he is a believer exactly as no deeds are of any profit without belief. Thus they are at one extreme and the Khawarij at the other who hold that with the commitment of any sin whatsoever, a man becomes an apostate, though some of them might qualify the sin as the major ones. The Mu`tazilah are close to them who say that with the commitment of a major sin, a Muslim loses his entire faith, nothing of it remaining with him. The Khawarij on the other hand are very specific. They say he comes out of the bounds of Islam and enters those of unbelief. The Mu`tazilah are one step behind. They say he comes out of the realm of faith but does not enter the realm of unfaith, rather, is stationed in between. Also, by saying he comes out of the realm of faith, they implied that he deserves to be in the Fire forever.

Nevertheless, some of the dialecticians, jurists and traditionists do not hold this kind of opinion with reference to deeds, rather, they do so in matters of innovatory faiths and beliefs alone, even if the one who commits those acts has an explanation for doing what he did. Rather, they would declare anyone an apostate who will say unacceptable things without distinguishing him from one who arrived at that point after research or due to error. Conversely, some others declare every innovator an apostate. Thus, these people seem to be overstretching things a bit in matters of such great importance. There is abundant text to the effect that whoever carries the littlest amount of belief in his heart will be ultimately brought out of the Fire. The texts of glad tidings that these people argue with, contradict the texts of threat on which the other group emphasizes.

In brief, what we are trying to say is that innovation is also one of those things (that requires a careful evaluation). Sometimes a man might be a believer both inwardly as well as outwardly, but he errs in his understanding: either despite making best efforts to find the truth, or exceeding the limits sinfully. It cannot be declared that he lost his belief because of that, unless (it were to be an affair of prime importance) over which there is a well established evidence from the *Shari`ah*. Indeed, this is the approach of the Khawarij and the Mu`tazilah. On the other hand, we do not also say that the man may never be declared an apostate. Rather, justice lies in hitting the middle of the road. To explain: false, innovatory, and unlawful statements that deny one of those things which were confirmed assertively by the Prophet (*saws*), or those that confirm what the Prophet rejected, or, commanding those that have been declared forbidden, or the other way round   in all such cases one may speak out the truth. The man involved might be told that he deserves those threats of punishment that the Qur`an and *Sunnah* have spoken. It might also be made clear to him that indulging in such things entails apostasy. It might also be said to him that whoever said such and such a thing will become an infidel, and so forth. But, when it comes to specific individuals, and if we are specifically asked, 'Do you testify that he deserves Divine punishment or that he is an unbeliever?' The answer then would be: 'We cannot testify any such thing without good grounds. It is a great transgression to testify against a specific individual to the effect that Allah (*swt*) will not forgive him, will not show him mercy, rather He will let him abide in the Fire forever. For the man could be one who did his best to reach the truth but couldn't and therefore is forgivable. Or, the man might not be in possession of the right evidences. Another possibility is that he might be a man of great faith and have earned quite a few good deeds on the strength of which he would be forgiven as, for example, the man who left behind him the testament that when he died his body should be burned and the ashes spread over the seas. He had thought that Allah (*swt*) won't be able to gather together his ashes and quicken him again. Yet, Allah (*swt*) forgave him his sins because of his fear of Him.

Nevertheless, our extreme care, so far as the Hereafter is concerned, does not prevent us from criticizing the man in this world or exhort him to repent. If he doesn't, we shall rule that he be killed.

Further, if what he utters be a word of unbelief, we shall rule that it is apostasy and that whoever said those words might be declared an apostate on certain other additional conditions and absence of everything that can prevent (such a declaration), as this cannot be imagined to be the case unless he became a hypocrite or a heretic. We cannot imagine anyone of the people of the *Qiblah*, such as those who profess to be Muslims, to be declared an unbeliever unless he be a heretic and a hypocrite. Allah's Book makes it plain. Allah Himself divided the people into three categories: first, unbelievers from among the polytheists and holders of a previous Book, those who do not testify to the truth of Islam, second, believers outwardly and inwardly, and a third kind, those who testified outwardly but not so inwardly. The three kinds have been spoken of at the beginning of the chapter *Al Baqarah*. As for anyone who denies the basics but testifies to the two testimonies of Islam, he can only be a heretic (*zindiq*). And a heretic is no different from a hypocrite.

This is where the error of the two at extremes becomes apparent. One who declared anyone an apostate for an innovation will have to treat many people as apostates although they might not be hypocrites at heart, rather at heart truly loving Allah and His Messenger, staunchly believing in Allah and His Messenger, despite their sins. (A case of this order appeared during the Prophet's time). Bukhari reports that there was a man during the time of the Prophet whose name was `Abdullah but nicknamed donkey. He used to joke with the Prophet. He had been once whipped for drinking wine. He was brought up a second time (in the state of intoxication). He was ordered whipped again. At that someone quipped: "Allah curse him. How often he is brought up for whipping?!" The Prophet told him: "Don't curse him, for, by Allah, from what I know, he loves Allah and His Messenger."

This is a confirmed opinion of a great majority of scholars. It is only the Jah-miyyah, the Murji'ah, the Qadariyyah, the Shi`ah or the Khawarij who have had different opinions and expressions about them. But, so far as the major scholars are concerned, they did not endorse all that they have expressed, but only agree only with a part here and a part there.

Indeed, it is the weakness of the innovators that some of them rush to declare others apostates. In contrast, those of knowledge allow for errors and do not rush with the declaration of apostasy.

Never the less, a doubt remains over what the author has stated. Hasn't Allah and His Messenger not declared as apostates those who commit certain kind of sins? For instance, Allah said (*Al Mā'idah*, 44): "Whoever did not judge by what Allah revealed, they, such indeed are the unbelievers." Or, the Prophet (*saws*) said in a report of the *Sahihayn*: "Calling a Muslim names is a major sin and attempting to kill him is infidelity." The Prophet also said in a *hadīth* of Muslim: "The Prayer is (the dividing line) between a Muslim and a non Muslim." He also said: "There are two among my *Ummah* who have unbelief residing in their hearts: Those who taunt over lineage and those who beat themselves over the dead (in mourning)." Examples of this sort can be multiplied.

The answer is: the *Ahl al Sunnah* are united over the opinion that the one who commits a major sin does not cross the bounds of Islam to enter into the folds of unbelief, as the Khawarij have said. Had he become an apostate altogether pushing him out of the bounds of Islam, he would have been declared an apostate outright. In that case monetary compensation would not be accepted from him (if he murdered), nor would capital punishment be ordered for adultery, theft or for drinking wine. These are well known facts. The *Ahl al Sunnah* are also not divided over the opinion that he (who commits a major sin) does not go out of Islam or faith (*imān*) nor does he enter into the state of unbelief. Further, he does not deserve to abide in the Fire forever along with the unbelievers. The opinion of the Mu`tazilah in this regard is obviously false. Allah Himself declared a sinner who committed a major sin a believer. He said:

$$\text{يَا أَيُّهَا الَّذِينَ آمَنُوا كُتِبَ عَلَيْكُمُ الْقِصَاصُ فِي الْقَتْلَى}$$

"Believers! Just retribution has been instituted for you in matters of murder." (Al Baqarah, 178)

The above verse is then followed by the words:

156

فَمَنْ عُفِيَ لَهُ مِنْ أَخِيهِ شَيْءٌ فَاتِّبَاعٌ بِالْمَعْرُوفِ

"Then, whoever is forgiven something by his brother, then its pursuance should be in a goodly manner." (Al Baqarah, 178)

It can be seen that Allah did not separate out the murderer from the believers. Rather, He called him a brother unto the heirs. And, the term brother is employed in the sense of brothers in the religion of Islam.

The Qur`anic and *hadīth* texts also tell us that an adulterer, a thief, or a slanderer might not be killed, rather a just retribution is to be ordered. This shows that the man did not commit apostasy by the sin. We also have a report from the Prophet (*saws*) that he said: "Whoever has a wrong upon himself committed against his brother, by way of honor or anything else, may seek to be absolved of it now before a Day when there will be no dealing in Dinar or Dirham. Rather, if he has good deeds, a quantity proportionate to the sin will be taken away from him (and given away to the man he wronged). But if he is not left with any good deed, the other man's sins will be off loaded from the wronged and loaded onto the wrong doer. Then he will be thrown into the Fire." (*Sahihayn*)

The above shows that sinners will have good deeds in their records to be given away in retaliation. Authentic reports also have the following. The Prophet asked: "Whom do you reckon a pauper?" They replied: "We reckon him a pauper who has neither Dinar no Dirham in his possession." He said: "A true pauper is one who will appear on the Day of Judgement with mountain size good deeds. But, he would have called somcone names, misappropriated the wealth of another, slandered another, or hit another. In retribution, his good deeds would be taken away and given to those he wronged. But, if his good deeds are exhausted before the others can be compensated, the sins of the wronged would be taken from them and loaded on to him. Then he will be consigned to the Fire." (*Muslim*)

The Mu`tazilah are one with the Khawarij in this regard. They are of the opinion that one who committed a major sin will abide in the Fire forever. The only difference between them is that the former call such a sinner an unbeliever while the latter call him a corrupt person (*fāsiq*). Thus, the difference between them is only verbal.

The *Ahl al Sunnah* hold the opinion that a sinner deserves the punishment that has been promised. The texts are very clear about it. They part ways with the Murji'ah who believe that no harm will come to a man if he is a believer nor any good will come to a man with disbelief. But, were a person to list down the text of glad tidings that are used by the Murji'ah and the text of threats that the Khawarij and the Mu`tazilah employ, the error of the two becomes manifest. And, there is no use in the pursuance of this or that group's thoughts and ideas save that you might discover in every group's arguments substance that will discredit the arguments of the other.

Coming back to the *Ahl al Sunnah*, we discover that after their agreement over the main issue, they disagree over the details. Nevertheless, the difference is not in the essence, rather it is verbal, viz., are their kinds and classes of disbelief, or is the difference only of degrees? That is, is it disbelief of a different nature altogether? Conversely, they also disagreed over the question of faith if it could be of classes? That is, faith of a different nature.

This disagreement has arisen between them because of the way they defined faith: whether it is merely a testification or is it testification plus deeds? And, whether it increases and decreases or does it not? This disagreement is despite their agreement over the issue that one whom Allah declared an unbeliever, is an unbeliever. For, it is unthinkable that Allah (*swt*) should declare one who does not judge by His command an unbeliever, and so should the Prophet, but we refuse to use the word infidel in describing such a person.

But what happened is that those who said that belief is the other name of testification and deeds, and that it increases and decreases, also asserted that (disobedience is) practical disbelief and not disbelief of the nature of beliefs. Thus, to such disbelief can be categorized, as also belief.

As for those who say that the term faith is simply testification: deeds not forming a constituent part of faith, and that, on the other hand, disbelief is to dispute the truth and that the two cannot increase or decrease such people said that the disbelief of the disobedient is only figuratively so, and not true disbelief. In contrast, disbelief of the true kind removes the man altogether from the folds of the nation of Islam. This is how they explain the word belief when used by Allah for certain acts, that is, they say the usage is only figurative. Such as, in the verse:

$$\text{وَمَا كَانَ اللهُ لِيُضِيعَ إِيمَانَكُمْ}$$

"Allah was not such as to waste away your faith (i.e., your Prayers facing Jerusalem)." (Al Baqarah, 143)

Here, the Prayers were termed as belief only figuratively. And there is a good reason. Prayers are an aspect and proof of faith. Hence, when an unbeliever prays like we pray, he will be called a believer. There is no difference of opinion among the scholars over a sinner so long as he testifies both inwardly as well as outwardly to what is proven to be, by persistent reports, what the Prophet brought that he is of those exposed to the dangers of falling into Hell. But, to say that they will be in Hell fire forever is an unacceptable opinion, such as what the Khawarij and Mu`tazilah say.

But, worse than the above is to be prejudiced against those who are opposed to their ideas, to fasten upon him what he does not deserve to be fastened upon, or to be disgusted with him. How come, when we have been ordered to be just even with the unbelievers while arguing out things with them, and that they are to be debated with in a goodly manner ... how can then, some of us don't do justice to each other in matters involving controversial opinions?

None the less, a point may be kept in mind. The failure to judge by what Allah has judged with could at times be declared as an unbelief of the kind that removes a man from the folds of the nation of Islam, or, at other times, it could simply be a major or even minor sin. In other instances, it could be so only figuratively, or, alternatively, a minor type of disbelief depending upon the opinions held by the man in question. If he thinks, for instance, that judging by what Allah has revealed is not binding, and that he has a choice, or, if he showed disrespect to Allah's rule when told about it, then this is the great infidelity.

On the other hand, if he believes that it is the requirement of faith to judge by what Allah has revealed, and has the knowledge of Allah's revelation pertaining to the particular case he is judging, yet does not judge by it but admits that he faces the risk of punishment, then he is an infidel in the figurative sense only, or, infidelity of the lower order.

In contrast, if the man is ignorant of the rule of Allah, despite having made an effort to locate the truth, then, in this case, it is only an error on his part. He shall be rewarded for his effort and his error would be forgiven.

As regards the words of the author: "We do not say that no sin will harm a man so long as there is faith" is to refute the Murji'ah. It is likely that they were led to this belief because of a few incidents taking place in early Islam. In a well known case (of some people drinking wine during the time of `Umar), the Companions agreed they should be killed if they did not repent. Qudamah b. `Abdullah had, for instance, drunk wine along with a few people. When asked why, they cited the following verse:

لَيْسَ عَلَى الَّذِينَ آمَنُوا وَعَمِلُوا الصَّالِحَاتِ جُنَاحٌ فِيمَا طَعِمُوا إِذَا مَا اتَّقَوْا وَآمَنُوا وَعَمِلُوا الصَّالِحَاتِ

"There is no sin upon those who believed and acted righteously in what they partook of, so long as they feared, believed and acted righteously." (Al Mā'idah, 93)

When their case was presented to `Umar ibn al Khattab, he agreed with `Ali and all other Companions that if they admit of its unlawfulness, they should be whipped, but if they insisted on its lawfulness, they were to be executed. At that time `Umar told Qudamah: "Had you feared, believed, and acted righteously, you would not have drunk wine." As for the wordings of the Qur`anic text, it was because when wine was prohibited   which happened after the battle of Uhud   some Companions expressed their misgivings about some of their compatriots who died with wine in their stomachs. In response, Allah revealed this verse explaining that partaking of what was not prohibited until then was not sinful so long as they were fearful, believers, and acted righteously, as was the case with the change in the *Qiblah*.

Then it so happened that those who had drunk despaired. `Umar then wrote to Qudamah the following verse:

حم (١) تَنْزِيلُ الْكِتَابِ مِنَ اللهِ الْعَزِيزِ الْعَلِيمِ (٢) غَافِرِ الذَّنْبِ وَقَابِلِ التَّوْبِ شَدِيدِ الْعِقَابِ(٣)

"Ha mim. Revealing of the Book by Allah, the Powerful, the Knowing, For-giver of the sins, Accepter of the repentance, severe in chastisement." (Al Ghāfir, 1 3)

160

After that `Umar added: "I am not sure which of your two sins is greater: your treatment of an unlawful as lawful or your subsequent despair of Allah's mercy."

This is what the Companions agreed between themselves, and this is what the great Imams agree between themselves too.

و نرجوا للمحسنين من المؤمنين أن يَعْفو عنهم ويدخلهم الجنة برحمته، ولا نأمن عليهم، ولا نشهد لهم بالجنة، و نستغفر لمسيئتهم، و نخاف عليهم، و لا نُقَنِّطُهم

We hope His pardon for those of the believers who did well and that He will admit them into Paradise by His mercy. None the less, we are not in security about them nor shall we say they are the dwellers of Paradise. We seek forgiveness for their sins, yet, are apprehensive (that they might be questioned) but do not lead them into despair.

These should be the sentiments of the believers. Allah has said:

أُولَٰئِكَ الَّذِينَ يَدْعُونَ يَبْتَغُونَ إِلَىٰ رَبِّهِمُ الْوَسِيلَةَ أَيُّهُمْ أَقْرَبُ وَيَرْجُونَ رَحْمَتَهُ وَيَخَافُونَ عَذَابَهُ إِنَّ عَذَابَ رَبِّكَ كَانَ مَحْذُورًا

"It is these who supplicate and strive for a means of access to their Lord as to which of them is nearest (to his Lord). They hope for His mercy and fear His chastisement. Surely, Your Lord's chastisement is worth heeding." (Al Isrā', 57)

Musnad Ahmed and Tirmidhi have a report narrated by `A'isha. She said: "I said, 'O Messenger of Allah! Concerning the verse "Those who give out of what they have been given, but their hearts are fearful (*Al Mu'minūn*, 60)" is it talking about someone who commits adultery, drinks wine and steals?'" He replied, "No, O daughter of Siddiq. It is speaking of a man who fasts, Prays, gives in charity but is fearful that all that might not be accepted."

(Concerning the people in the verse quoted by `A'isha) Hasan al Busri said: "They acted, by Allah, obediently, striving hard, but feared that their efforts might be thrown back at them. The believer combines extreme piety with fear. On the contrary, the hypocrite combines evil acts with self satisfaction."

None the less, there have been differences in opinion among the scholars over what constitutes a major sin and what a minor. But, there is a point that demands a little attention, viz., occasionally a major sin is committed but is accompanied by shame, fear, and the feeling of having committed a heinous crime. That renders it a minor sin. In contrast, some minor sins are committed without shame, treated as an affair of no consequence, with a lack of fear, and accompanied by the act of belittling it all these are acts that would get it bracketed with major sins. Thus, what is involved is the condition of the heart and is in addition to the physical act. Every man learns about it both from within himself as also from others without.

Also, sometimes a virtuous person is forgiven what an evil person would not be forgiven.

Further, a man who commits evils may be forgiven punishment of the Fire for ten reasons. Worked out from the Qur`an and *Sunnah*, they are as follows:

1. Repentance: A pure repentance, also known as *tawbatu al nasūh*, is not related to a specific sin. But, a question: Does its acceptance depend upon a complete repentance so that if he repents of one sin but commits another, it wouldn't be accepted? The answer is, no. The repentance is still acceptable.

2. Seeking forgiveness: Allah Most High said:

وَمَا كَانَ اللهُ مُعَذِّبَهُمْ وَهُمْ يَسْتَغْفِرُونَ

"And He was not such as to punish them while they were seeking forgiveness." (Al Anfāl, 33)

3. Good deeds: Good deeds are rewarded tenfold, while a sin is punished with the like of it alone. Woe then unto him whose singles overcame his tens. Allah said:

إِنَّ الْحَسَنَاتِ يُذْهِبْنَ السَّيِّئَاتِ

"Verily good deeds obliterate the evil ones." (Hūd, 114)

And the Prophet said: "Follow up an evil deed with a good one. It will erase it."

4. Worldly hardships: the Prophet said: "The believer is not struck by a hardship, a sorrow, tension, or grief even a thorn that pricks him but they expiate his sins."

Thus, the hardships are by themselves a means of expiation. Furthermore, if the man bears them with patience and perseverance, he is additionally rewarded. On the contrary, if he reacts angrily, he sins.

5. Other believers' supplications and seeking of their forgiveness of the sinner: during his life time, or, after his death.

6. What is gifted to the sinner after his death: by way of charity on his behalf, recitation of the Qur`an, performance of Hajj, etc.

7. The horrors and pains of the Day of Judgement.

8. What has been reported in the *Sahihayn* that when the believers have crossed the Bridge (*Sirat*), they would be held up on a vault between Paradise and Hell fire. There they will have to undergo retribution with each other. Thus cleansed, they will be allowed to proceed to Paradise.

9. Intercession of the intercessors.

10. Forgiveness by Allah of the Most Merciful without any intercession, as He said:

وَيَغْفِرُ مَا دُونَ ذَلِكَ لِمَنْ يَّشَآءُ

"He will forgive anything less than that (sin of association) whom He will."
(Al Nisā', 48)

Nevertheless, whomsoever Allah will not forgive, because of the seriousness of his sins, there will be no escape for him from the Fire. He has to suffer it in order that his faith is cleansed of the stain of sins. In the final analysis, no one who had faith to the extent of the weight of a mustard seed will remain in the Fire. Even so, not even he who ever uttered the words: 'there is no deity save Allah,' as asserted by the *hadīth* of Anas.

Nevertheless, it is not possible to say with certainty about any individual, save for him about whom the Prophet himself bore witness, that he is of Paradise. But, we do fasten good hope for the righteous although, at the same time, we remain apprehensive of them.

و الأمن و اليأس ينقلان عن ملة الإسلام، وسبيل الحق بينهما لأهل القبلة

(False) security and despair are ways that lead out of the folds of the community of Muslims. The right attitude for the people of the *Qiblah* lies between the two.

That is to say, a slave should remain between fear and hope. For, the right and the approved kind of fear is that which acts as a barrier between the slave and the things forbidden by Allah. But, if fear is excessive, then the possibility is that the man will fall into despair and pessimism.

On the other hand the approved state of optimism is of a man who does good in the light of the *Shari`ah* and is hopeful of being rewarded for it. Or, conversely, if a man committed a sin, he repents sincerely, and is hopeful of being forgiven. Allah (*swt*) said:

إِنَّ الَّذِينَ أَمَنُوا وَالَّذِينَ هَاجَرُوا وَجَاهَدُوا فِي سَبِيلِ اللهِ أُولَئِكَ يَرْجُونَ رَحْمَتَ اللهِ وَاللهُ غَفُورٌ رَّحِيمٌ

"Verily, those who believed, and those who migrated and fought in the way of Allah, it is they who are hopeful of Allah's mercy. And Allah is very Forgiving, very Merciful." (Al Baqarah, 218)

In contrast, if a man indulges in sins and excesses, but is hopeful that he would be forgiven without doing anything good, then, this is self deception, dreaming, and false hope. Abu `Ali Rowzbari has said, "Fear and hope are like the two wings of a bird. If they are well balanced, the flight will be well balanced. But, if one is stunted, the flight would also be stunted. And, to be sure, if the two are lost, the bird will soon be in the throes of death." Allah has praised the people of hope and fear in the following verse:

أَمَّنْ هُوَ قَانِتٌ أَنَاءَ الَّيْلِ سَاجِدًا وَقَائِمًا يَحْذَرُ الْآخِرَةَ وَيَرْجُوا رَحْمَةَ رَبِّهِ

"Is one who worships devotedly during the night, prostrating himself or standing, fearing the Hereafter, and hoping for the mercy of his Lord (is equal to him who doesn't do these things)?" (Al Zumar, 9)

Hope then also demands fear. If that was not the case, one would be in a state of false security. Conversely, fear demands hope. Without that it would be despair.

ولا يخرج العبد من الإيمان إلا بجحود ما أدخله فيه

A man will not come out of the folds of faith save by denying what admitted him in.

By this the author intended to refute the Khawarij and the Mu`tazilah who said that a man comes out of the folds of faith by committing a major sin.

والإيمان: هو الإقرار باللسان، والتصديق بالجنان و جميعُ ما صح عن رسول الله صلى الله عليه وسلم من الشرَع و البيان كله حق و الإيمان واحد، وأهله في أصله سواء، و التفاضُل بينهم بالخشية و التقى، و مخالفة الهوى، و ملازِمَة الأُولى

As for faith, it is the confession of the tongue and testimony of the heart. And, all that is true which is authentically proven to have come down from the Prophet be it the Law (as dictated in the Qur`an) or elucidations and illustrations (by the Prophet). Further, faith is a single entity. Those who avow it are primarily equal in status, the superiority between them being only on the basis of fear, piety, opposition to the base self and adherence to what is preferable.

People have differed over what constitutes faith. Malik, Shafe`i, Ahmed, Awza`i, Is-haq b. Rahwayh, the *Ahl al Hadīth*, the people of Madinah Munawwarah, the Zahirites and quite a few of the dialecticians have said that it is testification of the heart, confession of the tongue and acts of the body. But most of our people (i.e., the Hanafiyyah) believe in what Tahawi has stated, that is, it is confession of the tongue and testification of the heart.

The Karamiyyah have held that faith is nothing but confession of the tongue. Accordingly, to them, the hypocrites are wholesome believers. Although, they also say that they deserve the punishment that Allah has promised them. The wrongness of their opinion should be apparent.

In contrast, Jahm b. Safwan has said that faith is the cognizance of the heart. This statement promises greater corruption than the previous one. It implies that Fir`awn and his folk were believers, for they knew at heart the truthfulness of Musa and Harun, but refused to believe in them. We find Musa telling Fir`awn:

لَقَدْ عَلِمْتَ مَا أَنْزَلَ هَؤُلَاءِ إِلَّا رَبُّ السَّمْوٰتِ وَالْأَرْضِ بَصَآئِرَ

"You know very well that these (signs) were not sent down but by Allah, the Lord of the heavens and the earth eye openers." (Al Isrā', 102)

In brief, faith is either what the heart, the tongue and the body testify to, as the great majority of the scholars of the first few generations and others have held, or, it is the testification of the tongue and the heart excluding the body acts, as Tahawi has reported as the opinion of Abu Hanifah and his disciples.

None the less, the difference between Abu Hanifah and other scholars is superficial. For the acts of the body are, in fact, expressions of the faith residing in the heart, or they are a part of it. They both agree that the one who commits major sins does not go out of the fold of faith, rather, his fate will depend on the will of Allah who might either forgive him or punish him. Thus the difference (between the two opinions) is verbal leading to no serious consequences.

As for those who declare apostasy of a man who gave up Praying, they have argued by evidences other than this. Otherwise, it should not be overlooked that the Prophet (*saws*) also denied the faith of an adulterer, a thief, one who drinks, yet, despite that, no one by consensus declared such a man without faith altogether. Further, there is no difference of opinion between the scholars that Allah (*swt*) demanded from his slave both the (utterance of the) word as well as the action. As for the "word," it is testification of the heart and confession of the tongue. This is what is meant when it is said: "Faith (*imān*) is word and deed." But, does this requirement constitute faith? Or, is one of them alone `faith?' That is, the `word' alone? Are deeds something different that cannot be

166

defined as faith when that alone is spelled out, even if that term is applied to it figuratively? This is where the differences have occurred.

Yet, they all agree that if a man testified with his heart and confessed with the tongue, but did not act with his body, then, he is merely a sinner in the sight of Allah who deserves the threats pronounced.

Therefore, it appears, although Allah knows best, that the author, may Allah (*swt*) show him mercy, added, "And those who avow it are primarily equal in status," to imply that the equality is in its primary meaning. It does not mean equality in all respects. Rather, the differences in the ranks of Light emanating out of the words *"Lā ilāha illa Allah"* in the hearts can be measured by none save Allah. So that there are people in whose heart its Light shines like the sun. Another's can be compared to a bright star. Yet another's has a flamboyant flame. Another's light could be like a burning lamp, while another's like a weak candle. It is following these differences here in this world, that their Lights will appear in various degrees on the Day of Judgement: on their right hand side and in front of them, in true proportion to the light of *Tawhīd* and faith that they have in their hearts now: of knowledge and of deeds. Whenever the Light of this testimony brightens up, it burns down doubts and animal desires: also in proportion to the intensity.

Evidences pertaining to the increase and decrease in faith are replete in the Qur`an, *Sunnah* and statements of the pious predecessors. For example, Allah (*swt*) said:

وَإِذَا تُلِيَتْ عَلَيْهِمْ آيَاتُهُ زَادَتْهُمْ إِيمَانًا

"When its verses are recited to them, their faith is increased." (Al Anfāl, 2)

And Allah's words:

وَيَزْدَادَ الَّذِينَ آمَنُوا إِيمَانًا

"And, in order that Allah may cause increase in the faith of those who believed." (Al Muddaththir, 31)

And His words:

هُوَ الَّذِىْ اَنْزَلَ السَّكِيْنَةَ فِىْ قُلُوْبِ الْمُؤْمِنِيْنَ لِيَزْدَادُوْٓا اِيْمَانًا مَّعَ اِيْمَانِهِمْ

"It is He who sent down tranquility into the hearts of the believers in order that they may add faith to their faith." (Al Futh, 4)

The Prophet (*saws*) has informed us that anyone with the littlest of faith will be removed from the Fire. How then can it be said that the faith of all those who inhabit the heavens and the earth is of the same measure and quality, or that the difference between them are to be understood in a different sense.

We also have numerous statements from the Companions. `Umar used to say to them: "Come on. Let us work to increase our faith." `Abdullah ibn Mas`ud used to say in his supplications: "O Allah. Grant us increase in our faith, conviction and understanding." Mu`adh ibn Jabal would say to one of his friends: "Let us sit down for a few moments and refresh our faiths."

As for deeds being part of faith, there are plenty of textual proofs for that. Authentic reports tell us that the Prophet told the delegation of `Abd al Qays: "I enjoin you to believe in Allah the One. Do you know what is belief in Allah? It is to testify that there is no deity save Allah, the One. He has no associates; to establish the Prayers; to pay the *Zakah* ; and that you should pay a fifth of the booty (to the state)." Obviously, he didn't mean that these deeds are faith per se without there being faith in the heart, whereas, he had on several occasions pointed out that there was no recourse to any good without faith in the heart. Therefore, we can conclude that these deeds, along with the right belief residing in the heart, constitute faith. What better proof there can be than this to the statement that deeds apart of faith? Further, with the knowledge that faith has been defined as deeds, without the mention of testification, it is for us to deduce that deeds are worthless if one disputes (with the articles of faith).

With regard to the author's statement: "All that is true which is authentically proven to have come down from the Prophet be they aspects of the *Shari`ah* or elucidations and illustrations," it is meant to refute the Jahmiyyah and the Mu`tazilah who say that of the reports that the Prophet (*saws*) brought, there are two kinds: those that have come from multiple sources (*mutawātir*) and those that came from a single source (*āhād*). As for that which has emanated from multiple sources, even if it has a reliable chain of narrators, it is not a definitive proof. For, they say, verbal proofs do not lead to certainty. Accordingly, they reject those Attributes that are implied from the Qur'anic texts. As for those that have a single source, they reject them altogether on grounds that they do not lend a firm knowledge, and therefore cannot be relied upon for argument: neither the text contained in them, nor because of the strength of the chain of narrators involved in it. Thus they prevented the hearts from acquiring the knowledge of their Lord's Names, Attributes and Acts: those that come from the Prophet (*saws*). Instead, they filled the heads of the people with conjectural ideas and fictitious issues.

In contrast, the methodology followed by the *Ahl al Sunnah* is to accept a proven report and not subject it to their personal reasoning, nor treat it in the light of the opinion of this or that person, as the author has implied in the above statement.

Bukhari, may Allah show him peace, said: "I heard Humaydi say, 'We were with Shafe`i, may Allah show him mercy, when a man came up and asked a question. Shafe`i told him that the Prophet had decided in such a case in such and such a way. The man asked, "What's your own opinion?" He replied, "Glory to Allah. Do you think I am sitting in a Church. Do you think I am sitting in a Synagogue? Do you think I am sitting between a Zoroastrian and a Christian? I say to you, 'the Prophet (*saws*) ruled in such and such a manner.' And you ask me, 'What's your own opinion?!'"

As regards a report originating from a single reporter, when the Muslims in general accepted it, practicing it and confessing it, then, according to the majority of the scholars, it lends out certain knowledge. Indeed, it is considered as the second of the two kinds. That is, a report through multiple sources (*mutawātir*). There was never any dispute over that among the earliest scholars. As example we might quote `Umar's report: "Deeds are by their intentions." Or, Abu Hurayrah's report: "A woman and her paternal or maternal aunts may not be brought together in one marriage." Or, another report: "What is forbidden by kinship is forbidden by fosterage." They are all of the same class as the famous incident of a single man informing the people of Masjid Quba that the *Qiblah* had been changed, and they all turned around toward Makkah.

the Prophet himself used to send a single messenger with verbal messages or written ones. Those that they were sent to, didn't say that they wouldn't accept a single reporter.

It is perhaps following this scheme that Allah humiliated anyone who tried to fasten a lie on the Prophet (*saws*), whether during his life time, or after him. Sufyan b. `Uyaynah said: "Allah never let go a man but exposed him who fastened a lie on the Prophet." `Abdullah ibn Mubarak said: "If a man in the seas tried to fasten a lie on the Prophet (*saws*), the people will surely say about him one day: 'So and so is a liar.'"

Now, reports that originate from a single narrator can both be true or false, but, the knowledge and understanding of what is trustworthy of the reports and what is otherwise, is not the share of anyone but he who spends a great part of his time studying the *hadīth*, the life of the narrators in order to know their ways and words, and to realize how tough they were against any wrong step. They would rather die than allow anyone to fasten a lie upon the Prophet (*saws*), far from themselves doing it. They passed on to us accurately what was passed on to them. They were the pillars of faith, critical evaluators of reports and treasurers of the *hadīth*.

But those who denied (the *āhād* reports) used the verse, "there is nothing like unto Him," to reject many authentic *ahādīth*. Whenever a report reached them that did not go well with their ideas, principles and philosophies, they rejected it on the pretext of the verse "there is nothing like unto Him," by such subterfuge they convinced only those who are more blind of heart than themselves, and fastening a meaning upon the verses out of context. They derived meanings from those verses concerning Allah's Attributes that neither He nor His Messenger ever intended, nor did any of the great Imams ever understood in a way that they could lead to a likeness with His creation. Then they used a perverted meaning of the words, "there is nothing like unto Him," to distort (other parts of) the two texts (Qur`an and *Sunnah*).

As for the author's words: "of the *Shari`ah* or elucidations and illustrations," it is to indicate that essentially there are two kinds of reports coming from the Prophet (*saws*): the one that pertains to the Law as originated and enunciated by the Prophet himself, and that which is the explanation of what Allah (*swt*) commanded in His Book. Both of them are true and deserve to be followed.

و المؤمنون كلهم أولياء الرحمن

The believers are all the Favorites of the Compassionate.

The above is based on the text:

اَلَا اِنَّ اَوْلِيَآءَ اللهِ لَا خَوْفٌ عَلَيْهِمْ وَلَا هُمْ يَحْزَنُوْنَ (٦٢)الَّذِيْنَ اٰمَنُوْا وَكَانُوْا يَتَّقُوْنَ (٦٣)

"Lo! The Favorites of Allah: they have nothing to fear nor to grieve   those who believed and were fearful." (Yūnus, 62-63)

The word *waliyy* of the text has its root in *walāyah*, whose antonym is *`adāwah* (enmity). Hamzah has read another verse where, in his belief, this word occurs as *wilāyah* although others have read it as *walāyah* only. The verse is as follows:

مَا لَكُمْ مِّنْ وَّلَايَتِهِمْ مِّنْ شَيْءٍ

"You owe no duty of protection to them." (Al Anfāl, 72)

Some linguists say that these are two different words. It is also said that *walāyah* stands for "help" (or "protection") whereas *wilāyah* stands for "rule" or "governorship." Zajjaj has ruled that reading the word as *wilāyah* is also allowable.

(Note: In this book when the word *waliyy* is used for Allah, it will be translated as Protector or Friend. But when it is used for believers it will be translated as Favorites.)

However, what it all amounts to is that all the believers are Allah's Favorites and He is their Protector. He said:

ذٰلِكَ بِأَنَّ اللهَ مَوْلَى الَّذِيْنَ اٰمَنُوْا وَأَنَّ الْكٰفِرِيْنَ لَا مَوْلَى لَهُمْ

"That is because Allah is the Protector of the believers, while the unbelievers have no protector." (Muhammad, 11)

He also said:

إِنَّمَا وَلِيُّكُمُ اللهُ وَرَسُولُهُ وَالَّذِينَ آمَنُوا الَّذِينَ يُقِيمُونَ الصَّلوةَ وَيُؤْتُونَ الزَّكوةَ وَهُمْ رَاكِعُونَ (٥٥)وَمَنْ يَتَوَلَّ اللهَ وَ رَسُولَهُ وَالَّذِينَ آمَنُوا فَإِنَّ حِزْبَ اللهِ هُمُ الْغَلِبُونَ(٥٦)

"Surely, your true Protector is Allah, His Messenger, and the believers: those who perform the Prayers, spend in charity and are humble. And whosoever makes Allah his Protector, His Messenger and the believers, (should rest assured that) it is the party of Allah that is victorious." (Al Māʾidah, 55, 56)

These texts establish that there is help, support and friendship between believers, that they are all Favorites of Allah, and that Allah is their Friend and Protector. Therefore, whoever fell in feud with the believers, invited Allah to a fight. This favoritism (*wilāyah*) is a mercy and blessing from Allah. It is not the kind of relationship that prevails between men with needs at the back of their mind. Allah said:

وَقُلِ الْحَمْدُ لِلّهِ الَّذِى لَمْ يَتَّخِذْ وَلَدًا وَّلَمْ يَكُنْ لَّهُ شَرِيكٌ فِى الْمُلْكِ وَلَمْ يَكُنْ لَّهُ وَلِيٌّ مِّنَ الذُّلِّ وَكَبِّرْهُ تَكْبِيرًا

"Say, 'Praise be to Allah who did not take a son, does not have a partner in the dominion, nor did He take a Friend out of weakness. And magnify Him for His greatness." (Al Isrā, 111)

Thus, Allah does not have a friend out of a need, rather all glory is for Him, in contrast to the kings and others who take friends out of humiliation and out of needs so they can be helped out. *Wilāyah* is also equivalent of faith. The author, thus, could be intending to say that basically all the believers are equal, but, it (that is, favoritism) is of different order: perfect and imperfect. Perfect favoritism is for sincere believers, the truly pious. Allah said:

أَلَا إِنَّ أَوْلِيَآءَ اللهِ لَا خَوْفٌ عَلَيْهِمْ وَلَا هُمْ يَحْزَنُونَ (٦٢)الَّذِينَ آمَنُوا وَكَانُوا يَتَّقُونَ (٦٣) لَهُمُ الْبُشْرَى فِى الْحَيوةِ الدُّنْيَا وَفِى الْأَخِرَةِ (٦٤)

"Lo! The Favorites of Allah: they have nothing to fear nor shall they grieve: those who believed and were pious. For them is good news in the life of this world and in the Hereafter." (Yūnus, 62-64)

To be sure, Protection and enmity may both happen to be the share of a single believer at the same time: protection and friendship from one angle and enmity from another. Exactly as belief and unbelief may combinedly exist in him, or *Tawḥīd* and *Shirk*, or piety and corruption or sound faith and hypocrisy, etc.

172

The Prophet (*saws*) has said: "Whosoever possesses three (qualities) will be a pure hypocrite, and in whomsoever one of the three exist, will have one degree of hypocrisy in him, until he gets rid of it: when he talks, he lies, when he promises, he breaks it and when he quarrels, he speaks foul."

Further, obedient acts are branches of faith and sins are branches of infidelity. Although, to dispute with the (well established) truth is the principal disbelief, and the principal belief is to testify.

وأكرمهم عند الله أطوعُهم وأتبعُهم للقرآن

The most honored of them in the sight of Allah are the most obedient and the most meticulous followers of the Qur`an.

What the author meant when he said "the most obedient" is that the most obedient of them to Allah. Further, the most meticulous follower of the Qur`an is the most pious, and the most pious is the most honored.

Allah has said:

اِنَّ اَكْرَمَكُمْ عِنْدَ اللهِ اَتْقٰكُمْ

"The most honored of you in the sight of Allah is the most pious of you." (Al Hujurāt, 13)

the Prophet has said: "There is no superiority of an Arab over a non Arab, nor of a non Arab over an Arab, or a white over a non white, or a non white over a white, save by piety. People are from Adam, and Adam was made of dust."

The above renders redundant the argument of the people over whether the patient and persevering poor man is better or the rich but grateful. The dispute is solved this way. The superiority of one over the other is not dependent on wealth or poverty. It depends entirely on deeds and inner states. Superiority in the sight of Allah is on the basis of piety and quality of faith: not on the basis of richness or poverty. Therefore `Umar said although Allah knows best "Poverty and wealth are two mounts and I don't care which one of the two I ride."

و الإيمان: هو الإيمان بالله، وملائكته، وكتبه، ورسله، و اليوم الآخر، والقدر خيره وشره، وحلوه ومُرّه، من الله تعالى

And faith is: Faith in Allah, His angels, His Books, His Messengers, the Last Day, the Divine Decree and Predestination: the good of it and the evil of it, the sweet of it and the bitter of it   all from Allah Most High.

In what preceded, we have stated that these are the essentials of Islam. This is how the Prophet answered in the famous trustworthy report known as "*Hadīth of Jibril*," when Jibril showed up in the form of a stranger to ask the Prophet about Islam, faith (*imān*) and excellence (*ihsān*).

The Qur`an and the *Sunnah* carry abundant texts that prove that a man's faith cannot be testified to, without deeds accompanying the testification. Further, the term deed goes in application beyond Prayers and charity. This has been made clear by the *Sunnah*. As to what constitutes faith, both the Book as well as the *Sunnah* have explained it.

Allah's Book said:

إِنَّمَا الْمُؤْمِنُونَ الَّذِينَ إِذَا ذُكِرَ اللهُ وَجِلَتْ قُلُوبُهُمْ وَإِذَا تُلِيَتْ عَلَيْهِمْ آيَاتُهُ زَادَتْهُمْ إِيمَانًا

"Verily, believers are those who, when Allah is mentioned, their hearts quake, and when they hear His revelations recited to them, it increases them in faith." (Al Anfāl, 2)

And Allah's words:

فَلَا وَرَبِّكَ لَا يُؤْمِنُونَ حَتَّى يُحَكِّمُوكَ فِيمَا شَجَرَ بَيْنَهُمْ ثُمَّ لَا يَجِدُوا فِي أَنْفُسِهِمْ حَرَجًا مِّمَّا قَضَيْتَ وَيُسَلِّمُوا تَسْلِيمًا

"No, by your Lord, they will not (truly) believe until they accept you (to the exclusion of all else) as the judge in matters of dispute between themselves, and then, find no displeasure in their hearts at your judgement, and submit themselves in total submission." (Al Nisā, 65)

The denial of faith in the above verse until that level (of submission) is achieved, points to the fact that that level of submission is obligatory on the people. Whoever failed to come up with it deserves the threats of punishments pronounced and has not complied with the faith that is obligatory on him.

It might be asked: If, for faith to be of any value, the deeds declared obligatory by Allah were to be more than five that the Prophet (*saws*) counted in the famous "*Hadīth of Jibrīl*," why did the Prophet (*saws*) say that these five constitute the pillars of Islam?

Some scholars have answered that the five spoken of by the Prophet are the well known and the most important of the obligations of Islam. His submission is incomplete without them, and their giving up would be an indication of degeneracy.

But speaking more accurately, the answer is as follows. the Prophet spoke of that part of religion which is the absolutely essential aspect of a man's surrender to his Lord: that which is incumbent upon every individual, upon everyone who is capable of meeting with these obligations we mean the five that the Prophet (*saws*) spoke of. As for the rest, they become obligatory depending upon circumstances and situations. They are not binding on everyone as a general rule. Some of them are either conditional community obligatory (*fard al kifayah*) such as *Jihad*, ordering the good and preventing the evil and the extensions of these such as leadership, judgement between the people, deliverance of legal opinions, studying, coaching, and so forth. There are others whose obligatoriness arises out of a man's relationship with others. They might be applicable to one as a demand on him because of certain rights of others, but might drop off from another for the absence of those reasons, such as, for e.g., paying back of the dues, honoring the trusts, justice in case of transgressions, retribution of the blood, wealth or honor, rights of the spouse and children, joining of the kin, and so forth. In all these cases, what is obligatory on, say Zayd, might not be obligatory on Bakr in contrast to the fasts of Ramadan, Pilgrimage of the House, five daily Prayers and *Zakah*.

The author's words, "the good of it and the evil of it, the sweet of it and the bitter of it: all from Allah Most High," corroborate with the word of Allah:

قُل لَّن يُصِيبَنَا إِلَّا مَا كَتَبَ اللهُ لَنَا

"Say, `Nothing will strike us, save what has been written for us." (Al Taw-bah, 51)

Allah also said:

وَإِن تُصِبْهُمْ سَيِّئَةٌ يَقُولُوا هَٰذِهِ مِنْ عِندِكَ قُلْ كُلٌّ مِّنْ عِندِ اللَّهِ فَمَالِ هَٰؤُلَاءِ الْقَوْمِ لَا يَكَادُونَ يَفْقَهُونَ حَدِيثًا

"And if a good thing happens to them, they (the hypocrites) say, 'This is from Allah.' But when an evil befalls them, they say, 'This is from you (O Muhammad).' Tell them, 'Everything is from Allah.' What then is the matter with these people that they come nowhere near to understanding the discourse." (Al Nisā, 78)

He also said:

مَّا أَصَابَكَ مِنْ حَسَنَةٍ فَمِنَ اللَّهِ وَمَا أَصَابَكَ مِنْ سَيِّئَةٍ فَمِنْ نَفْسِكَ

"Whatever good happens to you (O man), it is from Allah (as a blessing). And whatever evil befalls you, it is from yourself (as a retribution)." (Al Nisā, 79)

If it is asked, how can the two statements be reconciled: one saying (verse 78 above), "everything is from Allah," and the other (verse 79), "from yourself?" The answer is, everything is from Allah, superabundance as well as drought, victory as well as defeat, all of them. As for the words "from yourself" what it means is that whatever strikes you of the evil is because of a sin from you and is a punishment to you. As Allah said:

وَمَا أَصَابَكُم مِّن مُّصِيبَةٍ فَبِمَا كَسَبَتْ أَيْدِيكُمْ

"And what strikes you of a calamity is because what your hands earn." (Al Shurā, 30)

The above meaning derives its strength from what is reported of Ibn `Abbas as its explanation. He read the above verse, "And what strikes you of a calamity is what your hands have earned," and said, "And I (i.e., Allah) decreed it for you."

By the word al hasanah of the text, it is blessings that is meant, and with *al sayyi'ah* the allusion is to misfortunes. That seems to be the appropriate interpretation. None the less, some have interpreted al hasanah as obedience and *al sayyi'ah* as disobedience.

176

Also, there are some points hidden in Allah's words "from your own self." Let not a man be in security from his own self, for evil remains hidden in it. It does not appear but from that as the place of origin. One should not bother about the censure of the people, nor blame the people when they treat him ill. For the misfortunes that struck him were caused by his own sins. So, let him think back on his sins and turn to Allah seeking His protection from the evil hidden in his self, and from the evil consequences of his deeds. He should supplicate for Allah's help for the performance of good deeds. This way, all that is good will become his share and all that is evil will be kept at bay.

Accordingly, the best of supplications is that which is stated in the opening chapter of the Qur`an: "*Show us the right path: the path of those whom You favored and not of those who earned Your anger, nor of those who lost the way.*"

If Allah guides him to this path, then surely He will help him on to obedience and avoidance of disobedience. No evil will touch him: neither in this world nor in the Hereafter. Sins are a natural component of a man's soul. Therefore, he needs guidance every moment. Indeed, his need for guidance is greater than his need for food and water. The situation is unlike what some of the commentators have said, to the effect, that since he has already been guided, what other guidance should he seek? Then they reply that the allusion is to a firm footing on the guidance and an increase in the quality of guidance. Rather, the correct explanation is that a man is in need of being taught by Allah (*swt*), the details of what he is required to do in every situation, and the details of what he is required to abstain from. That is his requirement every new day. Further, he also requires that he be inspired to do what he knows as the right thing to do. Mere knowledge does not suffice if Allah will not inspire him to accomplish what he has the knowledge of. Otherwise, that knowledge is against him in the other pan of the Balance, and he cannot be reckoned a guided one. Furthermore, the man is also in need of being given the power to perform the deeds that he wishes to perform.

What has to be kept in mind is that of those that are unknown to us of the truth far exceed what we know about them. And, of what we know, what we do not wish to act in accordance with because of laziness or heedlessness, or whatever other reason is of the same magnitude, or maybe ever more than what we wish to act upon. Similarly, what we do not have power over, is far greater in aggregate than what we have the power to perform. Finally, what we are ignorant of the several major requirements as well as those others whose details we lack, is simply immeasurable. (Thus, the deeds finally attempted are reduced to an infinitesimally small quantity). Therefore, we need a comprehensive guidance. Whoever has mastered these things, might ask for a firm footing upon the path: which is the last of the requirements. After all these comes the ultimate guidance: the guidance to the path of Paradise. Hence, people have been ordered to supplicate for it in everyone of their five daily Prayers.

All these things the Prophet (*saws*) used to combine together in his own Prayers, as the authentic reports tell us. We are to learn that when he raised his head from the *ruku`*, he would say,

ربَّنا لكَ الحَمدُ حمداً كثيراً طيّباً مباركاً فيه ملءُ السَّماواتِ، وملءُ الأرض ، وملءُ ما شِئتَ من شيءٍ بعد،
أهلُ الثناء والمجد، أحقّ ما قال العبد ، وكُلُّنا لكَ عبدٌ.

"O our Lord. For You is the Praise. Praises: plentiful, pure, blessed by itself, filling the heavens and the earth, and filling all that You wish (to create) after this. You are deserving of praises and exaltation; deserving all that the slave can say and we are all Your slaves."

The above then is the praise. It is to thank Allah Most High and to declare that what the slave says, Allah deserves it. the Prophet (*saws*) used to say after that:

لا مانعَ لِما أعطيتَ ، ولا مُعطيَ لِما مَنَعتَ ، ولا يَنفَعُ ذَا الجَدِّ منكَ الجَدُّ

"None there is to withhold what You give nor anyone to give what You withhold. And of no use before You, anyone's resources against Your resources."

This then, is *Tawhīd* of Lordship: in point of creation, in point of pre determination, whether it be the beginning of things, or the end of them. So He is the Bestower and the Withholder. There is none to withhold what He will give. And none to give what He will withhold. This is also the *Tawhīd* of Divinity: in point of Law, command or forbiddance. 'Even if the slaves are given kingdom,

178

power and rule, their being in possession of these resources is of no use against Your resources,' that is, it will not help him escape or achieve salvation.

Whoever knew this in the manner he should know, will have the door of *Tawhīd* opened up for him. He will know that there is no point in asking other creations besides Him, far from worshipping them; there is no point in placing one's trust in anyone nor in fastening hopes on any.

و نحن المؤمنون بذلك كله، لا نفرق بين أحد من رسله، و نصدقهم كلهم على ما جاءوا به

We believe in all this. We do not distinguish between any of His Messengers, rather, we attest them all in reference to what they brought.

That is, we do not distinguish between them by believing in some and rejecting others. Rather, we believe in all and testify everyone of them. For he who believed in some but rejected others, rejected all. Allah said:

وَيَقُولُونَ نُؤْمِنُ بِبَعْضٍ وَنَكْفُرُ بِبَعْضٍ وَيُرِيدُونَ أَن يَتَّخِذُوا بَيْنَ ذَلِكَ سَبِيلاً , أُولَٰئِكَ هُمُ الْكَافِرُونَ حَقًّا

"They say, 'We shall believe in some and deny others,' wishing to take between this and that a way. Such are the true unbelievers." (Al Nisā', 150-151)

This is because, the reasons of belief that the believers in some of them found, are also to be found in those they didn't believe in. Further, the Messenger in whom they believed, confirmed the rest of the Messengers. Therefore, if a person didn't believe in other Messengers, in actual fact, disbelieved in him he thinks he believes.

وأهل الكبائر من أمة محمد صلى الله عليه وسلم في النار لا يخلدون، إذا ماتوا وهم مُوَحِّدون، وإن لم يكونوا تائبين، بعد أن لقوا الله عارفين، وهم في مشيئته وحكمه، إن شاء غفر لهم وعفا عنهم بفضله، كما ذكر عز وجل في كتابه: (وَيَغْفِرُ مَا دُونَ ذَلِكَ لِمَنْ يَشَاءُ)، وإن شاء عذبهم في النار بعدله، ثم يخرجهم منها برحمته وشفاعة الشافعين من أهل طاعته، ثم يبعثهم إلى جنته، ذلك بأن الله تعالى تَوَلَّى أهل معرفته، ولم يجعلهم في الدارين كأهل نَكِرَته، الذين خابوا من هدايته، ولم ينالوا من ولايته. اللهم يا وليَّ الإسلام و أهله، ثَبِّتْنا على الإسلام حتى نلقاك به

Those of the followers of Prophet Muhammad who committed major sins will not abide in the Fire forever: provided they died believing in the oneness of Allah, even if they did not repent, so long as they met Allah well acquainted (with His oneness). They are under the will and judgment of Allah. If He wished, He will forgive them altogether by His grace, as He said in His Book: "He will forgive whomsoever He will besides that (i.e. besides the sin of association)." Or, following His (rules of) justice, He might punish them in the Fire and then bring them out of it by His mercy, or by the intercession of the intercessors: those who led a virtuous life, and then admit them into Paradise. This is because Allah is the Friend and Protector of those who know (and admit) Him as One. Therefore, He will never let them ― either in this world or the next ― be treated equal to those who denied Him: those who did not receive His guidance and did not get any share of His Friendship and Protection. 'O Allah, O Protector of Islam and its followers: give us steadfastness in Islam until we meet You with it.'

The most accurate definition of a Major Sin (*kabirah*) is as follows. It is one of those that (i) deserves a capital punishment, (ii) that has been threatened with a punishment with the Fire, or (iii) for which a curse has been pronounced, or (iv) has been threatened with Allah's anger.

And the nearest about Minor Sin (*Saghirah*) is that it is that sin which entails neither a capital punishment in this world nor a threat of punishment in the Hereafter.

With regard to the term 'threat' used above, it is either the threat of punishment in the Fire, or a curse, or anger that is implied. For a specific 'threat' that will be realized in the Hereafter, is similar in some ways to the punishments specified (for crimes) in this world. Similarly, the punishment handed down in this world (by the courts, involving crimes for which a specific punishment has not been pronounced by the *Shari`ah*, i.e., *ta`zirat*), can be equated with the threats of punishment in the Hereafter ― but not of Fire, or one accompanied by a curse or expression of anger.

Whatever the definition, (it must be kept in mind that) all that has a text behind it is a Major sin. Such as, Association (*Shirk*), murder, adultery, sorcery, slandering chaste innocent women and others of this sort. Or, they could be the other kind, such as, running away from the battle field, devouring orphan's property, usury, misbehaving with the parents, false oath, false testimony and others.

The definition itself, as above, is following the opinions of renowned scholars such as Ibn `Abbas, Ibn `Uyaynah, Ahmed b. Hanbal and others. Secondly, we have a verse of the Qur`an which can be cited in support. It says:

اِنْ تَجْتَنِبُوْا كَبَآئِرَ مَا تُنْهَوْنَ عَنْهُ نُكَفِّرْ عَنْكُمْ سَيِّاٰتِكُمْ وَنُدْخِلْكُمْ مُّدْخَلاً كَرِيْمًا

i..e, "If you will avoid the major (sins) that you are forbidden, We shall obliterate from you your (minor) evil deeds and allow you a noble entry (into Paradise)" Al Nisā, 31.

Thirdly, the above is to rule out the definition of those who said that the Major Sins are those over which there is consensus between all the previous religions. Such an idea is erroneous. It would imply that intoxication, marriage with certain close kin, illegality of marriage with foster relations etc., are not Major Sins. In the like manner, those opinions are also wrong which have it that Major Sin is anything that closes that acts as a barrier to the perception of God. Some have said that anything is a Major Sin that leads to loss of life or property. All these are incorrect definitions.

ونرى الصلاة خلف كل بَرٍّ و فاجر من أهل القبلة، وعلى من مات منهم

We see Prayers (as allowable) behind every pious and the corrupt of the people of the *Qiblah*, and (similarly, Prayers) over every one of them who died.

This is derived from the words of the Prophet who said: "Pray behind every pious and corrupt." Mak-hul has narrated it from Abu Hurayrah. Dara Qutni also recorded it adding as his assessment: "Mak-hul never met Abu Hurayrah. Further, there is one in the chain called Mu`awiyyah b. Saleh about whose integrity some have raised doubts. However, Muslim has narrations through him in his Compilation.

Dara Qutni has recorded another report, and so has Abu Da'ud that narrates Mak-hul narrating Abu Hurayrah again, that the Prophet said: "Prayers are obligatory on you behind every Muslim, whether he be a pious person or corrupt, and even if he committed major sins. So also, *Jihad* is obligatory on you under the leadership of every leader of the Muslims, be he pious or corrupt, even if he committed major sins."

It is reported in Bukhari that `Abdullah ibn `Umar used to pray behind Hajjaj b. *Yūsuf* Thaqafiyy as would also Anas b. Malik, although, as is well known, Hajjaj b. *Yūsuf* was a thoroughly corrupt person and a tyrant.

Bukhari has also recorded the Prophet's words: "They (the corrupt ones) will lead you in Prayers. If they do it right, both you and they will be rewarded. If they commit errors (in the Prayers), you will be rewarded and they will be punished."

You should also know, O reader, may Allah show you and us mercy, that according to all Imams, it is permissible to pray behind one whose innovation and corruption is not known. It is not a requirement that a follower should know the faiths and beliefs of his Imam, or that he should make inquiries about it, asking him, for instance, "What are your beliefs?" Rather, he can pray behind one whose personality is in dark. Similarly, one might even pray behind an Imam who commits innovations and invites others to it, or behind one whose corrupt ways are well known, on condition that the Imam is an employee and there is no recourse but to Pray behind him. Such as the (state) Imam of the Friday and `Eid Prayers, or the Imam at `Arafah in Hajj. Whoever gave up the Friday Prayers, or other congregational Prayers because of a corrupt Imam, is himself an innovator. This is the opinion of the great majority of the scholars. Also, he need not repeat the Prayers in private. For the Companions would do the congregational and Friday Prayers behind corrupt Imams without repeating them in private: such as `Abdullah ibn `Umar who prayed behind Hajjaj b. Yūsuf, or Anas b. Malik. It is also reported of `Abdullah ibn Mas`ud and some others that

182

they used to Pray behind Al Walid b. `Uqbah b. Abi Mu`ayt although the man used to drink wine.

Indeed the Prayers of the innovator or the corrupt of character are by themselves acceptable. Therefore, if someone Prays behind such a person, his Prayers cannot be invalidated. But those who disliked Prayers behind them have done so because they say that (in such a situation) enjoining the good and preventing the vice becomes obligatory.

The details are as follows. Whoever openly committed innovations and corruptions does not deserve to be employed as the Imam of the Muslims, rather, he needs to be delivered a punishment by the state authorities until he repents. Now, if it is possible to abandon him until the time he will repent, then, that should be alright. If some people did not Pray behind such a person, doing those Prayers behind another Imam, their act would be considered as a kind of disapproval of the Imam. The door will be open for him to repent, or for his removal, and, the people are warned that he may not be followed in his corrupt ways. Thus, there is wisdom in the action, so long as the person does not miss his congregational or Friday Prayers (by refusing to Pray behind a corrupt Imam). But no one can refuse to Pray behind a corrupt Imam, (which entails missing congregational or Friday Prayers) unless the man refusing be himself an innovator, opposed to the ways of the Companions. So also, when the State authorities have appointed an Imam. There is no religious wisdom in not Praying behind him.

In short, Prayers behind the most virtuous around is better. Therefore, if it is possible for one to prevent him to lead who openly commits sins, he might do it. But if someone takes charge, and his replacement is not possible, or the evil feared in his removal be greater than the evil contained in the man leading in the Prayers, then, it is not allowed to fight a lesser evil at the cost of a greater evil at hand. Nor is it advisable to drive out a lesser evil but end up with a greater evil. For the (Islamic) laws have been designed to promote the good and lessen the evil so far as possible. Non attendance of the Friday Prayers is of a greater evil than contained in the leadership of a corrupt person, especially when staying away will not help to chase off the evil. The result would be nullification of religious good without the removal of the cause of evil.

However, wherever it is possible to offer the Friday and other Prayers behind a virtuous person, then, surely, that is preferable over offering them behind a corrupt man. Therefore, if someone did that, that is, offered Prayers behind a corrupt person who sins openly, without a good reason, then, there are some scholars who have said that he might repeat the Prayers, while others have opined that he need not.

In contrast, if the Imam forgets (during the Prayers) or commits an error, but the followers do not know about it, then the follower may not repeat the Prayers, in view of the preceding *hadīth*. `Umar once led in the Prayers having forgotten that he was in the state requiring major ablution. He repeated his Prayers but did not ask the congregation to re-do it. Nonetheless, if a man learns that his Imam was without ablution, a follower should, according to Imam Abu Hanifah re-do his prayers. But Malik, Shafe`i and Ahmed have said that it is not necessary. That applies also to an Imam doing what is not acceptable to the followers. However, these things require detailed discussion which are proper for *Fiqh* books. Nevertheless, if the follower knows before hand that the Imam is offering Prayers without ablution, then, he might not Pray behind him as the man is a joker and not a devotee.

The Qur`anic and *Sunnah* texts as well as the consensus of the earliest scholars tells us that the ruler, the Imam who leads in Prayers, the governor, the commander in chief, the *Zakah* collector, each of them must be obeyed in matters that require a fresh juridical reasoning (*ijtihad*). He (the ruler and others) is not required to necessarily follow the opinion of those under him. Rather, they (those under him) should obey him abandoning their own opinion in favor of his opinion. For, the general good of the community, its harmony, and the evil of division and disagreement is of greater repercussion than the minor issue at hand. Following the same principle, it is not desirable for the rulers to cancel out each other's commands and instructions. These few points should lead us to the right conclusion concerning the correctness of Prayers of some behind the others.

As for the report that Bukhari has narrated that the Prophet (*saws*) said: "They will lead you in Prayers. If they do it right, it will be good for them and for you. But, if they do it wrong, then it will be 'for you' and 'upon them.'" (That is, rewards for you and punishment upon them: tr.). This is clear text to prove our point that if an Imam leading in the Prayers commits an error, the error is upon him and not upon the followers. It allows us to deduce another point. The worse that a reputed scholar (*mujtahid*) can do is to commit the error of dropping off something obligatory because in his opinion it is not obligatory, or, does something prohibited because in his opinion it is not prohibited. In such an event, it is not allowable for someone who believes in Allah and His Messenger that he should oppose this clear *hadīth*. This is also a strong argument against some of the followers of the Hanafiyy, Shafe`i or Hanbaliyy schools of thought who have ruled that if the Imam drops off what the follower thinks is obligatory, it is not right to follow him. Unity and harmony demand the abandoning of that which leads to division and disagreements.

As for the words of the author, "(Prayers) over everyone of them who died," he means to say that we believe we ought to pray over everyone of them, whether they be virtuous or corrupt, although excluded are the rebels and thigh way robbers, or one who commits suicide, notwithstanding the fact that Abu *Yūsuf* has a different opinion over this issue, also, not over the martyr, as against the opinions of Malik and Shafe`i. Nonetheless, the author has primarily placed this note in order to impress that we do not refuse to pray over the innovators and the open sinners. He didn't mean to include all and sundry. To explain: of the believers in Islam there are two kinds: the true believer and the hypocrite. Now, when the hypocrisy of a person is known for certain, it is not allowable that he be prayed over, or supplicated for, for forgiveness. But if his hypocrisy is not confirmed, then he might be prayed over. So too, if a certain person has confirmed knowledge of another person's hypocrisy, he might not pray over him. Only those might pray over him who did not have a personal knowledge of his hypocrisy. `Umar for instance would not pray over one Hudhayfah would not pray. This is because (during the Tabuk expedition) Hudhayfah had gained the knowledge of the hypocrisy of certain people. Further, Allah Most High forbade the Prophet (*saws*) to pray over the hypocrites who died, informing him that He would not forgive them, even if he sought forgiveness for them, stating their disbelief in Allah and His Messenger as the reason. Therefore, whoever believes in Allah and His Messenger, may not be denied that he be prayed over when dead: even if he were to commit a few innovations that affect his faith or some sins in his everyday life. Rather, Allah has ordered that forgiveness be sought for the believers. He said:

فَاعْلَمْ أَنَّهُ لَا إِلٰهَ إِلَّا اللهُ وَاسْتَغْفِرْ لِذَنْبِكَ وَلِلْمُؤْمِنِينَ وَ الْمُؤْمِنٰتِ

"Know, therefore, that there is no deity save Allah, seek forgiveness for your sins and for the sins of the believing men and women." (Muhammad, 19)

Belief in the oneness of Allah then, is the core of religion. Now, with regard to seeking of forgiveness, it is in practice of two kinds: the general and the specific. As for the general, it is well known, such as in this verse. As for the specific, one of them is prayers over the dead. So, no believer dies but the other believers have been ordered to pray over him as part of burying ritual. And, while doing the prayers, they are required to seek forgiveness for him. This is following a report in Abu Da'ud and Ibn Majah, narrated by Abu Hurayrah, who said: "I heard the Prophet say, 'When you do Prayers over a dead man, make supplications for him.'"

ولا نُنَزِّلُ أَحدًا منهم جنة ولا نار

We do not say about anyone that he belongs either to Paradise or the Fire.

What the author means is that we do not say about a specific person of the people of the *Qiblah* that he is of the Fire or Paradise, unless the most truthful himself, peace be upon him, informed us about someone that he is of Paradise, such as, the ten who were given the glad tidings of Paradise, may Allah be pleased with them. We believe that those who committed major sins have to necessarily enter into the Fire if Allah wills so. But they will be brought out by the intercession of the intercessors. However, so far as a specific individual is concerned, we remain silent: neither consigning him to the Fire, nor to Paradise, unless we have received knowledge. No one is aware of the truth in the hearts. And we cannot circumspect the events and situation immediately preceding the death. Rather, we hope the best for those who do good and are apprehensive of the evil doers.

Nonetheless, one might assert about someone that he will enter Paradise if the believers generally think so. This is in view of a *hadīth* in the *Sahihayn* wherein it is said that a bier passed by. The people spoke well of the dead man. the Prophet (*saws*) said: "It became obligatory." Then another bier was being taken across but the people spoke ill of him. the Prophet (*saws*) said: "It became obligatory." According to a report he repeated these words. `Umar enquired: "O Messenger of Allah, what became obligatory?" He replied: "When you spoke well of the first, Paradise became obligatory for him. And when you spoke ill of the second, the Fire became obligatory for him. You are Allah's witnesses on the earth."

the Prophet also said: "It is possible that you will know the people of Paradise from the people of Hell fire." They asked him: "How could we do that, O Messenger of Allah?" He replied: "By the praises and censure (of the dead person)." Thus, the Muslims can know about a person if he is of the Fire or of Paradise.

ولا نشهد عليهم بكفر ولا بشرك ولابنفاق، مالم يظهر منهم شيء من ذلك، ونَذَرُ سرائرهم إلى الله تعالى

Further, we do not bear witness to their disbelief, association or hypocrisy, so long as something clear is not manifest. We leave their secrets to Allah.

This is because we have been ordered to go by what is apparent and have been prohibited from thinking evil of someone or to follow that train of thought which has no knowledge in its support. Allah said:

يَآ أَيُّهَا الَّذِينَ آمَنُوا اجْتَنِبُوا كَثِيرًا مِّنَ الظَّنِّ إِنَّ بَعْضَ الظَّنِّ إِثْمٌ

"O believers! Avoid suspicion as much as possible, for some suspicion is sin."
(Al Hujurāt, 12)

ولا نرى السيف على أحد من أمة محمد صلى الله عليه وسلم إلا مَنْ وَجَبَ عليه السيف

We also do not approve of a death sentence for anyone of the *Ummah* of the Prophet unless it became mandatory on him (because of a crime he committed).

This follows a authentic tradition in which the Prophet said: "The blood of a Muslim who testified that there is no deity save Allah and that I am His Messenger, is not lawful save under three conditions: 'A married adulterer, life for life and the apostate who separated out from the community.'"

ولا نرى الخروج على أئمتنا وولاة أمورنا، وإن جاروا، ولا ندعوا عليهم، ولا ننزع يدا من طاعتهم، ونرى طَاعتهم من طاعة الله عز وجل فَريضة، مَا لم يأمروا بِمَعْصية، وندعو لهم بالصَّلاح والمعافاة

We also do not allow rebellion against our rulers or those in charge of our affairs even if they oppress. We do not pray (for Allah's wrath) against them nor do we withdraw our hand of obedience from them. Rather, we believe that their obedience is the obedience of Allah an obligation, so long as they do not command a sin. Otherwise, we pray for them a turn toward the better and for forgiveness.

This is based on the words of Allah Most High:

يَا أَيُّهَا الَّذِينَ آمَنُوا أَطِيعُوا اللهَ وَأَطِيعُوا الرَّسُولَ وَأُولِي الْأَمْرِ مِنْكُمْ

"Believers! Obey Allah, obey the Messenger and those of you who are in charge of the affairs." (Al Nisā', 59)

There is a report in authentic compilations that the Prophet (*saws*) said: "Whoever obeyed me, obeyed Allah. And whoever disobeyed me, disobeyed Allah. And whoever obeyed the Amir, obeyed me and whoever disobeyed the Amir, disobeyed me."

Abu Dharr has also reported: "My friend (i.e., the Prophet) admonished me that I hear and obey even if the Amir be an Abyssinian with ...'"

Another trustworthy report says: "To hear and obey is obligatory upon a Muslim in all matters involving the liked and the disliked, unless he were to be ordered a sin. If he is ordered a sin, then there is no hearing, no obeying."

Further, `Awf b. Malik has reported the Prophet: "The best of your rulers are those whom you love and who love you. They pray for you and you pray for them. And the worst of your rulers are those whom you hate and who hate you. You curse them and they curse you." We asked: "Should we not destroy such of them with our swords?" He replied: "No. So long as they establish the Prayers among you. Except for him who was appointed a deputy by a ruler. One of you sees him committing a sin against Allah (*swt*). He disapproves of that, but does not withdraw his hand of obedience."

Thus, the Book and the *Sunnah* have both declared the obedience of the rulers obligatory, so long as they do not order a sin.

Also, give a second thought to the words of Allah: "Obey Allah, obey the Messenger, and those of you who are in charge of the affairs." Allah (*swt*) said, "Obey Allah and obey the Messenger." But He didn't say, "Obey those of you who are in charge of the affairs." That is because, those in charge of the affairs cannot be obeyed unconditionally. Their obedience is conditional to themselves obeying Allah and His Messenger.

As for obeying them even if they oppress, this is because, the evil that rebellion against them will give rise to, will be of greater magnitude than the evil resulting from their oppression. Indeed, in observing patience against their oppression, there is the advantage of forgiveness of one's sins, and increase in rewards. Allah did not place them upon us but because of our evil deeds. And the recompense is of the same kind. Therefore, it is upon us to do the best, seek Allah's forgiveness, turn to Him in repentance and reform ourselves.

ونتَّبِعُ السنة والجماعة، ونجتنب الشُّذُوذَ والخلاف والفُرقة

We follow the *Sunnah* and the community, sidestepping disputes, disagreements and divisions.

As regards the *Sunnah* of the above usage, it is the ways of the Prophet (*saws*). As for the community (*Jama`ah*) it is the community of Muslims but specifically applicable to the Companions and those who followed them in good stead until the day of Judgement. Following them is right guidance and opposing them is to go astray.

A *hadīth* declared authentic by Tirmidhi has `Irbad b. Sariyyah as saying: "Once the Prophet (*saws*) admonished us in such an effective manner that it brought tears into our eyes and the hearts became soft. Somebody said: 'This was a parting admonition. So what kind of pledge would you suggest us?' He replied: 'I advise you to hear and obey. For, whoever of you lives for some time will witness a lot of disputes. (For such a situation), it is incumbent upon you to follow my *Sunnah* and the *Sunnah* of the rightly guided caliphs after me. Hold fast unto it with your teeth. And beware of innovations, for every innovation is a misguidance.'"

the Prophet also said: "The peoples of the two Books divided themselves into seventy two sects. This *Ummah* will divide itself into seventy three sects, following their carnal desires. All of them would be in the Fire except for one. This is the *Jama`ah*." According to another version they enquired: "Which one is it, O Messenger of Allah?" He replied: "That upon which I and my Companions are." Thus the Prophet (*saws*) made it clear that all the differing people are to meet with destruction, except for the *Ahl al Sunnah wa al Jama`ah*.

How apt then the statement of `Abdullah ibn Mas`ud who said: "Whoever wishes to follow the ways of another, let him follow the ways of those who are dead. For, the living cannot be sure of coming out unscathed from the trials. They, indeed, they are the Companions of the Prophet. They were the best of this *Ummah*, the most pious of heart, deepest of knowledge, the least of affected manners a people whom Allah chose for His Messenger and for the establishment of His religion. Therefore, learn their greatness, follow them in their ways, and acquire what you can of their character and religion. For they were on a guidance even and true."

ونحب أهل العدل والأمانة، ونَبغض أهل الجور و الخِيَانة

We love the just and the trustworthy and hate the tyrannous and the treacherous.

This is the perfection of faith and completeness of humility. For worship includes the perfectness of love to its maximum extent and perfection of humility to its maximum extent. That has to be so because the love of Allah's Messengers and Prophets is because of the love of Allah: although no one else deserves this love. Other than Allah are loved for the sake of Allah: and not along with the love of Allah. For the lover loves what his beloved loves and hates what his beloved hates. He bids what his beloved bids and forbids what his beloved forbids. In short, he agrees with his beloved in every sense. Allah (*swt*) loves those who do good, the pious, the repentant, the pure, and we love those whom Allah loves. Allah does not love the treacherous, the corrupt, nor the haughty. We too do not love them, rather, hate them, agreeing totally with Allah Most High.

و نقول: الله أعلم، فيما اشتبه علينا علمه

And we say, in matters of doubt, "Allah knows best."

The author has earlier stated that only he saved his religion who submitted whole heartedly to Allah and His Messenger, leaving that which he does not comprehend to the one who has its knowledge. Allah said:

قُلْ إِنَّمَا حَرَّمَ رَبِّيَ الْفَوَاحِشَ مَا ظَهَرَ مِنْهَا وَمَا بَطَنَ وَ الْإِثْمَ وَالْبَغْيَ بِغَيْرِ الْحَقِّ وَأَنْ تُشْرِكُوا بِاللهِ مَا لَمْ يُنَزِّلْ بِهِ سُلْطَانًا وَأَنْ تَقُولُوا عَلَى اللهِ مَا لَا تَعْلَمُونَ

"Say, 'Verily, my Lord has only forbidden indecencies be they open or concealed sin, high handedness without justice; that you should associate with

Allah that for which He has not sent you down an authority; and that you should fasten upon Allah what you have no knowledge of." (Al A`rāf, 33)

Indeed, Allah taught the Prophet to leave the knowledge of that which he does not posses to Allah. (That is, attribute the knowledge to Him). Allah (*swt*) said:

قُلِ اللهُ أَعْلَمُ بِمَا لَبِثُوا لَهُ غَيْبُ السَّمٰوٰتِ وَالْأَرْضِ

"Say, Allah knows how long they tarried. To Him belongs the unknown of the heavens and the earth." (Al Kahaf, 26)

Accordingly, when the Prophet was asked about pagan children (whether they woll be in Paradise or Hell fire), he replied, "Allah knows best what they were going to do (when they grew)," a proof of his authenticity.

و نرى المسح على الخُفَّيْن، في السفر والحَضَر، كما جاء في الأثر

And we believe in the wiping of (thick) socks both in journey as well as during residence, in accordance with what is related in the traditions.

The Prophet's *Sunnah* of wiping on the socks (during ablution) or washing the two feet is a well proven one. But the *Shi`ah* oppose this.

As for the verse concerning the ablution, there are two readings. The verse itself is as follows:

يَا أَيُّهَا الَّذِينَ أَمَنُوا إِذَا قُمْتُمْ إِلَى الصَّلٰوةِ فَاغْسِلُوا وُجُوهَكُمْ وَأَيْدِيَكُمْ إِلَى الْمَرَافِقِ وَامْسَحُوا بِرُءُوسِكُمْ وَأَرْجُلَكُمْ إِلَى الْكَعْبَيْنِ

"Believers! When you prepare for Prayer, wash your face, arms up to (and including) the elbows, wipe your heads (with water) and (wash) your feet up to (and including) the ankles." (Al Mā'idah, 6)

The two readings are either in the accusative (*fat-ha*) or genitive (*kasra*) of the textual word "*arjul.*" The reasons for such diacritical marks can be seen in larger works. But it might be noted that when it comes to major ablution, the diacritical mark can only be an accusative.

192

و الحج و الجهاد ماضيان مع أولي الأمر من المسلمين، بَرِّهم و فاجرهم، إلى قيام الساعة، لا
يُبْطِلُهما شيء ولا ينقضهما

Hajj and *Jihad* will remain (as obligations, to be performed) under the leadership of the Muslim rulers, the pious of them or the corrupt until the Day of Judgment; nothing will nullify the two nor abolish them.

This is because Hajj and *Jihad* are both related to travel. Therefore, it is necessary that a leader lead the people and face the enemy. This can be achieved under a pious leader as well as a corrupt leader.

ونؤمن بالكرام الكاتبين، فإن الله قد جعلهم علينا حافظين

We believe in the honorable scribes. Allah has appointed them as guardians over us.

Allah said:

وَإِنَّ عَلَيْكُمْ لَحَافِظِينَ (١٠) كِرَامًا كَاتِبِينَ (١١) يَعْلَمُونَ مَا تَفْعَلُونَ (١٢)

"And upon you are guardians. The honored Scribes. They know what you do." (Al Infitār, 10-12)

And,

إِذْ يَتَلَقَّى الْمُتَلَقِّيَانِ عَنِ الْيَمِينِ وَعَنِ الشِّمَالِ قَعِيدٌ (١٧) مَا يَلْفِظُ مِنْ قَوْلٍ إِلَّا لَدَيْهِ رَقِيبٌ عَتِيدٌ (١٨)

"When the two (angels) meet together, positioning themselves on either side of the man. Not a word he utters but by him is an observer ready (to write down)." (Qāf: 17, 18)

And also,

أَمْ يَحْسَبُونَ أَنَّا لَا نَسْمَعُ سِرَّهُمْ وَنَجْوَاهُمْ بَلَى وَرُسُلُنَا لَدَيْهِمْ يَكْتُبُونَ

"Or, do they think We do not hear their secret and their whispers? Nay, Our messenger angels are with them writing down." (Al Zukhruf, 80)

In authentic compilations there is a report that the Prophet (*saws*) said: "You are followed up by the evening angels and the morning angels. They meet together at the time of dawn and after noon Prayers. As those that were with you ascend (to the Heavens), He asks   and He knows better than them   `In what state did you leave My slaves?' They reply, `When we went to them, they were Praying, and when we left them, they were Praying.'"

Thus, the above texts prove that the angels write down our words and deeds. They also write down the intentions. For that is the deed of the heart and is covered by the words above: "They know what you do." This can also be substantiated by the words of the Prophet who said: "Allah (*swt*) said, `If My slave happens to intend an evil, don't write it down. If he commits it, then write down a single evil against him. But if My slave intends a good deed, but does not perform it, then write it down in his favor as a single good deed. But, if he commits it, then write it down as ten good deeds.'"

The Prophet also said: "The Angels said, `There is a man there who intends to commit an evil.' Although He is better seeing than him. He replied, `Follow him. If he goes ahead and commits it, write down its equivalent. But if he gives it up, write down a good deed in his favor. For he gave it up for My sake.'" This *hadīth* is in the *Sahihayn* and the words here are those of Muslim.

ونؤمن بِمَلَكِ الموت، المُوَكَّل بقبْض أرْواح العالمين

We believe in the angel of death, responsible for the withdrawal of the people's souls.

Allah said:

قُلْ يَتَوَفَّىكُمْ مَّلَكُ الْمَوْتِ الَّذِى وُكِّلَ بِكُمْ ثُمَّ إِلَى رَبِّكُمْ تُرْجَعُونَ

"Say, `The angel of death assigned over you withdraws your souls, and then to your Lord you are returned.'" (Al Sajdah, 11)

The above does not contradict the words of Allah:

حَتَّى إِذَا جَاءَ أَحَدَكُمُ الْمَوْتُ تَوَفَّتْهُ رُسُلُنَا وَهُمْ لَا يُفَرِّطُونَ

194

"Until, when death arrives upon one of you, Our angels withdraw the souls, and they do not commit excesses." (Al An`ām, 61)

Nor the words of Allah:

اللهُ يَتَوَفَّى الْأَنْفُسَ حِينَ مَوْتِهَا وَالَّتِي لَمْ تَمُتْ فِي مَنَامِهَا فَيُمْسِكُ الَّتِي قَضَىٰ عَلَيْهَا الْمَوْتَ وَ يُرْسِلُ الْأُخْرَىٰ إِلَىٰ أَجَلٍ مُّسَمًّى

"Allah withdraws the soul (of men) at the time of their death, and of those who die not in their sleep. Then He holds back those for whom He had decreed their death but sends back the other until an appointed term." (Al Zumar, 42)

The explanation is that it is primarily the angel of death who is assigned the role of withdrawal of souls. When he has done that, either the angels of mercy or the angels of punishment take over. The command and decree of Allah accomplish all this. Therefore, it is right to attribute the whole affair to Him.

و بعذاب القبر لمن كان له أهلاً، وسؤال مُنْكَر و نَكير في قبره عن ربه و دينه ونبيه، على ما جاءت به الأخبار عن رسول الله صلى الله عليه وسلم، وعن الصحابة رضوان الله عليهم والقبر روضة من رياض الجنة، أو حفرة من حفر النّيران

We also believe in the punishment in the grave, of him who deserved it; in the questioning in the graves by the angels called Munkar and Nakir concerning his Lord, religion and Prophet in accordance with the narrations attributed to the Messenger of Allah, on whom be peace, as well as those attributed to the Companions, may Allah be pleased with them. And (we believe) that the grave is either a patch of Paradise or a pit of Fire.

The above is substantiated by what Bukhari has reported through Anas, that the Prophet said: "When a slave is placed into his grave and is left behind, he hears the noise of the receding footsteps of his departing friends. Two angels come in and sit him up. They ask him, `What was your opinion about this man, Muhammad, on whom be peace?' He replies, `I bear witness that he is Allah's slave and Messenger.' They say, `Look at your abode in the Fire which has been exchanged for  that in Paradise.' the Prophet  said, `He sees both the places.' As for the unbeliever or the hypocrite, he replies, `I don't know. I only used to repeat what the people said.' He would be told, `You neither knew nor learned.' Then he is hit with an iron hammer between his two ears (that is, on the forehead). He cries out at that so loudly that everyone around hears except the Jinn and mankind."

Qatadah added, "It has been narrated unto us that (for the believer) the grave is widened."

Ibn `Abbas has also been recorded in the *Sahihayn* as saying that: "The Prophet (*saws*) passed by two graves whose occupants were being punished. He said, `They are being tortured. And they are not being tortured for something very serious. One of them would not cover himself up when he urinated. The other used to carry people's reports around sowing dissension.' Then he took a fresh branch, split it into two and pitched them each on the graves.' They enquired, `Why did you do that, O Messenger of Allah?' He answered, 'Hopefully, their torture would be reduced until the branches dry up."

Innumerous reports have come to us from the Prophet regarding questioning in the grave and either blessings or torture therein. Therefore, it is obligatory to believe in these things without asking how they take place. Reason has no entry upon affairs of this sort. It may also be kept in mind that religion does not always speak of things that the reason can appreciate. In fact, most of the time it speaks of things that leave the reason in a puzzle. The return of the soul, for instance, never happens in this world. But, it will be returned to the bodies, in a manner that does not happen anytime in this world.

Furthermore, it is not the soul alone that will be subject to the questioning in the grave, as Ibn Hazm and others have thought, nor will it happen to the body alone, as conjectured on a line worse than that. Authentic traditions refute both the ideas. So also, both the body and the soul will be subjected to punishment in the grave. There is no difference in opinion over this among the *Ahl al Sunnah wa al Jama`ah*. However, a person might be punished or blessed in both ways: only the body, or both body and soul.

Also, it must be understood that the torture in the grave is the torture of the isthmus between this world and the next: the Hades (*barzakh*). Anyone who dies deserving punishment, will receive his share of the torture whether he is

196

buried or not, whether the animals devoured his body, is burned and the ashes dispersed in the air, is left hung on the cross, or is sunk deep in the seas. His soul joins up with his body to taste what the buried are destined to taste. As for the other details that have been spoken of in the traditions such as making the man sit up or pressing together of the ribs, etc., these are to be understood without addition or deletion. Those words should not be given the meaning they were not intended. Neither should one deny them the purpose they were intended for: to warn and guide. After all, how many people have not been led astray by unwarranted interpretations, while only Allah (*swt*) knows the true interpretation?! Indeed, poor understanding of what Allah and His Messenger spoke is at the root of all destructive innovation that rose up in Islam, leading to all kinds of errors in the understanding of the principles as well as the derivatives, especially, when evil intentions were added up to ignorance. Allah's help do we implore.

To recapitulate, there are three stages: (i) this world, (ii) the Isthmian Hades (*barzakh*), and (iii) the Hereafter. Allah has set separate laws specific to each of them, placing in them Man as composed of the body and the soul. He has made the laws of this world applicable only to the body (that is, physical laws on the material body), although the soul is also affected by them. That of the Hades is applicable in principle to the soul, although they also affect the body. Finally, when people are brought out of their graves and gathered on the plain of the Hereafter, the laws of that state of existence, as well as the torture or the blessings, will apply in equal measure to the body as well as to the soul. If you can reach up to the true meaning of this statement, you will realize with the help of reason and logic   that the grave is either a patch of Paradise or a patch of Fire. This is the truth one cannot argue with. And, by this acceptance, do the believers in the Unseen are distinguished from the unbelievers.

It might also be kept in mind that the blessings or the Fire of the grave are not akin to the blessings of this world or its Fire. Although Allah heats up the dust and the rocks over and under the man in the grave to the degree higher than any kind of fire in this world, yet, if anyone (of this world) touched it, he would feel nothing at all. Indeed, two people can be buried side by side, with one in the pit of Fire, while the other on a patch of Paradise, without one being affected in the least by his neighbor. Yet, Allah's power is greater than this.

But the problem is, people are inclined to disbelieve in something that cannot be comprehended by reason. Hasn't Allah, after all, not demonstrated to us wonders greater than this in this world itself? Had Allah willed, He could have shown some of His slaves a few of those wonders, at the same time concealing them from the others. Had He shown them to everyone, man's trial could not take place and the wisdom in the requirement to believe in the Unseen and Unknown would be lost and the people would have stopped burying the dead as said the Prophet: "If it would not discourage you from burying the dead, I would have supplicated to Allah that He allow you to hear the torture in the grave."

A question: will the torture in the grave last until the Day of Judgement, or is it discontinued? The answer is, of the torture there are two kinds. One of them will last. Allah said:

النَّارُ يُعْرَضُونَ عَلَيْهَا غُدُوًّا وَعَشِيًّا وَيَوْمَ تَقُومُ السَّاعَةُ أَدْخِلُوا آلَ فِرْعَوْنَ أَشَدَّ الْعَذَابِ

"The Fire, to which they are exposed morning and evening. And, when the Hour strikes, (it will be ordered), `Admit the folks of Fir`awn in the severest chastisement.'" (Al Ghāfir, 46)

The tradition reported by Al Bara' b. `Azib, preserved in Ahmed, has to say the same thing concerning the unbelievers. The words therein are: "Then a door to the Fire is opened up for him so that he might look at his place in the Fire until the Hour strikes."

The other kind of torture would be for a period to be discontinued thereafter. That is the torture of those who would have committed minor sin.

There have been differences too over the resting place of the souls during the interval between death and the striking of the Hour. Evidences lead us to the opinion that in the isthmian world various souls would be stationed at various places. Some will be in the highest places in the company of the companions on high. Those will be souls of the Prophets, Allah's peace and blessing on them. Yet, they too are of various status. As for the others, there are some who will be in the form of green birds perched up in their cages, flying about in Paradise at will. Those will be some of the martyrs, not all. Indeed, some of the martyrs would be prevented from entering Paradise because of debts on them, as in the

198

hadīth of *Musnad Ahmed* reported by `Abdullah ibn Jahash: "A man came up to the Prophet and asked: 'Messenger of Allah! What will I get if I am killed in Allah's cause?' He replied, 'You will be in Paradise.' But, as the man turned to go, the Prophet added, 'Except for debts. Jibril interjected this just now.'"

Some of the souls will be held up at the gates of Paradise, as in the *hadīth* of the Prophet (*saws*) in which he said: "I saw your companion held up at the gate of Paradise." Some souls will be held up in the grave itself. Some will be inside the earth. Some souls will be in the oven prepared for the adulterers and adulteresses. Yet other souls will be in the rivers of blood, swimming in it and devouring stones. All these have been detailed out in the traditions. Allah knows best.

As for the martyrs, Allah said about them:

وَلَا تَحْسَبَنَّ الَّذِينَ قُتِلُوا فِى سَبِيلِ اللهِ أَمْوَاتًا بَلْ أَحْيَاءٌ عِنْدَ رَبِّهِمْ يُرْزَقُونَ

"And think not about those killed in the way of Allah as dead. Rather, they are alive, being fed, near their Lord." (Āl `Imrān, 169)

That is a kind of life that is special to them. Allah has placed their souls in green birds as in the *hadīth* narrated by Ibn `Abbas. He said, "the Prophet (*saws*) said, 'When your brothers were afflicted, that is, those at Uhud Allah placed their souls in the body of green birds. They drink from the waters of the springs of Paradise and feed on its fruits. Then they return to the golden lanterns hanging by the shade of the `*Arsh*." Imam Ahmed and Abu Da'ud have preserved it. It is also preserved in *Muslim*, as a narration of `Abdullah ibn Mas`ud, in somewhat different words.

ونؤمن بالبعث وجزاء الأعمال يوم القيامة، والعرض والحساب، وقراءة الكتاب، والثواب والعقاب، والصراطَ و الميزان

We also believe in the Resurrection, in the requital of the deeds on the Day of Judgment, in the Presentation of the deeds, in the Reckoning, reading from the Record (of deeds), in rewards and punishments, in the Bridge and in the Scales.

Belief in the Hereafter is on the one hand proven by the Book and the *Sunnah* and, on the other, a demand of uncorrupted reason. Allah (*swt*) informed us about it in His revelation, presented proofs, and refuted the skeptics, over much of the Qur`an. That is because belief in God is invested in every soul. It is something natural. But not that of the Hereafter. And hence, plenty of people deny it. Therefore, since the Prophet (*saws*) was the Final Messenger, and since he was sent very close to the Day of Judgement, details concerning the Hereafter were presented as abundantly as never before in any of the earlier revelations.

The Qur`an spoke of the return of the soul (to the Next world) at the time of death, and then resurrection of the body on the Day of Judgement. The philosophers deny that any of the earlier Prophets spoke of the Hereafter. But they lied. The Qur`an informed us about the earlier Prophets' knowledge of the Hereafter. First of them was no less than Adam himself. Allah said:

قَالَ اهْبِطُوا بَعْضُكُمْ لِبَعْضٍ عَدُوٌّ وَلَكُمْ فِي الْأَرْضِ مُسْتَقَرٌّ وَمَتَاعٌ إِلَى حِينٍ

"He said, `Go down, some of you enemies unto the others. You shall have a respite on earth and sustenance until an appointed term." (Al A`rāf, 24)

Ibrahim said:

وَالَّذِي أَطْمَعُ أَنْ يَغْفِرَ لِي خَطِيئَتِي يَوْمَ الدِّينِ

"And He, I hope, will forgive me my faults on the Day of Judgement." (Al Shu`arā, 82)

And Musa said:

وَاكْتُبْ لَنَا فِي هَذِهِ الدُّنْيَا حَسَنَةً وَفِي الْآخِرَةِ

"And write down for us (O Allah) in this world (all that is) good, and in the Hereafter (too)." (Al A`rāf, 156)

As for Tahawi's words: "in the requital of deeds," they are based on Allah's words:

جَزَاءً بِمَا كَانُوا يَعْمَلُونَ

"A just requital for what they were doing." (Al Sajdah, 17)

And in Allah's words:

مَنْ جَاءَ بِالْحَسَنَةِ فَلَهُ خَيْرٌ مِنْهَا وَمَنْ جَاءَ بِالسَّيِّئَةِ فَلَا يُجْزَى الَّذِينَ عَمِلُوا السَّيِّئَاتِ إِلَّا مَا كَانُوا يَعْمَلُونَ

"Whoever brought forth a good deed, he shall have (as rewards) better than that. And whoever brought forth an evil deed, then (he should know that) those who do evil will not be requited but for what they were doing." (Al Qasas, 84)

With regard to the author's words: "the Presentation of the deeds, in the Reckoning, reading from the Record (of deeds), in rewards and punishments," they have their basis in the words of Allah:

فَيَوْمَئِذٍ وَقَعَتِ الْوَاقِعَةُ (١٥)وَانْشَقَّتِ السَّمَاءُ فَهِيَ يَوْمَئِذٍ وَاهِيَةٌ (١٦)وَالْمَلَكُ عَلَى أَرْجَائِهَا وَيَحْمِلُ عَرْشَ رَبِّكَ فَوْقَهُمْ يَوْمَئِذٍ ثَمَانِيَةٌ (١٧)يَوْمَئِذٍ تُعْرَضُونَ لَا تَخْفَى مِنْكُمْ خَافِيَةٌ (١٨) فَأَمَّا مَنْ أُوتِيَ كِتَابَهُ بِيَمِينِهِ فَيَقُولُ هَاؤُمُ اقْرَءُوا كِتَابِيَهْ (١٩) إِنِّي ظَنَنْتُ أَنِّي مُلَاقٍ حِسَابِيَهْ (٢٠)

"On that Day, the Great Event shall come to pass. The heaven will be rent asunder, for it will be flimsy that Day. The angels will be on its sides, and eight will that Day bear the `Arsh of their Lord above them. The Day you will be presented for judgement, not a secret of yours will remain hidden. Then, as to he who is handed over his record in his right hand, will say, `Here! Read my record. I did really believe in encountering my account." (Al Hāqqah, 15-20)

Bukhari, may his soul rest in peace, has recorded in his compilation a *hadīth* of `A'isha. She narrates the Prophet (*saws*) as having said: "No one will be taken up for reckoning in the Hereafter, but he will be condemned to perdition." I asked, `Messenger of Allah! Hasn't Allah (*swt*) said, "Whoever is handed over his Book (of deeds) in his right hand, will be given an easy reckoning?"' He replied, `That will be at the time of the Presentation (before the Lord). But, there is no one taken up for detailed accounting on the Day of Judgement except that he will be punished.'"

What he meant is that if a person is taken up for a detailed questioning, then, surely, he will be condemned to punishment. Allah will not do any injustice to them. Rather, He forgives and pardons.

The author's words, "(we believe in) the Bridge," refer to the Bridge over Hellfire. When the people would have been through rest of the affairs (of reckoning) they will end up at a dark place with the Bridge ahead of them, as `A'isha reported of the Prophet (*saws*) when he was asked, "Where will the people be when this earth and the heavens will be changed for another?" He answered, "They will be in a darkness with the Bridge just ahead."

In this place, the hypocrites will be separated from the faithful, falling behind, with the believers overtaking them. A partition will be placed between them so that they will never be able to join up with the believers again.

Nonetheless, the commentators have differed over the words (*Maryam*, 71): "And there is none among you, but has to arrive there," as to which place is alluded to? The most likely answer is that it would be at the Bridge. Allah said:

ثُمَّ نُنَجِّي الَّذِينَ اتَّقَوا وَّنَذَرُ الظَّالِمِينَ فِيهَا جِثِيًّا

"Then We shall deliver the god fearing and abandon the transgressors therein, on their knees." (Maryam, 72)

Authentic reports record the Prophet's words: "By Him in whose hand is my soul, those who pledged their hands under the Tree would never enter the Fire." Hafsah says, `I asked: "Messenger of Allah! Didn't Allah say, `And there is none among you but will arrive thereat?'" He replied, "Haven't you heard Him saying, "Then, We shall deliver the god fearing, and abandon the transgressors thereat, on their knees?"'"

By the above, the Prophet hinted that just arriving at the spot doesn't necessary entail an entry into the Fire, and that deliverance from an evil does not necessarily entail falling into it first. For example, if someone was wished destruction by his enemies, but they couldn't bring it about, it would be said, "He was delivered of their evil." Hence we find Allah (*swt*) saying:

وَ لَمَّا جَاءَ أَمْرُنَا نَجَّيْنَا هُودًا

"When Our command came, we delivered Hud." (Hūd, 58)

And,

فَلَمَّا جَآءَ أَمْرُنَا نَجَّيْنَا صَلِحًا

"When Our command came, we delivered Saleh." (Hūd, 66)

And, also,

وَلَمَّا جَآءَ أَمْرُنَا نَجَّيْنَا شُعَيْبًا

"When our command came, we delivered Sho`ayb." (Hūd, 94)

Although, in all the above cases, they never tasted any punishment, we came upon others besides them. Obviously, hadn't Allah prepared grounds for their deliverance, they would have been afflicted with the same punishment as others. That's what applies to those that will arrive at the Fire. They shall pass by it over the Bridge, Allah will deliver them and leave the unbelievers on their knees therein.

As for the "Scales," it derives its substantiation from the following verses:

وَنَضَعُ الْمَوَازِينَ الْقِسْطَ لِيَوْمِ الْقِيَمَةِ فَلَا تُظْلَمُ نَفْسٌ شَيْئًا وَإِن كَانَ مِثْقَالَ حَبَّةٍ مِّنْ خَرْدَلٍ أَتَيْنَا بِهَا وَكَفَى بِنَا حَسِبِينَ

"Then We shall set up the Scales on justice for the Day of Judgement and no soul shall be dealt with injustice in the least. And, if there be (a deed) equal to a mustard seed, We shall bring it up. Sufficient We are as a Reckoner." (Al Anbiyā, 47)

And,

فَمَن ثَقُلَتْ مَوَازِينُهُ فَأُولَٰئِكَ هُمُ الْمُفْلِحُونَ (١٠٢)وَمَنْ خَفَّتْ مَوَازِينُهُ فَأُولَٰئِكَ الَّذِينَ خَسِرُوٓا أَنفُسَهُمْ فِى جَهَنَّمَ خَلِدُونَ (١٠٣)

"Then he whose Scales (of good deeds) are heavy, they, indeed, they are the successors. And he whose Scales are light, they indeed are those who lost their souls, abiding in Hellfire forever." (Al Mu'minūn, 102, 103)

Qurtubi has stated the opinion of the scholars that the deeds will be weighed after the reckoning. This weighing would be to determine the magnitude of rewards and hence it is logical that it should take place after the reckoning. The reckoning will be to determine the nature of the deeds. Whereas the weighing will be to determine their worth, since the magnitude of the rewards will depend upon their worth.

Prophetic traditions give us more details, such as that the two pans of the Scale would have a physical appearance, and that the man himself will be weighed along with the deeds. This has the following *hadīth* of Bukhari in its support. Abu Hurayrah reports the Prophet (*saws*) as having said: "A man will appear tall and massive but will weigh with Allah the equal of a gnat's wing." Then he added: "Read if you wish Allah's words (*Al Kahaf*, 105), '*We shall not assign any weight to them on the Day of Judgement.*'"

Ahmed has reported that Ibn Mas`ud was attempting to break branches to fabricate a few miswak. His calves were pretty thin. The winds began to sway him and the people laughed. the Prophet (*saws*) said: "What are you laughing about?" They said: "Over the slimness of his legs." He said: "By Him in whose hands is my life, they will be heavier than (Mount) Uhud on the Day of Judgement."

Traditions also speak of the deeds being weighed. *Sahih Muslim* records Abu Malik al Ash`ari as saying that the Prophet (*saws*) said: "Cleanliness is one half of faith. And *Al hamdulillah* will fill the Scales."

At the end of Bukhari's compilation we have the words of the Prophet: "There are two words that are light on the tongue, but dear to Al Rahman, weighty in the Scales: *Subhana Allahi wa bi hamdihi, subhana Allahi al `Azim*."

Therefore, one need pay no attention to the atheist who says that the deeds are immaterial objects, how can they be weighed? It is only material body that can be weighed. The answer is, Allah will assign them weight.

Further, it is upon us to believe in the Unknown, exactly in terms we have been told by the Prophet: neither less nor more.

والجنة و النار مخلوقتان، لا تَفْنِيَان أبدا ولا تبيدان، فإن الله تعالى خلق الجنة والنار قبل الخلق، وخلق لهما أهلا، فمَن شاء منهم إلى الجنة فضلا منه، ومن شاء منهم إلى النار عدلاً منه، وكل يعمل لما قد فرغ له، وصائر إلى ما خُلِقَ له والخير والشر مُقَدَّران على العباد

Paradise and Hellfire are created abodes. They will never pass away nor perish. Allah created Paradise and Hellfire before He created the creations. He created creations for the two. Then, whomsoever of them He wishes, He will usher into Paradise: by His grace. And whomsoever of them He wishes, He will usher into Hellfire: justly. Everyone works in accordance with what has been destined for him, and moves towards what He has been created for. Good and evil are predestined for the slaves.

The *Ahl al Sunnah* are unanimous that Paradise and Hellfire have both been created and are in existence now. The *Ahl al Sunnah* were always on this faith until a group of people appeared among the Mu`tazilah and the Qadariyyah who denied this. They claim that Allah (*swt*) will create them on the Day of Judgement. The basis for such a deviation is nothing but their fanciful belief that Allah should be doing things in this order and not in that order. They liken Him to His creations in acts. They are basically anthropomorphists in matters involving acts. Subsequently, as they evolved they began to deny Allah His Attributes. They reasoned out that it was a useless thing to create Paradise before reckoning as it would lie waste, unused. Thus they denied the texts on the basis of self made rules and principles and declared those who disagreed with them as the misguided ones.

As for the texts, Allah said:

$$ أُعِدَّتْ لِلْمُتَّقِينَ $$

"It has been prepared for the god-fearing." (Āl `Imrān, 133)

About the Fire, He said:

$$ أُعِدَّتْ لِلْكَافِرِينَ $$

"It has been prepared for the unbelievers." (Al Baqarah, 24, Āl `Imrān, 131)

Allah also said:

$$ وَلَقَدْ رَآهُ نَزْلَةً أُخْرَىٰ (١٣) عِنْدَ سِدْرَةِ الْمُنْتَهَىٰ (١٤) عِنْدَهَا جَنَّةُ الْمَأْوَىٰ (١٥) $$

"And surely He saw him another time; near the farthest end of the Lote Tree. Near it is the Garden of Abode." (Al Najm, 13-15)

The Prophet witnessed the farthest end of the Lote Tree and saw Paradise by it. A narration of Anas b. Malik in the *Sahihayn* says, while describing the Night Journey and Ascension: "Then Jibril moved on with me until the farthest end of the Lote Tree. It was engulfed by colors that I couldn't make out what they were." After that he added: "Then I entered Paradise. I found its domes of pearls and its soil of *misk*."

As for the doubt raised by some people that were Paradise to be in existence now, it would also be destroyed on the Day of Judgement in view of Allah's words:

$$كُلُّ شَىْءٍ هَالِكٌ إِلَّا وَجْهَهُ$$

"Everything will be destroyed except His Face." (Al Qasas, 88)

Allah also narrated to us the words of Fir`awn's wife:

$$رَبِّ ابْنِ لِي عِنْدَكَ بَيْتًا فِي الْجَنَّةِ$$

"O my Lord. Build for me a house by You in Paradise." (Al Tahrīm, 11)

The answer to the above is that if you say that Paradise has not been created at all until the Trumpet would be blown and people would be resurrected, it stands rejected in view of the texts quoted. But if you say that it has been created but Allah adds to it whatever He will, from time to time, then, that is an undeniable truth. With regards to your argument with the verse: *"Everything will be destroyed except His Face,"* surely, you haven't given the meaning the verse deserves to be given. The basis of your denial of the present existence of Heaven and Hell is similar to the basis of your denial of their ultimate destruction. Our scholars have understood the verse in question as speaking of only those things that are destined to be destroyed at the blow of the Trumpet. As for Heaven and Hell, they have been created to remain in existence and not to be destroyed. Indeed, the `*Arsh* would also not be subjected to destruction since it is the roof of Paradise. The texts are unambiguous about the non destruction of the Heaven and Hell at any time.

The author's words, "they shall never pass away nor perish," is the echoing of the belief of the great majority of scholars of the earliest and later epochs, although, a section of the pious predecessors have spoken about the eternity of Paradise but ultimate destruction of Hellfire. Their opinions are recorded in commentary books as also in others. It was only Safwan b. Jahm who first spoke about the destruction of the Fire as well as of Paradise. Safwan by the way, is the leader of those who deny Allah's Attributes. He has no one else of the Companions or their followers with him in this opinion. Most Muslim scholars have refuted him and censured him.

As for the belief that Paradise will not pass away nor will it ever perish in the future, this is derived from the primary knowledge of the texts. The Qur`an said:

اِنَّ هَذَا لَرِزْقُنَا مَا لَهُ مِنْ نَّفَادٍ

"This is Our bounty. It shall not cease to be." (Sād, 54)

He also said:

اُكُلُهَا دَآئِمٌ وَّظِلُّهَا

"Perpetual is its fruits and its shades." (Al Ra`d, 35)

As for evidences from the *Sunnah*, they are in abundance. Such as the Prophet's words: "A crier will cry out: `People of Paradise! It is your share that you shall remain healthy and never be sick, remain young and never grow old, and that you shall live and never die.'"

Nevertheless, insofar as the eternity of the Fire goes, there are various opinions. There are some who have believed in its ultimate destruction. Such as, `Umar, Ibn Mas`ud, Abu Hurayrah, Abu Sa`id al Khudri and others. They said that Fire is the manifestation of Allah's anger, whereas Paradise is the manifestation of His mercy. And the Prophet (*saws*) has said:

"When Allah had created His creations, He inscribed a writing, which is with Him above the `Arsh, (in words), 'My mercy shall prevail over My anger.'" These are the words of Bukhari. Further, Allah (*swt*) has told us about the Fire that it would be the punishment of 'a great day,' or, of 'a painful day,' or, of 'a barren day.' But He did not use the words 'of a day' even in one instance for the blessings of Paradise. In contrast, He said:

عَذَابِيّ أُصِيبُ بِهِ مَنْ أَشَآءُ وَرَحْمَتِي وَسِعَتْ كُلَّ شَيْءٍ

"(That's) My punishment wherewith I shall punish whom I will. And My mercy has encompassed everything." (Al A`rāf, 156)

It is indispensable therefore, that His mercy should be the share of those subjected to torture. If they remain in the Fire, forever, without His mercy ever reaching them, then His mercy could not be said to encompass everything. Further, there is no wisdom in the Ultimate Sovereign creating a creation for no other purpose than to torture them forever. In contrast, if He creates beings for no other purpose than to do them good and bless them forever, then, surely, that is entirely in tune with His mercy. The people who hold this opinion have also explained that whatever has been reported of those in the Fire remaining therein forever, and never coming out, that also is true. There are no two opinions about that. The texts demand that this is how the words about their eternity in the Fire be understood, viz., so long as the Fire itself remains in existence. The monotheists would be removed from it during its existence. Thus, there is a difference between him who will be removed from the prison, while the prison remains in existence, and him whose prison term will be annulled because of the destruction of the prison itself.

As for those who have believed in its eternity and non perishability, they have judged by the words of Allah Most High :

وَلَهُمْ عَذَابٌ مُّقِيمٌ

"And for them will be an eternal punishment." (Al Mā'idah, 37)

Or,

خَالِدِينَ فِيهَا

"Remaining therein forever." (Al Mā'idah, 85)

The *Sunnah* is very specific about the removal of anyone therefrom who had the slightest faith in the oneness of God. Again, there are traditions that are emphatic about the removal of sinners from it through intercessions. This too is specific to them (i.e., the faithful). Now, if the unbelievers also leave the place then the two (believers and unbelievers) would be on par.

Now, Tahawi's words: "He created beings for the two (Heaven or Hell)," has its basis in Allah's words:

$$وَلَقَدْ ذَرَأْنَا لِجَهَنَّمَ كَثِيرًا مِّنَ الْجِنِّ وَالْإِنسِ$$

"Surely, We have created many of the mankind and the Jinn for the Hellfire."
(Al A`rāf, 179)

And the Prophet has said: "Allah created some people for Paradise. He destined them for it while they were yet seeds in the loins of their fathers. And He created some people for the Fire. He destined them for it while they were yet seeds in the loins of their fathers." The report is in Muslim and Abu Da'ud.

As for the author's words: "Then, whomsoever of them He wishes, He will usher into Paradise: by His grace. And whomsoever of them He wishes, He will usher into Hellfire: justly," it must be understood in this connection, that Allah will not deny the rewards unless its means are missing, which is good deeds, for:

$$وَمَن يَعْمَلْ مِنَ الصَّالِحَاتِ وَهُوَ مُؤْمِنٌ فَلَا يَخَافُ ظُلْمًا وَّلَا هَضْمًا$$

"Whoever worked righteousness, and he be of the believers, will not fear injustice nor oppression." (Tāhā, 112)

In the like manner, no one will be punished but after its cause has been obtained. Allah (*swt*) says:

$$وَمَا أَصَابَكُم مِّن مُّصِيبَةٍ فَبِمَا كَسَبَتْ أَيْدِيكُمْ وَيَعْفُو عَن كَثِيرٍ$$

"Whatever afflictions strike you are because of what your hands earn, although He forgives a lot." (Al Shurā, 30)

Allah is the Bestower, the Withholder. There is none to withhold if He will give and none to bestow if He will withhold. None the less, if He blesses a man with faith and good deeds, then there is no rule that can prevent that. In fact, He might reward him with that which no eye has seen and no ear has heard. But, when He withholds, then there has to be good ground for that: in this case, the absence of good deeds. Surely, He guides whom He will, and leads astray whom He will: all justified by His wisdom and justice. His withholding of the means

209

in this case good deeds   is in line with his wisdom and justice. But, once the means are there, then there is no reason why the ends should be missing, unless the means were to be wrong, such as, some kind of corruption in the deed, or, for reasons that came in the way of the appearance of the desired ends. Then, in such a case, the ends would be considered as the demand of the situation, or, something else preventing it. Now, if His withholding, and hence, punishment, was because of lack of faith and good deeds, and that because He did not initially bestow upon someone, in view of His wisdom and justice, then, to Allah praises for all situations. He is the Praised One at all events. Everything that He bestows is by His grace. And every punishment from Him is justice. Allah is the Wise who places things where they rightly belong. As He said:

وَإِذَا جَاءَتْهُمْ آيَةٌ قَالُوا لَنْ نُؤْمِنَ حَتَّى نُؤْتَى مِثْلَ مَا أُوتِيَ رُسُلُ اللَّهِ اللَّهُ أَعْلَمُ حَيْثُ يَجْعَلُ رِسَالَتَهُ

"Whenever a sign came to them they said, 'We shall not believe until we are given the like of what the Messengers of Allah were given.' Allah knows best where to place His Message." (Al An`ām, 124)

الاستطاعة التي يجب بها الفعل من نحوِ التوفيق الذي لا يجوز أن يوصَف المخلوقُ به – تكون مع الفعل. و أما الاستطاعة من جهة الصحة والوُسْع، والتَّمَكُّن و سلامة الآلات فهي قبل الفعل، وبها يَتَعَلَّقُ الخطاب، وهوكما قال تعالى: (لا يكلف الله نفسا إلا وسعها)

The ability necessary for action which can also be called as an impulse of divine origin   which no human can be qualified with (as having power over it)   accompanies the act. As to the ability by way of health, abundance, mastery and the availability of the means, these can be there before the act. They are related to the command. Allah said: "Allah does not charge a soul but what it can bear." (*Al Baqarah*, 286)

Ability, strength, power etc., (for an action) are words that are synonymous. This ability (to perform a deed) can itself be divided into two kinds, as the author points out. This also happens to be the opinion of the scholars in general. It is an opinion that avoids the extremes. Nevertheless, the Qadariyyah and the Mu`tazilah have speculated that the ability (to perform a deed) will not be there 'before' the action. However, the *Ahl al Sunnah* hold the opinion that it does not come along but with the action. That is, it accompanies it.

What the scholars have said in reply is that every man has a general kind of ability, on which is based the demanded of action on him. This can be there even before the action is performed. It is not necessary that it should accompany the deed. In contrast, the power to perform the deed has to accompany the deed. It is not possible to bring a deed into existence when its power is non existent.

But the other ability, that of health, wealth, mastery, possibility, the availability of means, etc., these can be in prior existence to the actions. This is the 'ability' that has been spoken of in the following verse:

وَلِلّٰهِ عَلَى النَّاسِ حِجُّ الْبَيْتِ مَنِ اسْتَطَاعَ إِلَيْهِ سَبِيلًا

"And people, who can afford the passage to it, owe to Allah pilgrimage to the House." (Āl `Imrān, 97)

In the above verse, Allah declared Hajj obligatory on him who has the 'ability' to perform it. If there was no ability prior to Hajj, none would be bound to perform Hajj, except one who has already performed it. Consequently, no one could be blamed for not attempting the pilgrimage. This is of course well known and understood about Islamic injunctions.

So also Allah's words:

فَمَنْ لَمْ يَسْتَطِعْ فَإِطْعَامُ سِتِّينَ مِسْكِينًا

"Then, whosoever does not have the ability, let him feed sixty poor souls." (Al Mujādalah, 4)

The allusion in this case by the word "ability" is to the availability of power and the means.

As to the 'ability,' which in truth is the power to act 'independently', the scholars have said that it has been alluded to in the following verse:

مَا كَانُوا يَسْتَطِيعُونَ السَّمْعَ وَمَا كَانُوا يُبْصِرُونَ

"They could not bear to listen, nor could they see." (Hūd, 20)

What 'ability' is this? Well, it is the 'ability' and the power to perform the deed independent of Allah. The allusion is not to the unavailability of material and physical means. They were there.

In similar sense are the words of Musa's companion:

إِنَّكَ لَنْ تَسْتَطِيعَ مَعِيَ صَبْرًا

"You do not have the power to bear with me." (Al Kahaf, 67)

What is meant is the strength to bear and not the means of it, which he surely possessed.

As against that, the Qadariyyah surmise that Allah's Decree is the same in favor of a believer as well as an unbeliever. They do not admit that Allah's choice fell on the subservient believer for help wherewith he gained faith. Rather, they say, this one (i.e., the believer) preferred to believe and the other (i.e., the unbeliever) preferred to disbelieve, similar to a father giving a sword to each of his two sons: one of them chose to fight in the way of Allah, while the other took it for highway robbery.

In contrast, there is no difference in opinion among the *Ahl al Sunnah* those who believe in the Divine Decree that the Qadariyyah contention is incorrect. The Sunni scholars believe that the obedient believer enjoys a special religious favor from Allah which was specific to him, in contrast to the unbeliever (who missed it), and that He helped him in obedience the way He did not help the unbeliever. Allah (*swt*) said,

وَ لَكِنَّ الله حَبَّبَ إِلَيْكُمُ الإِيْمَانَ وَزَيَّنَهُ فِي قُلُوبِكُمْ وَكَرَّهَ إِلَيْكُمُ الكُفْرَ وَالفُسُوقَ وَالعِصْيَانَ أُولَئِكَ هُمُ الرَّشِدُونَ

"But Allah endeared the faith to your heart and has made it beautiful to you and He made unbelief, wrong doing and rebellion hateful to you, such indeed are the righteously guided." (Al Hujurāt, 7)

He also said:

فَمَنْ يُرِدِ اللهُ أَنْ يَهْدِيَهُ يَشْرَحْ صَدْرَهُ لِلْإِسْلَامِ وَمَنْ يُرِدْ أَنْ يُضِلَّهُ يَجْعَلْ صَدْرَهُ ضَيِّقًا حَرَجًا كَأَنَّمَا يَصَّعَّدُ فِى السَّمَآءِ كَذَلِكَ يَجْعَلُ

اللهُ الرِّجْسَ عَلَى الَّذِينَ لَا يُؤْمِنُونَ

"Whomsoever Allah intends to guide, He opens up his heart for Islam. And whomsoever He intends to lead astray, He closes his heart, constricted, as if he were engaged in sheer ascent toward the heaven. That is how Allah lays abomination on those who do not believe." (Al An`ām, 125)

و أفعال العباد هي خلق الله، وكسبٌ من العباد

And people's deeds are Allah's creation but their own acquisition.

People have disagreed over the deeds of a man in which he has a choice. The Jabariyyah, whose leader was Safwan b. Jahm, have conjectured that the means adopted in connection with the deeds are all creations of Allah. They are all compulsive, in the same fashion as someone's body movements who is shivering, or the sweat of a man in fear, or the movements of the leaves on the tree. They are only figuratively attributed to the one who or which performs those acts. The Mu`tazilah confronted them by saying that all the actions involving choice, are the creations of the living souls. They are independent of Allah's will. Then they disagreed among themselves in subsequent details, such as, over the individual's deeds, whether they are predetermined by Allah or not.

The *Ahl al Sunnah* have said that the deeds of the people, by virtue of which they become either the obedient or the sinners, are the creations of Allah (*swt*). Allah alone is the creator of all that is in existence. There is no Creator save Him. The Jabariyyah, in contrast, committed excesses in the question of *Qadr* and denied men any part in the creation of deeds. As for the Qadariyyah, they went to the other extreme of denying *Qadr* any part and declare man as the sole creator of all his deeds. By dint of that, they became the "Zoroastrians of this *Ummah*." In fact, worse than the Zoroastrians because the Zoroastrians believe in only two creators (one of good and the other of evil). Whereas these people believe in numerous creators. In comparison, by saying that Allah (*swt*) is the creator of men's deeds (but the deeds are their acquisition) the *Ahl al Sunnah* were again rightly guided. Surely, this is by the grace of Allah, He guides whom He will to the straight path.

Indeed, every proof that the Jabariyyah furnish, goes to prove correctly that Allah is the creator of men's deeds, that He has power over everything, that the deeds of men are part of His creations, that what He willed happened, and what He didn't did not. Nevertheless, this does not lead to the conclusion that the slave is not the doer, that he did not wish, that he did not choose. The fact of Allah's creation of men's deeds, does not go to prove that the movements of the doer are similar to the movements of a shivering person or like the air bubbles.

So too, every evidence that the Qadariyyah proffer actually goes to prove that a man is himself the doer of his deeds, that it is he who intends them, and that it is he who chooses. Therefore, to attribute them to him is fully justified. Yet, they do not prove that they haven't been pre destined by Allah and that they take place without His will and approval. Thus, whatever truth there is in the statements of either of the two (the Jabariyyah and the Qadariyyah), if you put them together, you will arrive at the point that is stated not only in the Qur`an, but also in various other revelations of Allah, to the effect that in general it is by Allah's power and will that everything happens in this universe, and yet, it is the creations in fact who are the doers of their deeds and who deserve to be commended or censured for those deeds.

This then is the truth. Evidences of truth do not contradict each other. One piece of fact confirms another. We would have taken up the proofs and evidences furnished by the two sects and discussed them in a most thorough fashion but for the length. We shall, therefore, take up just one or two as an example to show how they are wrong in using them for their purposes.

The Jabariyyah have substantiated their arguments with the words of Allah:

$$\text{وَمَا رَمَيْتَ إِذْ رَمَيْتَ وَ لَكِنَّ اللهَ رَمَى}$$

"And you did not throw (O Prophet) when you threw. It was Allah who threw." (Al Anfāl, 17)

In this verse, Allah Most High denied that His Prophet threw (the pebbles at Badr over the heads of the pagans). He took the credit for it Himself, proving

214

that a slave cannot bring an action into existence. Therefore, they conclude that the deeds are not the basis of recompense in the Hereafter. They also present the following *hadīth* to bolster their argument. the Prophet (*saws*) said: "No one will enter Paradise on the strength of his deeds." They enquired: "Not even you, O Messenger of Allah?" He replied: "Not even me, unless Allah were to cover me up with His grace and mercy."

As for the Qadariyyah, they argued with the following verse:

فَتَبَارَكَ اللّٰهُ أَحْسَنُ الْخَالِقِيْنَ

"Glorified is Allah, the best of creators." (Al Mu'minūn, 14)

The Qadariyyah also said that the recompense in the Hereafter will be a complete replica of the deeds, as Allah said:

وَتِلْكَ الْجَنَّةُ الَّتِيْ أُوْرِثْتُمُوْهَا بِمَا كُنْتُمْ تَعْمَلُوْنَ

"This is the Paradise that you inherited for what you were doing." (Al Zukhruf, 72)

Now, as for the argument of the Jabariyyah with the verse, "*You did not throw what you threw ..*" it is refuted by the verse itself which attributes the throwing to the Prophet (*saws*) by saying, "when you threw." His act of throwing was not denied, rather, it was confirmed that the act had a beginning and an end. Its beginning was the act and its end was its hitting the target. Both could be called as "throwing." The meaning then although Allah (*swt*) knows best is that it was not you who hit the target when you threw, rather, it was Allah who did it. If we do not accept this meaning, then a logical conclusion would be: "It was not you who prayed, rather, it was Allah who prayed," and, "It was not you who fasted, rather, it was Allah who fasted." The error should be obvious.

So too, both the Jabariyyah and the Qadariyyah erred over the question of the relationship of the deeds with the rewards. The *Ahl al Sunnah* were rightly guided, Allah be praised. To explain: the *"bā"* of a negative sentence has a different meaning than the *"bā"* of a positive sentence. The *"bā"* of the Prophet's *hadīth* in the word *"bi `amalihī"* stands  for "equivalent, substitute, or a full return." In simpler words, the acts would not be the "price" one would pay to enter Paradise, as the Mu`tazilah have alleged. They have said that it is binding upon Allah that He admit a person into Paradise in return of his deeds. But that is not how it is. Rather, as the *hadīth* says, that would happen by Allah's grace and mercy. On the other hand, the article *"bā"* in the words *"bima kuntum ta`malun,"* lends the meaning of "by virtue," "cause," or "reason." In other words, the verse means, "you have entered Paradise by virtue of your deeds." None the less, since Allah is the creator of the means, and is the Cause of all causes, both the evidences confirm that it is by Allah's mercy and grace that the people will enter Paradise.

As for the Mu`tazilah's argument with the verse:

فَتَبَرَكَ اللّٰهُ اَحْسَنُ الْخَالِقِيْنَ

"So, blessed is Allah, the best of creators." (Al Mu'minūn, 14),

the meaning of the verse is, "Allah is the best of Molders," or, "the best of the Fashioners." That is, *"khalq,"* when used in the masculine, is used in the sense of "design" or, "pre molding." This argument relies upon another verse in which Allah (*swt*) said:

اَللّٰهُ خَالِقُ كُلِّ شَىْءٍ

"Allah is the creator of everything." (Al Zumar, 62)

That is, Allah is the creator of everything that has been created. Here "everything" includes the deeds of men. This is how the Mu`tazilah argue their point.

But, to refute, we might point out that there is no contradiction between two facts: that an individual causes to bring into existence his acts and deeds, and that those creations, (that is, the deeds) owe their existence to the will of Allah. Allah said:

وَنَفْسٍ وَّمَا سَوَّاهَا (٧) فَاَلْهَمَهَا فُجُوْرَهَا وَتَقْوٰىهَا (٨)

"And by the soul and Him who made it. Then He inspired in it its corruption and its piety." (Al Shams, 7,8)

In these verses both the decreeing has been confirmed by the use of the word "He inspired it," as well as man's own role in creation (of the deeds) by assigning the corruption or piety to his "self," so that it might be known that the "soul" itself is the corrupt or the pious.

And, interestingly, this has led them to another of their doubts that divided them between themselves, rather, tore them to pieces. They ask, 'How can you prove the correctness of your statements when you say on the one hand that Allah punishes people for their acts, while on the other hand, He is, as you claim, the creator of those deeds? How can He be justified in punishing over what He Himself created?'

This question has ever been on the lips. And the answers have varied, depending on the knowledge and understanding of those questioned. Consequently, with varied answers, people have split their ways. Some people, unable to reconcile the two, have refused that Allah has any power over men's deeds. Others have refused to acknowledge the relationship between cause and effect and have refused to answer the question altogether. Yet others have been led to the belief that men have no choice and freedom of the will. They will be punished for something that was beyond their power.

The right answer is as follows. When a man is tried with fresh sins although they are Allah's creation it is in consequence of sins committed earlier. Sins give birth to more sins. The consequence of an evil is another evil that follows it. They can be likened to contagious diseases. It might be asked, "What about the first sin that caused the later sins to appear?" The answer is, that sin was also the consequence of not doing what one was created for and nurtured on by his innate nature. Allah created His creations for His obedience and worship and none else. It is in man's nature therefore to acknowledge Allah, to love Him and to turn to Him. Allah (*swt*) said,

$$\text{فَأَقِمْ وَجْهَكَ لِلدِّينِ حَنِيفًا ۚ فِطْرَتَ اللهِ الَّتِي فَطَرَ النَّاسَ عَلَيْهَا}$$

"So set your face truly to the religion being upright, Allah's Original upon which He originated people." (Al Rūm, 30)

But when a man did not respond to what he was created for, and refused to heed to the call of nature from within, in response to his innate love of Allah and instinctive devotion to Him, then, in consequence, Satan decked out fair in his sight the acts of association or sins. Allah (*swt*) originated his heart clean and blank, ready to receive either good or evil. Had there been good in his heart, preventing its opposite, evil would not have got the better of him, as Allah (*swt*) said by the tongue of Iblis:

فَبِعِزَّتِكَ لَأُغْوِيَنَّهُمْ أَجْمَعِينَ (٨٢) إِلَّا عِبَادَكَ مِنْهُمُ الْمُخْلَصِينَ (٨٣)

"Then, by Your Power, I shall lead them all astray, save for your servants among them, purified (by Your grace)." (Sād, 82, 83)

As for the *ikhlas* of the text, when applied to a heart it denotes one that is free of everything except Allah. It is devoted to Allah alone. So Shaytan has no power over it. But, if he finds it empty, he will occupy it in proportion to how free it is. It is in that state that he stimulates him to sins and evils: a consequence of the lack of sincere devotion. This arrangement meets with the requirement of justice from Allah (*swt*).

ولم يكلفهم الله تعالى إلا ما يُطيقُون، ولا يطيقون إلا ما كَلَّفَهُمْ، و هو تفسير: لا حول ولا قوة إلا بالله نقول: لا حيلة لأحد، ولا تَحُوُّل لأحد، ولا حركة لأحد عن معصية الله، إلا بمَعُونة الله، ولا قوة لأحد على إقامة طاعة الله والثبات عليها إلا بتوفيق الله وكل شيء يجري بمشيئةِ الله تعالى وعلمه وقضائه وقدرته، غلبت مشيئَتُهُ المشيئاتِ كلها، وعكست إرادتُه الإراداتِ كلها، وغلب قضاؤه الحِيلَ كلها. يفعل ما يشاء، وهو غير ظالم أبدا. (لا يُسئل عما يفعل وهم يُسئلون)

Allah did not impose on them except for what they have the power for. And they do not have the power for any more than what has been imposed upon them. This is the meaning of the words: "There is no power nor strength save that of Allah". We say, there is no maneuvering, no escape, nor a movement possible against sins, save by Allah's succor. Conversely, no one has any power to be obedient to Allah, and to remain steadfast, save by Allah's inducement. Everything moves by the will of Allah, His knowledge and by the decree set by Him. His will overcomes all the wills, His wishes defeat all other wishes, and His pre determination overcomes all other schemes. He does what He will, without injustice: "He is not questioned about what He does, rather, they will be questioned."

218

The first sentence of the author's text above is in keeping with Allah's words:

$$\text{لَا يُكَلِّفُ اللهُ نَفْسًا إِلَّا وُسْعَهَا}$$

"He does not charge a soul with what it cannot bear." (Al Baqarah, 286)

As for Allah's words addressing the angels:

$$\text{أَنْبِئُونِي بِأَسْمَاءِ هَؤُلَاءِ إِنْ كُنْتُمْ صَادِقِينَ}$$

"Tell Me their names if you are true," (Al Baqarah, 31)

they are not making an unreasonable demand upon them, asking them about something that they hadn't been given the knowledge of. Rather, it was to impress upon them their ignorance.

The following prayer words of the faithful are to be understood in the same vein:

$$\text{رَبَّنَا وَلَا تُحَمِّلْنَا مَا لَا طَاقَةَ لَنَا بِهِ}$$

"O our Lord, do not charge us with what we do not have the strength for."
(Al Baqarah, 286)

Ibn al Anbari has said about the verse: "Do not lay a burden upon us that which will be too heavy for us to bear," that they could bear it with difficulty and resentment. In these words Allah spoke to the Arabs in a language which they understood. For, when one of them hated another he would say, "I can't bear to look at you." Although, obviously, he was quite able to look at him. But, it was detesting to him.

The author's words: "They do not have the power for anymore than what has been imposed upon them," meaning, they do not have the power to do but what He has empowered them with. This "power" (to do things) is the other name for Divine inducement, and does not refer to the state of their health, strength, ability or availability of the means. Further, the words, "there is no power, nor strength save that of Allah," are a proof of Divine Decree, which the author further elaborated in the following sentences.

However, a doubt could be raised because of the manner in which the author worded his statement. It is as follows: We know that, "the imposed" is not used in the sense of that which one has the power to do. Rather, imposition is generally used with reference to commandments and prohibitions. Whereas the author said: "He does not impose upon them what they have no power for, and they do not have power for any more than what has been imposed upon them." That is, the two sentence seem to be speaking of the same thing. But that is only apparently so, for the people have the power to do more than what He imposed upon them. But, Allah wishes ease for His slaves and a lessening of the burden. He said:

$$\text{يُرِيدُ اللهُ بِكُمُ الْيُسْرَ وَلَا يُرِيدُ بِكُمُ الْعُسر}$$

"Allah wishes ease for you. He does not wish hardship for you." (Al Baqarah, 185)

And,

$$\text{يُرِيدُ اللهُ أَنْ يُخَفِّفَ عَنْكُمْ}$$

"Allah wishes to lessen)the burden) on you." (Al Nisā', 28)

Had He imposed upon us something heavier, we could still have had the strength to do as ordered. But He was merciful with us and lessened the burden.

Now, the answer to the doubt raised above is that the word "power" as used by the author is referring to the power that comes with the Divine inducement. It is not referring to the physical and material means, such as good health, material means, etc. To be fair, the author's words are a bit ambiguous.

And, by his words: "Everything moves by the will of Allah, His knowledge, and the decree set by Him," the author means the universal Decree and not the legal decree. The word Decree can pertain both to the Universe as well as to the legal decrees. That is also true of the will and command, the authorization, what is written down, the judgement, the illegality , the words, and so forth. With regard to the decree of the universal nature (القضاء الكوني), Allah said:

فَقَضَاهُنَّ سَبْعَ سَمَوَاتٍ فِى يَوْمَيْنِ

"Then He decreed them into seven heavens." (Fussilat, 12)

As for the religious or legal decree (القضاء الديني الشرعي), He said:

وَقَضَى رَبُّكَ أَلَّا تَعْبُدُوا إِلَّا إِيَّاهُ

"And He decreed that you worship none but Him." (Al Isrā', 23)

As regard to the universal authority (الإذن الكوني), we might quote the following:

وَمَا هُمْ بِضَآرِّينَ بِهِ مِنْ أَحَدٍ إِلَّا بِإِذْنِ اللَّهِ

"And they harmed no one save by Allah's will." (Al Baqarah, 102)

The following is an example of legal authority (الإذن الشرعي):

مَا قَطَعْتُمْ مِّنْ لِّينَةٍ أَوْ تَرَكْتُمُوهَا قَآئِمَةً عَلَى أُصُولِهَا فَبِإِذْنِ اللهِ

"You did not cut down a tree nor left them standing on their stems, but by Allah's leave." (Al Hashr, 5)

With regard to the writing of the universal nature (الكتاب الكوني), we might quote:

وَمَا يُعَمَّرُ مِنْ مُّعَمَّرٍ وَّلَا يُنْقَصُ مِنْ عُمُرِهِ إِلَّا فِى كِتَبٍ إِنَّ ذَلِكَ عَلَى اللهِ يَسِيرٌ

"And not an aged one ages nor is his age decreased but is in a Book. That is easy for Allah." (Fātir, 11)

In contrast, as an example of the legal writing (الكتاب الديني الشرعي) note the following:

يَآأَيُّهَا الَّذِينَ آمَنُوا كُتِبَ عَلَيْكُمُ الصِّيَامُ

"Believers! Fasts have been written upon you." (Al Baqarah, 183)

As for universal judgement (الحكم الكوني), the following can be cited:

قُلْ رَبِّ احْكُمْ بِالْحَقِّ وَرَبُّنَا الرَّحْمَنُ الْمُسْتَعَانُ عَلَى مَا تَصِفُونَ

"He said, `My Lord, You judge in truth. Our Lord   the All merciful   His assistance is sought over what you ascribe." (Al Anbiyā', 112)

The legal judgement (الحكم الشرعي) is spoken of in the following:

ذَٰلِكُمْ حُكْمُ اللَّهِ يَحْكُمُ بَيْنَكُمْ

"This is Allah's judgement. He judges between you." (Al Mumtahanah: 10)

As for prohibition of the universal nature (التحريم الكوني), we have Allah's words:

قَالَ فَإِنَّهَا مُحَرَّمَةٌ عَلَيْهِمْ أَرْبَعِينَ سَنَةً يَتِيهُونَ فِي الْأَرْضِ

"(Allah) said, `Then it shall remain forbidden unto them for forty years, (during which time) they shall wander in the land." (Al Mā'idah, 26)

And legal unlawfulness (التحريم الشرعي) is in following words:

حُرِّمَتْ عَلَيْكُمُ الْمَيْتَةُ وَالدَّمُ وَلَحْمُ الْخِنْزِيرِ

"The carrion, blood and pork are forbidden unto you." (Al Mā'idah, 3)

وفي دعاء الأحياء وصدقاتهم منفَعة للأموات

(We also believe that) in the supplication of the living and in their charity, there is profit for the dead.

The *Ahl al Sunnah* are unanimous that the dead profit from the acts of the living in two ways. First, what the dead himself/herself initiated during his/her life and second, supplications for them by the Muslims and their seeking of forgiveness for their sins. Insofar as charity, Hajj and other acts are concerned, there are differences of opinion. Muhammad b. Hasan al Shaybani, one of the disciples of Abu Hanifah has said that what the dead gets out of Hajj performed on his behalf is the reward for the money spent on the affair, while the rewards for Hajj itself goes to the account of the one who performed it. However, most scholars have said that the reward for Hajj too goes to the one for whom it was performed. This is the correct position.

None the less, insofar as bodily acts of worship are concerned such as, fasts,

222

Prayers, recitation of the Qur`an, rosaries and others, differences in opinion have prevailed. Imam Abu Hanifah and Ahmed b. Hanbal believe they benefit the dead, but the better known opinion of Imam Shafe`i and that of Imam Malik is that they do not.

As for the dead profiting from acts not initiated by themselves, the proof can be found in the Qur`an, *Sunnah*, consensus of opinion, and by analogy. To take the Book, Allah (*swt*) said:

وَالَّذِينَ جَاؤُوا مِنْ بَعْدِهِمْ يَقُولُونَ رَبَّنَا اغْفِرْ لَنَا وَلِإِخْوَانِنَا الَّذِينَ سَبَقُونَا بِالْإِيمَانِ

"And those who came after them say, `Our Lord. Forgive us and our brothers who preceded us in faith." (Al Hashr, 10)

The context tells us that this verse praises those who seek forgiveness for themselves as well as those who went before them. This proves the legality of the act.

A further proof is provided by the supplication of the suppliants during funeral prayers, which is an accepted practice by consensus. So also their supplications at the time of visit to the graves. Buraydah b. Husayyib reports in Muslim's collection: "the Prophet taught them to say when they visited the graves: `Peace be upon you O people of the (other) world, the believers as well as ordinary Muslims. Verily, we shall soon join up with you. We seek Allah's protection both for ourselves as well as for you.'"

With regard to the rewards of charity dedicated to the dead, a *hadith* in Bukhari says that a man came up to the Prophet (*saws*) and said: "Messenger of Allah. My mother died while I was away. Will it profit her if I spent in charity on behalf of her?" He replied, "Yes." The man said, "Be a witness then that I have given away my orchard in Mikhraf as charity on her behalf."

With regard to fasts, the *Sahihayn* report the Prophet (*saws*) as saying: "Let the legal heir of that person fast on behalf of him who died with fasts due on him."

As for Hajj, Bukhari reports: "A woman from Juhaynah tribe went up to the Prophet and said, `My mother vowed that she would go on pilgrimage. But she

died and couldn't perform Hajj. May I perform the pilgrimage on her behalf?'
He replied, 'You might perform the Hajj on her behalf. Don't you think that if
your mother had left debts you would have paid them back? Pay back to Allah,
for Allah is more deserving that promises made to Him be kept.'"

Scholars also agree among themselves that the payment of debts on behalf
of the dead absolves the debtor even if paid by a non related person, and even
if paid from funds other than what he left behind. This is proven by the incident
involving Abu Qatadah who gave his word that he would pay two Dinars on
behalf of a dead debtor. When he paid out the amount, the Prophet (*saws*) told
him: "It is now that you have cooled his burning skin."

All the above follow the rules of the *Shari`ah*. It also stands confirmed by
analogy. For rewards are the ownership of the one who performed the deed.
Now, if he gives it away to a brother Muslim, there can be nothing against it.

The *Shari`ah* has led us to understand the profitability of the recitation of the
Qur`an for the dead, and other similar bodily acts of worship dedicated to the
dead, as similar in nature to fasts by explaining that a fast is nothing but absten-
tion from consumable items with a certain intention. The *Shari`ah* has told us
that the rewards of the fasts reach the one intended for. Why not the recitation
of the Qur`an then, which is the combination of an act and an intention?

To some people it has been difficult to reconcile the above with the words
of Allah:

$$وَأَنْ لَيْسَ لِلْإِنْسَانِ إِلَّا مَا سَعَى$$

"There is nothing for a man except what he earns." (Al Najm, 39)

The scholars have answered the doubts that spring up in this connection in
a variety of ways. The most appropriate are the following two. Firstly, the dead
person had, through his good deeds and proper treatment of the people, earned
friends who felt pity for him and performed a good deed on his behalf donating
him away the rewards. Thus, it was an effect of what he earned when was alive.

Secondly, the Qur`an did not deny a man benefiting from the acts of others.
Rather, it denied his ownership of other people's deeds. In this case, the one

who performed the deed is the owner of the deed. It is up to him to either gift it away to another, or keep it to himself.

Never the less, hiring someone for the recitation of the Qur`an and donating the rewards to a dead person is something that the earliest scholars did not do, nor has it been recommended by any of the great Imams. Insofar as offering oneself on hire for the recitation is concerned, there is no difference of opinion among the scholars that this is not permissible. They only differed over remuneration for teaching and other (religious services). The answer is, if someone recites the Qur`an and teaches it, and, in consequence is given something by way of help, then that would be a kind of charity and hence, acceptable. Nevertheless, it is stated in the book *"Al Ikhtiyar"* that if someone left a will that a part of his wealth be given away to the one who will recite the Qur`an over his grave, then such a testament is null and void, for it is a kind of wage. Indeed, Zahidi has written in his *"Al Ghaniyyah"* that if someone gave away to a trust naming it for someone who will recite the Qur`an on his grave then such a specification is null and void too.

As regards voluntary recitation of the Qur`an and donating its rewards to another, this is permissible in the like manner of Hajj, fasts etc. If it is said that this was not a practice among the pious predecessors, nor is there a behest by the Prophet to this effect, the answer is, if the questioner admits in the legality of the dedication of rewards of Hajj, fasts and supplications, then he might be asked: what is the difference between that and recitation of the Qur`an? As for the *Salaf* not having done it, how are we to pronounce a general impermissibility? If it is said that the Prophet (*saws*) allowed Hajj, fasts, etc., but did not allow the recitation of the Qur`an, the answer is, the permission for Hajj, fasts, etc., came up in response to inquiries. He did not initiate the topic. Someone asked about Hajj for a dead person and he said it was permissible. Another enquired about fasts and he said it was permissible. As for other acts, he did not rule them out.

On the other hand, if someone says that the dead profits from the Qur`an when it is recited by the grave, since he hears the Words of Allah, well, such a statement has not come from any of the great Imams. Accordingly, there are three opinions with regard to the recitation of the Qur`an near the graves. Is it to be discouraged? Or, is there no harm in it at the time of the burial? Or, is it to be discouraged after the burial? Among those who said it should be altogether discouraged is Abu Hanifah, Malik, and, according to one report Ahmed. They ruled that it is an innovatory practice since the *Sunnah* does not ratify it. One argument against it is that such a recitation is similar to Salah. And Salah is prohibited near the graves. Therefore, recitation by the grave follows the same rule. Yet, some have said that there is no harm in recitation by the graves. Muhammad b. Hasan al Shaybani, and, according to a second report, Ahmed, are those who are of this opinion. Their opinion is based on the testament left by Ibn `Umar that the first and the last few verses of *Surah Al Baqarah* be recited near his grave during his burial. Recitation of *Surah Al Baqarah* is also reported of some of the Immigrants. As for those who said there is no harm at the time of burial (but not at other times), among them is, according to one report, Ahmed, who perhaps relied on the reports coming from Ibn `Umar and some of the Immigrants, as stated above. As for all other practices, such as delegating someone to do the recitation by the grave, this is undesirable since the *Sunnah* did not say anything about it, nor has anything of that kind been reported of the Muslims of the first few generations. This seems to be the stronger opinion than the others. It reconciles the two evidences.

والله تعالى يستجيب الدعوات، ويقْضِي الحاجات

Allah responds to supplications and fulfills the needs.

This is following the words of the Qur`an:

وَقَالَ رَبُّكُمُ ادْعُونِي أَسْتَجِبْ لَكُمْ

"And your Lord said, `Call on Me, I shall answer you.'" (Al Ghāfir, 60)

And Allah's words:

وَإِذَا سَأَلَكَ عِبَادِي عَنِّي فَإِنِّي قَرِيبٌ أُجِيبُ دَعْوَةَ الدَّاعِ إِذَا دَعَانِ

"And when My slaves ask you concerning Me, (let them know), I am near. I respond to the call of the caller when he calls Me." (Al Baqarah, 186)

Most people of this *Ummah* as well as of others are one in opinion that supplication is one of the unfailing means of securing blessings and driving away adversities. Indeed, Allah (*swt*) has informed us about the unbelievers that when a calamity descends upon them in the seas, they too begin to call upon Him making the religion pure for Him.

The response to the supplications of a Muslim or a non-Muslim is of the nature of provisions for them: an obligation arising out of the Nourishing Attribute of the Lord toward His creations. However, the response can sometimes be a tribulation, or even harmful unto the supplicant especially when his disbelief and corruption demand it.

Ibn `Uqayl has said that Allah's exhortation to supplications has several connotations hidden in it.

First: (Allah's) existence, for a non existent is not called upon.

Second: Self sufficiency. The one himself in want is not called upon.

Third: Hearing. The deaf is not called upon.

Fourth: Generosity. The niggardly is not applied to.

Fifth: Compassion. The heartless is not appealed to.

Sixth: Power. The powerless is not sought help of.

Also, it is Allah Himself who moves His slaves to supplicate to Him. Thus this blessing is from Him and it is upon Him to respond to it as `Umar said: "I am not so much concerned about the response (to my supplications) as I am with the supplication itself. If I am inspired to supplicate, then the response will follow it." Allah has said:

يُدَبِّرُ الْأَمْرَ مِنَ السَّمَاءِ إِلَى الْأَرْضِ ثُمَّ يَعْرُجُ إِلَيْهِ فِي يَوْمٍ كَانَ مِقْدَارُهُ أَلْفَ سَنَةٍ مِّمَّا تَعُدُّونَ

"He directs the affairs from the heaven to the earth, then it ascends unto Him on a Day whose measure is a thousand years of your reckoning." (Al Sajdah, 5)

The above verse says that it is Allah who gives a start to the affairs. Then the affair that He had given a start returns to Him. (Applying that to our situation) it is Allah (*swt*) who provokes in a man the thought to resort to the supplications. He makes it a means to bestow on him something good that He had intended exactly as with any other deed and its reward. He it is then who impels a man to repentance. Consequently, He it is who accepts it. Exactly as it is He who impels a man to a good deed and then rewards him for it, in the like manner He induces him to supplications and then responds to them.

A doubt is often raised viz., there are people who supplicate but are not answered, or are given what they did not supplicate for. There are several answers. Firstly, the response to supplication is more general in nature than simply giving a man what he asked for. the Prophet has explained: "There isn't a man who supplicates to Allah, but not asking a sinful thing, or a severance of the blood ties, but He bestows on him one of the three: Either He gives the thing immediately, or, stores up for him the same amount of good, or turns away an evil of equal measure." At that, the Companions said: "If that is the case then we shall increase (our supplications)." He replied: "Allah is more (in giving)." The *hadīth* is from Ahmed but it has its basis in *Muslim*.

Another answer is that supplication is a means to achieve certain ends. Now the means also carry certain conditions. A few prohibitive factors also go with them. Whenever the conditions are met and the prohibitive factors removed, the objective can be achieved. If not, the objective will not be achieved, rather, something else would be obtained. This applies equally to all those prayer words that the *Sunnah* has taught us on which depends the securing of the good or driving away of the evil. The words are like tools in the hands of an artificer: their effects will depend on how they are applied, and with what force. Sometimes an obstruction comes in the way. Apparently, the conflicting texts promising or threatening dire consequences are of this kind. Quite often we have seen people supplicating by certain prayer words, and they were answered. It might have so happen that the man's needs, or his keen inclination towards Allah, had coincided with his supplications, or alternatively, he had forwarded a good deed that evoked a good response from Allah, or yet, it is possible that the man supplicated at the right hour, and so on there can be so many reasons for the good response. But, another person imagines that the secret in response lay in the

228

words of supplication. Consequently, he adopts the words from the successful suppliant without meeting with the other conditions (and so does not achieve the same results).

ويملك كل شيء، ولا يملكه شيء، ولا غِنى عن الله تعالى طَرْفَةَ عَينٍ، ومن استغنى عن الله طرفة عين، فقد كفر و صار من أهل الحَيْن و الله يغضَب و يرضى، لا كأحد من الورى

He owns everything and nothing owns Him. There is not a moment when one does not need Allah. Whoever thinks that he can do away without Allah even for a moment disbelieved and became of the doomed. And, Allah gets angry and is pleased but unlike any of the creations.

The opinion of the pious first few generation scholars and that of all the great Imams is confirmation of the Attributes of Anger, Approval, Enmity, Protection, Love, Hatred and other such Qualities that have been stated in the Qur`an and the *Sunnah*. They also prohibit the seeking of further clarity or efforts to interpret them in any way that could be considered derogatory to Allah. Allah (*swt*) said:

لَّقَدْ رَضِىَ اللهُ عَنِ الْمُؤْمِنِيْنَ إِذْ يُبَايِعُوْنَكَ تَحْتَ الشَّجَرَةِ

"Allah was pleased with the believers when they were swearing fealty to you under the tree." (Al Futh, 18)

Allah also said:

وَغَضِبَ اللهُ عَلَيْهِ وَلَعَنَهُ

"Allah was angry with him and cursed him." (Al Nisā, 93)

The author added the words, "unlike any of the creations," to defeat the purposes of the anthropomorphists.

It might not be said either that being pleased is nothing but the intention to do good, or about anger, that it is the intention to punish. This kind of interpretation would deny Allah His Attributes.

One who interprets Anger and Pleasure (of Allah) as intention to punish or do good, might be asked: why do you interpret it that way? The man will have no recourse but to reply that since anger is nothing but the rushing of the blood from the heart, and pleasure an expression of carnal desire, and both being unbecoming of Allah, we give the Qualities those interpretations. He might be explained that the rushing of blood from the heart in humans is the result of anger (and not the other way round). The same can be said about our intentions. It is one's inclination towards what is more in line with one's requirements. None of us desires or intends anything but what will help him obtain a good thing or chase away an evil. For man is in need of that which he desires and depends on. His happiness increases with their acquisition and decreases with their denial. Thus, the meaning that you have given the words (anger and pleasure) is the same as which you have refused to accept. If one of them is true, the other is also true. If one is unlikely, then the other is unlikely too.

If they say in reply that the intentions attributed to Allah are at variance with the intentions attributed to His creations, for each has its own separate connotation, then, it will be said in answer that you have to admit that the Anger and Pleasure that Allah (*swt*) has spoken of for Himself are in their reality different from what are attributed to His slaves although both are realities in their own sphere of existence. In that event, what is said about intentions, equally applies to these Attributes. They do not need any interpretation. Rather, interpretations need to be dropped since by doing so you will get rid of contradictions. That way you will also get rid of the need to deny Allah His Names and Attributes. To drop out the apparent meaning of the Qur`anic text, in preference of an implied meaning, is forbidden. Further, everything that the intellect of a person does not accept does not call for an interpretation. Intelligence, after all, varies from person to person. It is quite possible that someone will say that his intelligence leads to exactly the opposite of what another man was led to.

This is what can be said to anyone who denies any of the Attributes of Allah because of its equivalent being existent although only in name among His creations. For, if that is done, then there is no escape from attributing to Allah what He did not attribute to Himself, in fact, including the Attribute of Being and Existence. The existence enjoyed by the humans is far different in nature from the Existence of Allah, which is of a kind that becomes of Him. Allah's

Existence for instance rules out His becoming non existent. On the other hand, the existence of the creations does not rule out their going into non existence. Consequently, what names Allah attributed to Himself, also attributing them to His creations, such as that of Life, Knowledge, Power, or what He attributed to Himself of the Attributes, while also attributing them to His slaves, such as, Anger, Approval, and so on, in all these cases, we know by necessity what the true meaning of these terms are when applied to Allah (*swt*). We also believe that those meanings are true and existing. We also realize instinctively that between the two meanings (as applied to Allah and as applied to His creations) there happens to be a similarity of some kind. Yet, (we feel that) the meaning as attributed to Allah (*swt*) is not found in other than Allah. In fact, a complete sharing of the meanings does not exist but in the minds, none of it is found outside of it anywhere but in a specific sense. Thus, to both (Allah and His creatures) the meanings are as it is deserving of each.

ونحب أصحاب رسول الله صلى الله عليه وسلم، ولا نُفَرِّط في حب أحد منهم، ولا نَتَبَرَّأ من أحد منهم، ونبغض من يبغضهم، وبغير الخير يذكرهم، ولا نذكرهم إلا بخير، وحبهم: دين وإيمان وإحسان، وبُغضهم: كفر ونفاق وطغيان

And we love the Companions of the Prophet. Nonetheless we do not go to extremes in the love of any one of them, nor do we forsake any one of them. But we hate him who hates them, and talks of them in an unseemly manner. As for us, we do not mention them but in good terms. Their love is religion, faith, and excellence. And their hatred is disbelief, hypocrisy and rebellion.

This is because Allah spoke well of them, as did His Messenger. Allah was pleased with them and promised them "the good." He said:

وَالسَّابِقُونَ الْأَوَّلُونَ مِنَ الْمُهَاجِرِينَ وَالْأَنْصَارِ وَالَّذِينَ اتَّبَعُوهُم بِإِحْسَانٍ رَّضِيَ اللَّهُ عَنْهُمْ وَرَضُوا عَنْهُ وَأَعَدَّ لَهُمْ جَنَّاتٍ تَجْرِي تَحْتَهَا الْأَنْهَارُ خَالِدِينَ فِيهَا أَبَدًا ذَٰلِكَ الْفَوْزُ الْعَظِيمُ

"And the Outstrippers from among the Immigrants and the Helpers and those who followed them in good deeds, Allah was pleased with them and they were pleased with Him. He has prepared for them gardens beneath which rivers

flow, abiding therein forever. That is the great triumph." (Al Tawbah, 100)

Allah also said:

مُحَمَّدٌ رَّسُولُ اللهِ وَالَّذِينَ مَعَهُ أَشِدَّآءُ عَلَى الْكُفَّارِ رُحَمَآءُ بَيْنَهُمْ تَرَىٰهُمْ رُكَّعًا سُجَّدًا

"Muhammad the Messenger of Allah, and those who are with him, are hard upon the unbelievers, compassionate among themselves, you see them bowing down, prostrating themselves." (Al Fath, 29)

The *Sahihayn* have a report narrated by Abu Sa`id al Khudri. It says that something happened between Khalid b. Walid and `Abdul Rahman b. `Awf. Khalid said a harsh word to `Abdul Rahman. the Prophet (*saws*) said: "Don't say harsh things to any of my Companions. If one of you were to spend gold equal to Mount Uhūd, he will not achieve in any measure what any one of them achieved not even half of that." Thus we see that the Prophet (*saws*) prohibited one who had latter companionship from speaking against one who had earlier companionship. This, when a person of the stature of Khalid ibn Walid is involved, who embraced Islam with the fall of Makkah. What about him who had no share of his companionship?

Incidentally, what is narrated of the Prophet's words, viz., "My companions are stars. Whomsoever you followed, you will be guided" is a weak report not to be found in any of the authentic collections.

However, the following is an authentic report from the Prophet. He said: "No one who pledged his hand under the tree will enter the Fire."

`Abdullah ibn Mas`ud put it very aptly when he said describing them: "Allah looked upon the hearts of the people and found the heart of Muhammad as the best among them. So He chose him for Himself, and sent him with His message. Then He looked at the hearts of the people, after the heart of the Prophet (*saws*), and found the hearts of his companions as the best among the people. Therefore, He made them helpers to His messenger."

Referring to Tahawi's words, "Their hatred is disbelief and hypocrisy," we have already spoken over the declaration of apostasy while speaking of the innovators. This disbelief (as used by Tahawi) is of the same nature as mentioned in the words of Allah:

وَمَنْ لَمْ يَحْكُمْ بِمَا أَنْزَلَ اللهُ فَأُولَٰئِكَ هُمُ الْكَافِرُونَ

"And whoever did not judge by what Allah has revealed, they, such are the unbelievers." (Al Mā'idah, 44)

وَنُثْبِتُ الْخِلَافَةَ بَعْدَ الرَّسُولِ اللهِ صلى الله عليه وسلم أولًا لأبي بكْرَ الصِّدِّيق رضي الله عنه تفضيلاً له
و تقديماً على جميع الأمة

We affirm that the caliphate after the Prophet was, first and foremost, deserving of Abu Bakr, believing in his superiority and seniority over the rest of the *Ummah*.

Although, such is our opinion, the *Ummah* has disagreed over the nature of Abu Bakr's succession. Was it by the Prophet's command, or was it simply a choice? Hasan al Busri and a group of people from the *Ahl al hadith* believe it was by dint of command, although subtle and indirect, coming from the Prophet (*saws*). Some of them in fact have said that it is proven by the texts. However, some others of the *Ahl al hadīth*, the Mu`tazilah and Ash`ariyyah have said that it was established by choice and consent.

As a matter of fact, we have some reports that suggest that the caliphate of Abu Bakr was by the dint of a command from the Prophet (*saws*). One of them is in Bukhari, narrated by Jubayr b. Mut`im who said: "A woman came up to the Prophet (*saws*). He told her to come back to him later. She asked, 'What if I came and didn't find you?' (She meant, if he was dead). He replied, 'If you didn't find me, go to Abu Bakr.'" There are other reports supporting this one which can be said to be the text in support of his succession.

Then there is the *hadīth* of Hudayfah b. al Yaman who reports that the Prophet (*saws*) said: "Follow the two that will come after me: Abu Bakr and `Umar." The traditionists have preserved this report.

The *Sahihayn* also have reports narrated by `A'isha about her father. She says:

"The day the Messenger of Allah took ill, he entered into my house and said, `Call in your father and brother so that I write down in favor of Abu Bakr, for Allah and the Muslims will not accept anyone but Abu Bakr."

Reports about the Prophet preferring Abu Bakr over others are well known. In one of them he said: "Ask Abu Bakr to lead in the Prayers."

Trustworthy compilations also have another report recording the Prophet as having said from his pulpit: "Were I to take someone a Friend from among the people of the earth, I would have taken Abu Bakr as the Friend. Let there not be a door opening into the (Grand) mosque. Close them all, except for Abu Bakr's door."

As for those who opined that the Prophet did not appoint Abu Bakr as his caliph, not at least through a proven *hadīth*, they have argued with the report of Ibn `Umar who reported `Umar ibn al Khattab as saying: "If I nominate a successor after me, then one who was better than me, that is, Abu Bakr, nominated a successor after him. But if I don't nominate, then one who was better than me, that is, the Prophet (*saws*), did not name a successor after himself." 'Abdullah ibn `Umar adds: "When he mentioned the Prophet, I knew that he was not going to nominate his own successor."

What seems likely, although Allah knows best, is that the Prophet (*saws*) did not issue a written edict to the effect that Abu Bakr would be the caliph after him. He did intend to do that, but changed his mind, saying, "Allah and the Muslims will accept none but Abu Bakr." This indeed was a stronger manner of appointing him his successor. the Prophet (*saws*) let know the believers his own preference of Abu Bakr as his successor, and led them to accepting his preference through his various words and deeds. He also spoke of his appointment in favorable terms, expressing his own satisfaction. Were his hints insufficient to announce where lay his choice, he would have spoken out more outspokenly, leaving no room for excuses and doubts.

Bukhari and Muslim have another report about the Prophet saying: "Allah commissioned me unto you. You responded by saying, `You lied.' But Abu Bakr said, 'You spoke the truth.' Thereafter he backed me with continuous material and moral support."

ثُمَّ لِعُمَرَ بن الخطاب رضي الله عنه

Then of `Umar ibn al-Khattab, Allah be pleased with him.

That is, we believe that after Abu Bakr it was `Umar who was the most deserving of the caliphate. This opinion rests on the fact that Abu Bakr himself nominated him, and the fact that the people unanimously accepted him. His virtues are of such order that no one can be ignorant of them, and more numerous than what can be recounted. Muhammad b. Hanafiyyah has reported that he asked his father `Ali ibn. Abi Talib, "Father. Who was the most virtuous man after the Prophet?" He answered, "Son. Don't you know?" I said, "No, I do not." He said, "Abu Bakr." I asked, "Who after him?" He replied, "`Umar." Ibn Hanafiyyah says I was afraid he would say "Then, after him, `Uthman," and therefore, I asked, "Then it must be you." He answered, "I am no more than a Muslim among the Muslims."

Sahih Muslim reports Ibn `Abbas as saying that when `Umar was laid on the cot (after he was stabbed in the mosque), "People surrounded him, supplicating for him, praising him and praying upon him, before he could be lifted (for burial). I was one of them. No one noticed me but for a man. He caught me by my shoulders from behind me. I turned toward him. It was `Ali. He expressed his grief over `Umar and then said, 'You (meaning `Umar) didn't leave anyone behind you against whom I would wish to do better in life than him before I met Allah. And, by Allah, I was sure Allah (*swt*) would place you with the two preceding you (the Prophet and Abu Bakr) for, I used to hear so often from the Prophet (*saws*), "I, Abu Bakr and `Umar came up", "I, Abu Bakr and `Umar entered", "I, Abu Bakr and `Umar left the place." I was sure that Allah (*swt*) will place you with the two.'

The *Sahihayn* have also preserved the report that the Prophet (*saws*) said: "O `Umar ibn al Khattab. By Him in whose power is my soul, Shaytan didn't find you passing through a gorge, but slipped off into another."

ثم لعثمان رضي الله عنه

And then of `Uthman, Allah be pleased with him.

That is, we declare that after `Umar, it was `Uthman who was most deserving of the caliphate. Bukhari has a long report, recounting the death of `Umar, the counseling after him and pledging of hands for `Uthman. Reported by `Amr b. Maymun, it runs as follows: "A few days before `Umar ibn al Khattab was struck down, I saw him detaining Hudhayfah b. al Yaman and `Uthman b. Hunayf and asking: "What have you two done? Are you fearful that the two of you have made the land bear more than what it can?" They replied, "We have only laid upon it what it could bear." (That is, have you taxed it unjustly).

He asked, "Are you sure you didn't burden her with what it cannot bear?" They replied, "No." `Umar said, "If Allah allowed me time, I would leave the widows of Iraq in a state in which they would not be in need of anyone after me."

`Amr says, "Not four days passed after that but `Umar was struck."

"Then," `Amr continued, "I found myself standing with no one between me and him but `Abdullah ibn `Abbas on the morning he was struck. He would pass by two rows and say, `Line up properly.' Until, when he didn't find anyone out of the line, he entered into the Prayer by saying, `Allahu Akbar.' Most often he recited chapters *Yūsuf* or *Al Nahal* or something like that in the first cycle in order that people coming late could join up. But he hadn't said *Allahu Akbar* that he shortly uttered, 'He killed me', or, 'he ate me   the dog.' That was when he had struck him. The man then struck at least thirteen other people, of whom seven died. When one of the Muslims saw that, he threw a cloak around him. When the foreigner realized that he was caught, he killed himself. `Umar pulled `Abdul Rahman by his hand and made him lead in the Prayer. Only those who were near him had seen what had happened. Those at the back knew nothing about what was going on, except that they missed `Umar's  voice. They began to say, "Glory to Allah, glory to Allah," (realizing that there was something wrong). `Abdul Rahman did a short prayer. When the people had left, `Umar said, `O Ibn `Abbas. See who killed me.'

He went around a bit and then said, 'Mughira's slave.'

He asked, 'Was it Al San`?' (That is, "the craftsman?")

He replied, 'Yes.'

`Umar said, 'May Allah destroy him. I had instructed that he be treated well. Allah be praised He did not afflict by me one of those who claims to be a Muslim. It was you and your father `Abbas who were in favor of more foreigners in Madinah. (It is said, adds the narrator), that `Abbas was the kindest of the people. He said (i.e., `Abbas), 'If you wish we could do that.' 'If you wish we would kill them.' `Umar replied, 'You lied. (Will you kill them) after they have learned to speak your language, pray facing your *Qiblah*, and make pilgrimage the way you do?'

'After that he was carried to his house. We also went along. The people's reaction was incredulous, as if they had never experienced a disaster before. Some were saying, 'It's not serious.' Another would say, 'I fear for his life.' He was offered a drink which he gulped down. But it came out of his guts. Then he was offered some milk which he drank too. But it also came out of his intestines too. With that they knew that he wouldn't survive. So we started to visit him and people began to praise him. Then a young man entered. He said, 'Be of good cheer O leader of the faithful, by the good news from Allah for you. He who enjoyed the companionship of the Prophet, then a precedence in Islam that is well known, then you were bestowed with caliphate and did justice to it, and, finally, martyrdom.'

`Umar replied, 'All that I wish is that the scales rest equal: neither anything for me nor anything upon me.'

When the man turned to go, his lower garment could be seen dragging on the floor. `Umar said, 'Call the young man back.' (When the man was brought back) he said, 'O my brother's son, pull up your garment. That will assure a longer life for your clothes, and a better demonstration of fear of your Lord.'

Then he addressed his son, 'O `Abdullah. Look into my debts."

They checked and found that he owed 86,000 or so.

He ordered, 'If the wealth of `Umar's family suffices, well and good. If it doesn't, then ask Banu `Uday b. Ka`b. But if that doesn't help, then you might ask the Quraysh (to help pay up). But do not go to others. So, take charge of my debts. Now, go to `A'isha, the mother of the believers and tell her, "`Umar greets you"  but don't say, "the leader of the believers," since I am no longer the leader of the believers,  rather, say, `Umar ibn al Khattab requests that he be buried with the two of his companions.'

Accordingly, he greeted her and asked to be let in. When he entered upon her he found her crying. He said, "`Umar ibn al Khattab says *Salam* to you and seeks your permission for burial along with his two companions."

She replied, "I had reserved the place for myself. But today I shall give him preference over myself."

When he returned, the people told `Umar, "Here is `Abdullah, returning." He said, "Lift me up." Someone gave him support. He asked `Abdullah, "What have you brought?" He replied, "What you would love to hear O leader of the faithful. She has given her consent."

`Umar said, "Allah be praised. Nothing was more important to me than this. When I am dead, carry my body there. Then, when you arrive at her place, tell her, `Umar ibn al Khattab seeks your permission.' If she agrees bury me there. If she refuses, bury me in the common cemetery.

Then the mother of the believers Hafsah arrived. Other women were covering her. When we saw her we moved away from there. She entered upon him and cried for a while. Then other people sought permission to enter. She went into the inner quarters from where we could hear her cries.

The people said: "O leader of the faithful, express your will. Appoint your successor."

He replied, "I don't find anyone better suited than these people for this affair those with whom the Prophet was pleased until he died. Then he named them: `Ali, `Uthman, Zubayr, Talha, Sa`d and `Abdul Rahman."

Then he added: "`Abdullah ibn `Umar although he should not be considered for this affair (i.e., caliphate) be present during this issue. It would be a kind of a mourning for him. If Sa`d is given the caliphate, then, let that be. If not, let whoever that is chosen seek his help (in state affairs). I didn't remove him from his post (as a governor) because of a weakness or dishonesty on his part."

He also said: "I urge the caliph after me to be good to the first batch of Immigrants. He should know their rights and guard their honor. I also urge him to do good to the Helpers. Those before them who had homes (in Madinah) and adopted the Faith. I urge that their good behavior be appreciated and bad behavior ignored. I also urge him to be good to the general body of Muslims of the outlying areas, for they are the helpers of Islam, a source of wealth, and cause of anger to the enemies. I also urge him not to take away their wealth but what is in excess, and that too by their consent. Finally, I urge him to take care of the Bedouins. For they are the true Arabs and the raw material of Islam. I urge him therefore, not to take away from their cattle but what is excessive, yet to be returned to their poor alone. I also urge my follower, by Allah's trust and that of His Messenger, that he keep promises made to them, be at their rear during the battles, and that they be not burdened with anything except what they can bear."

When he was dead, we carried him and began to head (for `A'isha's house). When we arrived there, `Abdullah ibn `Umar greeted her and said: "`Umar ibn al Khattab seeks your permission."

She said, "Bring him in."

He was taken in and placed by the side of his two companions. When we were done with the affair, those people whom `Umar had named got together. `Abdul Rahman suggested: "Let the affair be decided between three of you."

Zubayr responded by saying, "I withdraw in favor of `Ali."

Talha said, "I withdraw in favor of `Uthman."

Sa`d said, "I withdraw in favor of `Abdul Rahman ibn `Awf."

`Abdul Rahman himself said: "Would one of you two like to withdraw so that the other can be nominated? And, by Allah, let him look at the better of the two." The two `Uthman and `Ali remained silent.

So `Abdul Rahman asked: "Would the two of you allow me to decide? By Allah, I shall not overlook the better of you."

The two agreed. At that he took the hand of one of them and said: "You are related to the Prophet (*saws*). Also, you enjoy seniority in Islam of the kind you are aware. I adjure you in Allah's name, will you do justice if I made you the caliph, and will you listen to `Uthman and obey if I made him the caliph?"

Then he spoke to the other in the same manner. When the two had given their promises he said: "Stretch out your hand O `Uthman." (When he did that), he pledged his own hand. Then `Ali pledged his hand. Then the people of the house came in to pledge their hands.

Bukhari has added in his report on the authority of Humayd b. `Abdul Rahman b. `Awf that Miswar b. Makhramah told him: "The people who were nominated by `Umar ibn al Khattab got together and consulted each other. `Abdul Rahman ibn `Awf said at that time, "Isn't it true that I was one of the contestants? But, if you wish, I will choose one of you (and withdraw myself). They agreed to his mediation. And when they had agreed to his mediation, the people gave up following the others. They followed `Abdul Rahman around those days advising him. It went on until the night in which he gave his decision and we pledged hands to `Uthman.

Miswar b. Makhramah said: `Abdul Rahman surprised me with a knock on my door deep in the night. He kept banging the door until I woke up. He said, "Probably you were asleep. By Allah, I haven't slept much these last three nights. Come out and bring me Zubayr and Sa`d."

So I went out and brought them forth. He consulted with them. Then he called out to me again saying, "Get `Ali here." I brought him up. He counseled him through much of the night. Then `Ali left him. He seemed to be in a hopeful state. `Abdul Rahman was apprehensive of `Ali's responses. However, he asked me to get `Uthman. So I went out and brought him in. `Abdul Rahman spoke to him until the Prayer call separated them. When the morning Prayers were over, these (six) people assembled near the mimber of the mosque. `Abdul Rahman sent for the Immigrants and the Helpers who were then around in Madinah. He also got in the commanders of various forces. They had come (from their fronts) to perform Hajj with `Umar. When they had all gathered, `Abdul Rahman said the customary words of supplication and then went on to say: "O `Ali. I have tried to read the people's mind. I don't find them but preferring `Uthman. Therefore, let there be no hard feeling in your heart. Then he (turned to `Uthman and) said: "I pledge my hand unto you on the *Sunnah* of Allah, His Messenger, and the two caliphs after him." Thus `Abdul Rahman pledged his hand and the people followed him: the Immigrants, the Helpers, the commanders of the forces and the rest of the people.

By way of `Uthman's virtues, we might mention that he was the son in law of the Prophet who had married two of his daughters.

Sahih Muslim has a narration of `A'isha: "Once the Prophet (*saws*) was lying in his bed, with his thighs bare   or the calves   when Abu Bakr sought to come in. He allowed him in. Remaining in the same position he conversed with him. Then `Umar sought to be let in. He allowed him in too, without changing his position, conversing with them. Then `Uthman came up. The Prophet sat up. He pulled down his clothes (to cover his legs). When he came in he chatted with him." When he had left, `A'isha remarked: "Abu Bakr entering in didn't move you and you didn't give a care. Then `Umar joined but you didn't move and didn't give him a care. But when `Uthman showed up you sat up and pulled down your clothes. Why was that?" the Prophet (*saws*) replied: "Should I not I feel shy of a person, in whose company even the angels feel shy?"

ثم لعلي بن أبي طالب رضي الله عنه

Then of `Ali ibn Abi Talib, Allah be pleased with him.

That is, we confirm `Ali's caliphate after `Uthman. When `Uthman was killed and the people pledged their hands to `Ali he became the leader of the faithful deserving obedience. In his time, he was the caliph on the pattern of the prophetic *Khilafah* ; as had predicted the Prophet (*saws*): "Prophetic caliphate will last 30 years. Then Allah will bestow the kingdom to whom He will."

Abu Bakr's caliphate lasted 2 years and 3 months. `Umar's caliphate lasted 10 years and 6 months. That of `Uthman lasted 12 years. Finally, that of `Ali lasted 4 years and 9 months. First of the Muslim kings was Mu`awiyyah. Nevertheless, he became the true ruler, in the complete sense, only after Hasan b. `Ali renounced his own caliphate in his favor. For the people of Iraq had pledged their hands to Hasan b. `Ali after the martyrdom of `Ali. In six months he stepped down in favor of Mu`awiyyah. That made it 30 and the Prophet's words came true who had said (about Hasan): "This my son is a (true) leader. Two great forces of Muslims will be reconciled to each other by him."

`Ali's caliphate was established after that of `Uthman by the allegiance of the people, except for Mu`awiyyah who had the Syrians with him. In that conflict truth was on the side of `Ali. When `Uthman was martyred, rumors floated aplenty concerning `Uthman and plenty of lies were spun about senior companions such as `Ali, Talha and Zubayr. Those who did not have a first hand information of what had happened were beset with doubts and fell into suspicions. Lust of power also crept in the breasts of those who followed their carnal desires, especially those who were away in the Syrian lands. To complicate matters, some of the rebellious Khawarij who had killed `Uthman were hiding in the forces commanded by `Ali. But no one could point an accusing finger at any one of them specifically, because of lack of definite proofs, without which their respective tribes would have risen in protest and rebellion. There were hypocrites too, who did not have the courage to come into the open. In this situation, Talha b. `Ubaydullah and Zubayr b. al `Awwam felt that if no one stood up against the assassins and demanded justice, Allah's anger and punishment would be provoked. That led to the battle of Jamal without `Ali being able to avoid it. Nor could Talha and Zubayr do anything to avert it. It was fired up by the corrupt without the senior Companions playing any role in it. Then erupted the battle of Siffin because of an opinion   to the effect that justice was not done to the people of Syria, or it didn't seem possible to deliver justice to them.

And they were demanding justice in order that unity be enforced, as also because they were fearful of the rebels hiding themselves in the forces of `Ali, that they would be encouraged to mischief just as  they had done against `Uthman. Obviously, `Ali was the rightly guided caliph whose obedience was binding on all and under whose banner all should have assembled. Therefore, he believed that obedience to (the ruler) and remaining united with the community of believers which was binding on them was only possible through the declaration of war on them. It didn't occur to him that to tolerate them for the moment was in keeping with the same spirit that was displayed during the Prophet's time and even during the time of Abu Bakr and `Umar after him. So, he felt, from what he was observing to the effect that what Islam demanded was the handing down of punishment and preventing them from mischief, and not the spirit of reconciliation that the declaration of war against them was the demand of the religion of Islam. But most of the senior Companions stayed away from the confrontational situation, especially when they heard of the Prophet's traditions instructing them to stay away from seductions of the sort involving fighting between two groups of Muslims, and also, because they saw that the confrontation would create more problems than solve them.

Whatever, our general reaction to what happened is to have good faith in them all and say:

رَبَّنَا اغْفِرْ لَنَا وَلِإِخْوَانِنَا الَّذِينَ سَبَقُونَا بِالْإِيمَانِ وَلَا تَجْعَلْ فِي قُلُوبِنَا غِلاًّ لِّلَّذِينَ آمَنُوا رَبَّنَا إِنَّكَ رَءُوفٌ رَّحِيمٌ

"O our Lord! Forgive us and those of our brothers who preceded us in faith and leave not in our hearts any rancor toward those who have believed. O our Lord! Truly, you are the Most Caring, the Most Kind." (Al Hashr, 10)

Allah preserved our hands from the strife that took place during the caliphate of `Ali. We pray to Allah (*swt*) that He preserve our tongues too from it: by His grace and generosity.

As for the virtues of the leader of the faithful, `Ali ibn Abi Talib, many have been passed on to us. One of them is in the *Sahihayn*, narrated by Sa`d ibn. Abi Waqqas. He said: "the Prophet (*saws*) said to `Ali, 'Does it not please you that you should be to me what Harun was to Musa?'"

Bukhari has recorded the Prophet as having said (at the time of the Khayber assault): "I shall hand over the command to a man to whom Allah will grant victory." At that Sahl b. Sa`d al Sa`idi said: "The people spent the night in discussions wondering who would be given the command the next day." When it was morning, they flocked to the Prophet (*saws*) in the hope of the command. The Prophet asked: "Where is `Ali ibn Abi Talib?" They said, "He has a problem with his eyes, Messenger of Allah." He said, "Let someone go and bring him to me." When he came the Prophet spat in his eyes and supplicated for him. He became alright  as if he had suffered from nothing. Then he gave him the banner. `Ali asked, "Do I fight them until they are like us (i.e., enter into Islam)?" He answered, "Take it easy. When you are in their territory invite them to Islam and tell them what are Allah's rights upon them. By Allah, that Allah should guide a single man by you to Islam is better for you than that you should have a hundred red camels." Allah (*swt*) granted him victory.

وهُم الخلفاءُ الراشدون، و الأئمةُ المهديُّون

These were the rightly guided caliphs and the rightly guiding leaders.

This follows the words of the Prophet: "Incumbent upon you is my *Sunnah* and the *Sunnah* of the rightly guided caliphs after me. Hold fast unto it with your teeth. And, beware of innovations, for, every innovation is misguidance."

The four *Sunan* compilers have recorded it with Tirmidhi declaring it authentic.

The order of the caliphs in virtue is the order in which they became caliphs. This is the opinion of the great majority of the *Ahl al Sunnah. Sahih Bukhari* has recorded `Abdullah ibn `Umar as saying: "It was commonly said amongst ourselves, even while the Prophet (*saws*) was alive, that the most virtuous amongst us was Abu Bakr, after him `Umar and after him `Uthman."

وأن العشرة الذين سماهم رسول الله صلى الله عليه وسلم و بشرهم بالجنة: نشهد لهم بالجنه، على ما شهد لهم رسول الله صلى الله عليه وسلم، و قوله الحق، وهم: أبو بكر، وعمر، وعثمان، وعلي،

244

وطلحة، والزبير، وسعد، وسعيد، و عبد الرحمن بن عوف، وأبو عبيدة بن الجرَّاح وهو أمين هذه
الأمة، رضي الله عنهم أجمعين

We also testify that the ten the Prophet named and gave the glad tidings of entry into Paradise, are indeed of Paradise. This is based entirely on the Prophet's prophecy. His word is the true. They are: Abu Bakr, `Umar, `Uthman, `Ali, Talha, Zubayr, Sa`d, Sa`id, `Abdul Rahman ibn `Awf and Abu `Ubaydah ibn al Jarrah. The last mentioned is the `Amin' of this *Ummah* may Allah be pleased with them all.

In what has preceded, the virtues of the first four of the above list have been mentioned in brief. Here are a few reports about the rest of the six.

Sahih Muslim recorded `A'isha as saying: "One night the Prophet (*saws*) was a bit restless. He remarked, 'If only one of the righteous of the Muslims stood guard at my tent!' That moment we heard the clunk of steel. He enquired, `Who is this?' Sa`d ibn Abi Waqqas answered, `O Messenger of Allah, I have come to guard you.' the Prophet (*saws*) supplicated for him and then slept." The *Sahihayn* also report that the Prophet (*saws*) gathered arrows for Sa`d ibn Abi Waqqas on the occasion of Uhud saying, "Shoot, may my father and mother be sacrificed for you."

Sahih Bukhari has Qays b. Abi Hazim as reporting: "I have personally seen Talha's hand which was paralyzed because of his shielding the Prophet (*saws*) with it (against arrows and missiles aimed at him) on the day of Uhud."

The *Sahihayn* have Abu `Uthman al Nahdi saying: "On that fateful day (of Uhud), for a few hours none remained with the Prophet (*saws*) except Talha and Sa`d."

The *Sahihayn* also have the report that we reproduce from Muslim that has Jabir b. `Abdullah saying: "the Prophet (*saws*) exhorted the people (to a task) during the campaign of the Battle of the Ditch. Zubayr responded. Then the Prophet (*saws*) exhorted them a second time. Once again Zubayr responded. The Prophet remarked, `Every Prophet is given a Hawwari. Zubayr is my Hawwari."

About Abu `Ubaydah ibn al Jarrah, *Sahih Muslim* has preserved the Prophet's words: "Every *Ummah* has its *Amin*. Our *Amin*  O my people  is Abu `Ubaydah ibn al Jarrah."

Musnad Ahmed and Tirmidhi have recorded the following words of the Prophet (*saws*): "Abu Bakr is in Paradise. `Umar is in Paradise. `Ali is in Paradise. `Uthman is in Paradise. Talha is in Paradise. Zubayr ibn al `Awwam is in Paradise. `Abdul Rahman ibn `Awf is in Paradise. Sa`id b. Zayd is in Paradise. And `Abu `Ubaydah ibn al Jarrah is in Paradise."

The Sa`id mentioned above is Sa`id b. Zayd b. `Amr b. Nufayl, the Qurayshi. His father was of the Ahnaf who had chosen the path of Ibrahim (even in pre Islamic times).

The *Ahl al Sunnah* are unanimous over the position of veneration and honor to be accorded to these ten because of the Prophet's words and because of their special personal virtues.

وَمَنْ أَحْسَنَ القَوْلَ فِي أَصْحَاب رَسُول الله صَلَّى الله عَلَيْهِ وَسَلَّم، وَأَزْوَاجِهِ الطَّاهِرَات مِن كُلِّ دَنَسٍ، وَذُرياته المُقَدَّسِين مِنْ كُلِّ رِجْس، فَقَد بَرِئَ من النِّفاق

Whoever spoke well of the Companions of the Prophet, peace on him, his wives and children, declaring them free of every blemish, and his sublime offspring from every impurity, freed himself of hypocrisy.

This has the Prophet's following words as it basis which are in Muslim. He said: "I am leaving behind me two weighty things. One of them is the Book of Allah. It has Guidance and Light. Therefore, hold on to the Book of Allah most firmly." Thus, he emphasized the Qur`an and awakened interest in it. Then he added: "And the people of my house: I remind you by Allah of the people of my house."

وعلماءُ السَّلفِ من السابقين، و مَن بَعدهم من التَّابعين – أهلُ الخَبَرِ والأَثَر، وأهلُ الفِقْه والنَّظَر – لا

يُذْكَرون إلا بالجَميل، ومَن ذَكَرَهُم بسوءٍ فهو على غَيرِ السَّبيل

As for the early Muslim scholars and the followers after them: those of wide knowledge, understanding and perception they might not be mentioned but in good terms. Whoever spoke of them in a disparaging manner, is not on the right course.

This draws its strength from Allah's words:

وَمَنْ يُشَاقِقِ الرَّسُولَ مِنْ بَعْدِ مَا تَبَيَّنَ لَهُ الْهُدَى وَ يَتَّبِعْ غَيْرَ سَبِيلِ الْمُؤْمِنِينَ نُوَلِّهِ مَا تَوَلَّى وَنُصْلِهِ جَهَنَّمَ وَسَاءَتْ مَصِيرًا

"Whosoever makes a breach with the Messenger, after the guidance has become clear to him, and follows (a way) other than the way of the believers, We shall let him do what he chooses, then roast him in Jahannum: an evil destination." (Al Nisā', 115)

Therefore, it is binding upon a Muslim to seek, after his friendship with Allah and His Messenger, the friendship of the believers following the Qur'anic injunction. This will especially apply to those who are the inheritors of the Prophets and are unanimous over complete obedience of the Prophet. Yes, if someone is found among them whose words go against a proven *hadīth*, then there is no choice but to drop that off. However, that would require the absence of any of the following three:

(i) The scholar's lack of conviction that those are the Prophet's words,

(ii) his lack of belief that the Prophet (*saws*) was speaking of the subject on hand, and, finally,

(iii) his belief that what the Prophet said has been abrogated (by another of his traditions).

Otherwise, they (the early Muslim scholars) are superior to us and have the right of reverence because they preceded us in belief, transmitted to us the contents of the prophetic message, and clarified those issues that were of equivocal type for us. May Allah be pleased with them and please them (with His rewards).

ولا نُفَضِّلُ أحداً من الأولياءِ على أحدٍ مِن الأنبياءِ عليهم السلام ونقولُ: نَبِيٌّ واحد أفضل من جميع الأولياءِ

We do not declare any one of the Favorites (of Allah) superior to any of the Prophets of Allah, on whom be peace. We say rather, a single Prophet is superior to all the Favorites (of Allah) put together.

This is because, without any difference of opinion among the *Ahl al Sunnah*, the rank occupied by the Prophets is the highest of ranks.

ونُؤمنُ بما جاءَ من كَرَاماتِهم، وصَحَّ عن الثِّقَاتِ من رواياتِهم

Nonetheless, we believe in the thaumaturgies that manifested at their hands and in all that is narrated (about their accomplishments) by trustworthy transmitters.

The word *mu'jizah* in Arabic (translated as miracle) is a common word that covers any act of the supernatural type (produced by a believer or one of higher rank). To the earliest scholars *karamāh* was its synonym. But the latter day scholars have differentiated between the two. They use the word *mu'jizah* for the Prophets, while *karamāh* (thaumaturgy) for the Favorites of Allah (the *'awliyā'*). The connotation common between them is supernaturalness of the act.

Perfection has three constituents: Knowledge, power and self sufficiency. The perfection of these three is not the share of anyone but Allah. He circumscribes everything with his knowledge. He has power over everything. And He is not dependent upon the worlds in anyway whatsoever. Accordingly, He ordered the Prophet to deny to himself these three qualities by saying:

قُل لَّآ اَقُولُ لَكُمْ عِنْدِىْ خَزَآئِنُ اللهِ وَلَآ اَعْلَمُ الْغَيْبَ وَلَآ اَقُولُ لَكُمْ اِنِّ مَلَكٌ اِنْ اَتَّبِعُ اِلَّا مَا يُوْحَى اِلَىَّ

"Tell (them), 'I do not say, "I possess the treasures of Allah;" nor do I know the Unseen; nor do I say to you, "I am an angel." I only follow what is revealed to me.'" (Al An'ām, 50)

That is what Nuh said, the first of the Messengers and one of the chosen few. And this is what the last of the Messengers said, and last of the chosen few among them. Both of them absolved themselves of any such thing. This was necessary because sometimes they were demanded information about the Unseen and the Unknowable, such as:

يَسْـَٔلُونَكَ عَنِ السَّاعَةِ أَيَّانَ مُرْسِهَا

"They ask you about the Hour as to when will its appointed time be." (Al A`rāf, 187)

At other times, demands were made on them to produce some kind of miracles, such as,

وَقَالُوا لَنْ نُؤْمِنَ لَكَ حَتَّى تَفْجُرَ لَنَا مِنَ الْأَرْضِ يَنْبُوعًا

"And they said, `We shall never believe in you until you can cause a spring to gush forth from the earth." (Al Isrā', 90)

At other times, the people found fault in the Prophets for being in physical wants, as said Allah Most High :

وَقَالُوا مَالِ هٰذَا الرَّسُولِ يَأْكُلُ الطَّعَامَ وَيَمْشِي فِي الْأَسْوَاقِ

"And they say, `What's the matter with this Messenger? He eats food, and moves about in the market.'" (Al Furqan, 7)

the Prophet was ordered to inform them that he had no power over these things. He received of the three (knowledge, power and self sufficiency) only in measures that Allah (*swt*) decided. He knew what Allah let him know. He was self sufficient in only those affairs that were made so for him by Allah. And, he only had power over what Allah had given him power, especially those that were supernatural or, normally not possible for human beings.

Now, none of the miracles or the thaumaturgies is the outcome of these three qualities.

With regard to the preternatural acts, the following may be understood about them. If   by the act   a demand of religion is met, then it is a good act, either of the obligatory nature or the approved one, depending on the circumstances. On the other hand, if it helps to obtain something only desirable   of the non obligatory nature   then it is one of Allah's blessings of the worldly nature, demanding gratitude. But if it is one of those acts that result in an unlawful act, whether it is the forbidden type, or merely a strongly disapproved one, then it becomes the cause of a punishment, or strong disapproval.

Thus, from the religious point of view, preternatural acts are of three types: The praiseworthy one, the undesirable type and the permissible type. As for the permissible type, if it brings an advantage, it is a blessing, otherwise it follows the same rule as the rest of the permissible things in Islam that are of no profit.

Abu `Ali Al Jawzajani said: "Covet for consistency and do not covet for thaumaturgy. While your inner self is desirous of thaumaturgy, Allah is desirous of consistency."

Sheikh Suhrawardi has said in his "`Awārif ": "Many people have been led into the abyss by this door. When several of those who worked hard (in the path of Islam), heard of the pious predecessors and what preternatural acts they were granted, set their sight on it as an (additional) objective. They would have loved to be granted a few, even if it were a minor type. But when that didn't happen, some of them began to find fault with themselves   broken hearted wondering if their deeds were of the right sort. Had they known the secret of it, it wouldn't have bothered them much. It should be realized that Allah opens up this door in a certain measure for some of the sincere ones striving in His way. It is in order to increase their faith. With that objective it is granted that a few preternatural acts appear by their hand. That strengthens their resolve against the delights of this world and prevents them from falling prey to carnal desires. Therefore, the right conduct for a sincere seeker is to pray for steadfastness. That is the *karamāh* of the perfect kind."

It should also be realized that if nothing of the Unseen is made visible to a believer, or, if nothing of the world is subdued to him, it is no sign of his lower rank with Allah. On the contrary, not to be granted anything of the sort, could be of greater profit to him. For, if it comes along with adherence to Islam, then it is good for him. Otherwise, the man is destroyed in both the worlds. The issue of preternatural act is sometimes accompanied by adherence to religion and sometimes not. If one is religious, then the preternatural act is profitable to him.

We might cite as example the gaining of worldly governance, which can only be profitable if it is advantageous to one's religion. So is the case of beneficial wealth. If someone makes these the object, granting religion a second position and subservient to it or a means to obtaining those things, then he is like one who devours the worldly things at the price of his religion. He isn't like the one who becomes religious out of fear of Allah's punishment and in the hope of His rewards.

Nevertheless, it must also be understood that if one's practice of religion is of the right kind, from the point of view of knowledge as well as practice, then it is indispensable that thaumaturgies appear, whenever their need arises for the person involved. Allah Most High said:

$$\text{وَمَنْ يَتَّقِ اللهَ يَجْعَل لَّهُ مَخْرَجاً , وَيَرْزُقْهُ مِنْ حَيْثُ لَا يَحْتَسِبُ}$$

"And whosoever fears Allah, He finds a way out for him, and feeds him from sources he didn't reckon." (Al Talāq, 2,3)

Also,

$$\text{اِنْ تَتَّقُوا اللهَ يَجْعَل لَّكُمْ فُرْقَاناً}$$

"If you will fear Allah, He will grant you a Criterion." (Al Anfāl, 29)

And the Prophet is reported to have said in a narration of Tirmidhi: "Beware of the far sightedness of a believer. For he sees with the help of Allah's Light." Then he recited the following verse:

$$\text{اِنَّ فِى ذَلِكَ لَآيَتٍ لِلْمُتَوَسِّمِينَ}$$

"Surely, in this are signs for such as mark (the truth)." (Al Hijr, 75)

A *hadīth* narrated by the Prophet (*saws*) on behalf of Allah (*hadīth al Qudsi*) says: "Allah says, 'Whoever declared enmity for one of My Favorites, challenged Me to a duel. My slave does not gain nearness to Me through anything better than what I have declared obligatory on him. And My slave gets nearer to me with the supererogatory acts until I begin to love him. And, when I begin to love him, I become his hearing by which he hears, his sight by which he sees, his hand by which he holds and his foot by which he walks. Then, if he asks Me, I grant him. And if he seeks My protection, I grant him."

ونُؤمنُ بأشراطِ الساعةِ، من خروج الدَّجَّال، ونُزول عيسى ابن مَرْيَم عليه السلام من السماء، ونؤمنُ بطلوع الشمس من مغربها وخروج دَابَّة الأرض من موضعها

We believe in the signs of the Hour, such as the appearance of Dajjal and the descending down of ʿIsa ibn Maryam from the heavens. We believe in the Sun rising from where it sets and in the emergence of the beast from its (appointed) place in the earth.

Hudayfah b. Asid al Ghifari has reported: "the Prophet happened to come upon us while we were discussing the Hour. He asked: "What are you talking about?" We replied: "About the Hour." He said: "It will not strike until you have witnessed ten signs." Then he mentioned them: "The smoke, Dajjal, the beast, the Sun rising from where it sets, descending down of ʿIsa ibn Maryam, Yajuj and Majuj, and three caving in of the Earth, one in the East, another in the West and one in the Arab peninsula. The last would be the fire that would start from the Yemen and drive men to the Field of Resurrection (*Sahih Muslim*)"

the Prophet also said in another authentic report: "There hasn't been a Prophet but he warned his followers of the one eyed Dajjal. Lo! He is one eyed. And your Lord is not one eyed. It will be written between his two eyes: K F R." In another version he explained the letters K F R as meaning "*Kāfir.*"

Bukhari has recorded Abu Hurayrah as reporting the Prophet: "By Him in whose hands is my soul, it is certain that ʿIsa ibn Maryam will descend amongst you, a just ruler. He will break the Cross, kill the pig and abrogate tribute. Wealth would be so abundant that there would be no one to take. Those days, a single prostration would be dearer than all that the Earth contains."

The Qurʾan also mentions the emergence of the beast from the earth:

وَ إِذَا وَقَعَ الْقَوْلُ عَلَيْهِمْ أَخْرَجْنَا لَهُمْ دَآبَّةً مِّنَ الْأَرْضِ تُكَلِّمُهُمْ أَنَّ النَّاسَ كَانُوا بِآيَاتِنَا لَا يُوقِنُونَ

"When the word is fulfilled against them We shall bring forth for them out of

the earth a beast that shall speak to them that mankind did not have faith in Our signs." (Al Namal, 82)

Bukhari has recorded Abu Hurayrah as narrating the Prophet: "The Hour will not strike until the Sun rises from where it sets. When people will see that, everyone would become a believer. But that would be a time when the belief of a person who hadn't believed earlier would be of no profit."

وَلَا نُصَدِّقُ كَاهِنًا وَلَا عَرَّافًا، ولا من يَدَّعى شيئا يُخالف الكتاب والسنة وإجماع الأمة

We do not testify the soothsayer, the diviner, nor anyone who claims something which disagrees with the Qur'an, the *Sunnah*, or the consensus of the *Ummah*.

the Prophet has said in a *hadīth* of Muslim: "Whoever went to a diviner to consult him will not have forty days of his Prayers accepted."

In another *hadīth* preserved by Imam Ahmed b. Hanbal, he said: "Whoever consulted a diviner or soothsayer and gave credence to what he said, disbelieved in what has been revealed to Muhammad."

The astrologer, it might be noted, is also included by definition in the term diviner.

We might ask ourselves: If such severe warning has been issued to those who consult them, then what about those who indulge in the practices?

The *Sahihayn* have recorded a *hadīth* by `A'isha. She said: "the Prophet (*saws*) was asked about the soothsayer. He replied, 'There is no truth (in what they say).' They inquired: 'Messenger of Allah. Sometimes they say things that prove true?' He replied: 'That could be a word that a Jinn snatched (from the heavens) and put it in the ears of his friend. To that they add up a hundred lies.'"

The divining with the arrows is also included in the prohibition, as well as throwing of the stakes, or drawing of lines on the sand (or paper). Unquestionably, whatever these people earn is forbidden as Baghwi and Qadi `Ayad have declared.

Sahih Bukhari reports that Abu Bakr had a slave who brought in something one day that Abu Bakr ate. The slave asked: "Do you know where it came from?" Abu Bakr asked: "Where was it from?" The slave explained: "I used to prophesy things to a man in the pre Islamic days. In fact, I didn't know much about astrology. I lied to him all the time. The other day I ran across him and he gave me the thing (you ate) as gift for those services." Abu Bakr inserted his finger into his throat and vomited out all that was in his stomach.

It is an obligation of the ruler, or whoever has the power to do so, to get the land cleared of the soothsayers, diviners, astrologers and others of the trade. They shouldn't be allowed to sit on the side walks, nor should the people be allowed to visit them in their houses.

The people who practice these type of things that run against the Qur'an and *Sunnah*, are several kinds. Some are outright phonies. They pretend that the Jinn are in their control, such as the Nassabi *Shuyukh* or the Turuqiyyah liars. They deserve severe punishment. Indeed, some of them might deserve a death penalty, such as one who says he can prophecy. Others are true magicians and the majority of scholars have ruled that the magicians deserve death punishment. That is also the opinion of Abu Hanifah, Malik and Ahmed. The same is reported of some Companions, such as, `Umar, `Uthman, and others.

The scholars differ among themselves over the truth behind magic as also over its kinds. Most of them hold the opinion that sometimes one under the spell could even die of the effects, without an outward physical cause. A few others believe that magic is nothing but phantasm and imagination. Nevertheless, they all declared that whoever invited to the reverence of the seven stars, or prostrations to them, or devised methods to seek closeness to them, with the help of certain kinds of apparel, or rings worn in the fingers, or with the help of smoke out of fumigators, or things like that, are all acts of disbelief. They are doors that lead to declaring Allah's equal and need to be firmly closed.

The scholars also unanimously ruled that charms, adjuring, or oaths involving words of association with Allah are disallowed to utter, even if that leads to the overpowering of the Jinn. So also, any utterance of disbelief is disallowed.

Hence the Prophet (*saws*) said: "There is no harm in the charms so long as words of association with Allah are not uttered."

It is also not allowed to seek the refuge of the Jinn in view of the following verse of the Qur`an:

وَأَنَّهُ كَانَ رِجَالٌ مِّنَ الْإِنسِ يَعُوذُونَ بِرِجَالٍ مِّنَ الْجِنِّ فَزَادُوهُمْ رَهَقًا

"There were persons of the mankind who sought refuge with the persons of the Jinn and they increased them in vileness." (Al Jinn, 6)

It is said in connection with the above verse that in pre Islamic times when some people descended into a valley they said: "I seek the refuge of the great Jinn of this valley from their foolish ones."

Allah said:

وَيَوْمَ يَحْشُرُهُمْ جَمِيعًا ثُمَّ يَقُولُ لِلْمَلَائِكَةِ أَهَٰؤُلَاءِ إِيَّاكُمْ كَانُوا يَعْبُدُونَ (٤٠)قَالُوا سُبْحَانَكَ أَنْتَ وَلِيُّنَا مِن دُونِهِمْ بَلْ كَانُوا يَعْبُدُونَ الْجِنَّ أَكْثَرُهُم بِهِم مُّؤْمِنُونَ (٤١)

"The day when We shall gather them all together and ask the angels, `Was it you that these (men) worshipped?' They will reply, 'Glory to You. You are our Protector apart from them. Rather, they worshipped the Jinn. Most of them were believers in them.'" (Saba', 40, 41)

As for those who claim that the angels come to them, they are a misguided lot. It is the Jinn that visit them.

In principle, the best thing is to apply the rules of the *Shari`ah* to the things they do. Whatever agrees with the principles may be accepted and whatever disagrees may be rejected. the Prophet (*saws*) has said: "Whoever came up in our religion with an innovation that does not agree with it, is rejected." There is no right way but the way of the Prophet (*saws*). There is no truth but the truth he brought. There is no faith but the faith he brought. No one is going to obtain Allah's nearness, His approval and win Paradise but by following what the Prophet (*saws*) has ordered, in all aspects: the open as well as the secret. Whoever did not believe in what the Prophet (*saws*) informed, did not obey in what he commanded, in the affairs involving the heart or deeds of the body, is not a believer, far from being a Friend of Allah notwithstanding what he achieves.

He might fly in the air, convert timber into gold, and accomplish all sorts of wondrous feats, but he will not be   if he failed to live by the commandments but one of the Devilish men.

Similar is the case of those who swoon at the hearing of beautiful songs. They are innovators and a misguided lot. There was none among the Companions or their Followers who swooned on any occasion   not even when they heard the Qur`an. Rather, they were, as Allah has worded:

اِذَا ذُكِرَ اللهُ وَجِلَتْ قُلُوبُهُمْ وَاِذَا تُلِيَتْ عَلَيْهِمْ اٰيٰتُهٗ زَادَتْهُمْ اِيمَانًا وَّعَلٰى رَبِّهِمْ يَتَوَكَّلُوْنَ

"When Allah is mentioned, their hearts quake, and when His verses are recited, they cause increase to their faith. And they place their trust in their Lord." (Al Anfāl, 2)

As for what some of them utter, when under the spell of musical songs, speaking out words of unknown languages, that is the Devil speaking by their tongue.

As regards those of the mad but rational persons, about whom the scholars have spoken in good words, they were a good people. But they lost their minds although not totally. Whenever for a brief period when normalcy touched them, they spoke intelligently because of the original faith that resided in their heart.

In contrast, those who seek penance by avoiding to eat, dress themselves shabbily, or torture themselves in a variety of ways, leading their lives in solitude, abandoning the Friday and other congregational Prayers, these are the people whose efforts are lost in this world, although they imagine that they are doing good. The Prophet has said: "Whoever did not do three consecutive Friday Prayers out of neglect, without a valid reason, will have his heart sealed by Allah."

With regard to those who turned away from the *Sunnah* of the Prophet (*saws*), if he were to be knowledgeable, he is of those who were angered upon. If he were to be ignorant, he is the one who lost his way. Accordingly, Allah (*swt*) has ordered us to seek guidance to the Straight Path in every Prayer: the Path of those whom He showed His favor, of the Prophets, the Truthful, the martyrs and the righteous. And a good company they are.

As for dispensing with the Revelation in favor of the so called divinely inspired knowledge ("*`Ilm al laduni*,") taking queue from the story of Musa and Khidr, well, those who utter such things are atheists of a sort who have been denied true divine inducement. Musa had not been sent to Khidr in the capacity of a Prophet, nor was Khidr ordered to follow Musa. That is why Khidr asked him, as the report in Bukhari states, "Are you the Musa commissioned to the Israelites?" Musa replied in the affirmative. But Prophet Muhammad has been sent to all the members of the two species: men and Jinn. Were Musa and `Isa to be alive, they would have had to follow him. When `Isa will descend down from the heavens, he will rule by the *Shari`ah* of the Prophet. Therefore, whoever claimed that he is, with reference to Muhammad, in the same kind of relationship as Khidr with Musa, needs to re affirm his faith in Islam. He has completely abandoned the religion of Islam. Far from being a Friend of Allah (*swt*), he is, in fact, a friend of Shaytan.

وَ نَرَى الْجَمَاعَة حَقاً وَصَوَاباً، و الْفُرْقَة زَيْغاً وعَذَاباً

We consider remaining with the (mainstream) as the true and right course, and disunity as a deviation leading to punishment.

This is based on Allah's words:

وَاعْتَصِمُوا بِحَبْلِ اللهِ جَمِيْعًا وَّلَا تَفَرَّقُوا

"Hold fast unto the Rope of Allah together, and divide not yourselves." (Āl `Imrān, 103)

He also said:

وَلَا تَكُوْنُوا كَالَّذِيْنَ تَفَرَّقُوا وَاخْتَلَفُوا مِنْ بَعْدِ مَا جَآءَهُمُ الْبَيِّنٰتُ وَأُولٰٓئِكَ لَهُمْ عَذَابٌ عَظِيْمٌ

"And be not like those who divided themselves (into sects and groups) and disputed (the truth) after the clear signs had reached them. For such indeed is a mighty chastisement." (Āl `Imrān, 105)

Allah also said:

اِنَّ الَّذِيْنَ فَرَّقُوْا دِيْنَهُمْ وَكَانُوْا شِيَعًا لَّسْتَ مِنْهُمْ فِىْ شَىْءٍ اِنَّمَآ اَمْرُهُمْ اِلَى اللّٰهِ ثُمَّ يُنَبِّئُهُمْ بِمَا كَانُوْا يَفْعَلُوْنَ

"Verily, those who created schism in their religion and broke into sects, you have nothing to do with them. Their affair is with Allah. He shall inform them of (of the truth of) what they were doing." (Al An`ām, 159)

The Prophet (*saws*) has said: "The people of the Book divided themselves on religious lines into seventy two sects. This *Ummah* will divide itself up into seventy three sects: all following their whims and fancies. All of them will be in the Fire, except for one. That is the *Jama`ah* (the main stream community)." Another version has it that the Companions asked, "Which one is that, O Messenger of Allah?" He replied, "The one upon which I and my Companions are." This makes it clear that all the will meet with their destruction, except for the people of the *Sunnah* and *Jama`ah*. Further, the *hadīth* implies that divisions and differences are bound to occur.

Imam Ahmed has transmitted through Mu`adh ibn Jabal reporting the Prophet's words: "Shaytan is man's wolf, as the wolf for the sheep. He snatches away the straying one. Therefore, beware of the ravines. Hold fast unto the *Jama`ah*, the mainstream Muslims, and the mosques."

With regard to the differences amongst the *Ummah*, whether they be in principles or derivatives if they are not referred to Allah and the Messenger, the truth will not become manifest. In that event, the differing people would not be on a clear line in their affairs. Instead of that, if by Allah's mercy, some of them agree with the others, rather than refute each other, as did the Companions during the time of `Umar and `Uthman, who, when they disagreed between themselves, some of them assented with the others, neither oppressing nor oppressed: if they did that it would be good for all. But, if they don't do that, and if Allah does not show them mercy, then, the disapproved type of differences will raise their head among them, with some oppressing the others, either in words, by way of denunciation of faith or calling the other man corrupt, or in acts, in the form of imprisonment, torture and even death. Those who, for instance, fell into discord over the creation of the Qur`an, were of this kind. They initiated an innovation, denounced the faith of those who opposed them in that affair and made lawful unto themselves the denial of their rights or their punishment.

258

It might be remembered that when some of that which the Prophet has brought is unclear to the people, they will either do justice or commit a wrong. The just among them, in that situation, are those who follow the lead given by the Prophets. They do not oppress anyone. In contrast, the unjust oppresses others. And most of them violate others' rights and are well aware that they are violators. Allah (*swt*) said:

وَمَا اخْتَلَفَ الَّذِيْنَ أُوتُوا الْكِتْبَ إِلَّا مِنْ بَعْدِ مَا جَآءَهُمُ الْعِلْمُ بَغْيًا بَيْنَهُمْ

"Verily the (true) religion with Allah is Islam. Those who were given the Book did not differ but after they had received the Knowledge in envy of each other." (Āl 'Imrān, 19)

Had they pursued the path of knowledge that leads to justice, they would have assented to each other. A fair example is that of those who followed the Imams in matters of jurisdiction. They are aware that they themselves are incapable of working out the Fiqh principles or the details of the law from the Qur'anic revelations or the Prophetic utterances. They considered their Imams as the deputies of the Prophet saying, about their own action: "This is the best we could do." The just among them do not oppress others either by word or deed, for e.g. by claiming that the opinion of his own Imam is the only correct opinion while he has no proofs of that and condemn him who opposes him, although being aware that the other man (being a commoner too: tr.) has no recourse (but to follow his own Imam: tr.).

It might also be pointed out that the differences are of two kinds: differences of the nature of diversity, and differences of the nature of contradiction.

Further, the differences of the nature of diversity can be of several kinds: one in which two opinions or acts could both be right. For example, the differences among the Companions over the readings of the Qur'an. When informed, the Prophet reproached both of the parties (for arguing with each other) and declared them both as correct. Other examples are the words of *adhān*, (the Prayer call) or *iqamah*, (call preceding the start of Prayers), the *thana'*, (opening supplication), the *sajdatu al sahw* (method of expiatory prostration) the *tashahhud, salatu al khawf*, (the Prayer in situation of fear), number of *takbirāt* in the 'Eid Prayers, and others of this sort. In the above examples, several methods are correct, although one or the other of the two opinions would be a preferred one. But you will find followers of this or that system crossing swords with each other, over such issues as whether to say the words once, or twice, in the call preceding the start of the Prayers. This is absolutely prohibited. Sometimes, two opinions are so worded that both affirm the other as true. The difference is only in the phrasing, as most people do when attempting definitions.

As regards the nature of contradictions, in any given situation, there could be two opinions, each of which rules out the other. It might be in principles or in derivations. This is a tougher case to deal with since the two opinions contradict each other. Yet, one thing is quite obvious. Quite often we notice that a man may hold a wrong opinion adulterated with the true one. Or, he may have an evidence that points to some truth in what he is adhering to. But people tend to reject the whole: the false as well as the true part of it. The result is that the man (assaulted, abandons the truth) but remains holding on to the untruth he was originally holding on to. This happens to many of the *Ahl al Sunnah*.

Insofar as the innovators are concerned, their fallacy is too apparent (for discussion). Whoever received guidance and the Light from his Lord, and gave their affairs a thought, will realize the advantage there is in the Qur`an and *Sunnah* prohibiting these kind of things, although, hearts that are pure will by instinct disapprove of them. If that be the case, then, it is Light upon Light.

In any case, with reference to the first kind of differences, that of the nature of diversity, only he deserves blame who oppresses another (differing with him) in that affair. The Qur`an declared both the two groups in this kind of situation praiseworthy, when none of them criticized the other, as in the words of Allah:

مَا قَطَعْتُمْ مِّنْ لِّينَةٍ أَوْ تَرَكْتُمُوهَا قَآئِمَةً عَلَى أُصُولِهَا فَبِإِذْنِ اللهِ

"You did not cut down a tree or left them standing on their stems, but by the leave of Allah." (Al Hashr, 5)

The verse was occasioned when two groups differed among themselves over the uprooting of trees during the invasion directed at Banu Nadir.

the Prophet has said: "When the judge does his best, then, if he arrives at the right opinion, he has two rewards, but if he committed error, despite his best efforts, then he is rewarded once."

As for the second kind of difference, that of the nature of contradiction, one of them has been praised while the other blamed in the following words of Allah:

وَلَوْ شَآءَ اللهُ مَا اقْتَتَلَ الَّذِينَ مِنْ بَعْدِهِمْ مِنْ بَعْدِ مَا جَآءَتْهُمُ الْبَيِّنْتُ وَلَكِنِ اخْتَلَفُوا فَمِنْهُمْ مَّنْ أَمَنَ وَمِنْهُمْ مَّنْ كَفَرَ

"Had Allah willed, those who came after them would not have slaughtered each other, after the clear signs had come to them. But, they differed, some believing, others rejecting." (Al Baqarah, 253)

With regard to the Qur`an, most of the differences involved therein occur in interpretations. The safe road then lies in keeping in view what the Prophet told us through the report of `Amr b. Shu`ayb who reports his father, and who narrates his father, saying: "One day the Prophet (*saws*) came upon his Companions who were disputing over the Divine Decree. One of them would quote one verse and the other, another. The Prophet's reacted as if a pomegranate juice had been sprinkled over his face. He asked: "Is this what you have been exhorted to? Or, have you been entrusted with this? That you should assault the Book of Allah with some of its own? Be on the look out for what you have been ordered to do, go ahead and do it; and stay away from what you have been prohibited (Ahmed in his *Musnad*)."

Another version has the following additional words: "People before you were not cursed until they disagreed among themselves. Any argumentation over the Qur`an is unbelief."

The above *hadīth* is a well reported one that is to be found in several *Musnad* as well as *Sunnah* collections. Muslim also has a report narrated by `Abdullah b. Rubah al Ansari, which says that `Abdullah ibn `Amr b. al ,`As said: "Once I went to see the Prophet. He heard voices of two people who were arguing over (the meaning of) a verse. He came out to us with anger writ large on his face. He said, `Those who went before you were destroyed because of their differences in their Book.'"

As expected, most of the innovatory groups differ over its interpretations, believing in a part of it and disbelieving in a part. They acknowledge as true verses that agree with their own opinions. As to what does not, they either interpret it by taking it wholly out of context, or will say, simply, 'We don't know whatever is being meant by these verses.' Now, to say that, is a kind of unbelief too, since, to believe merely in the words without any meaning is the kind of attitude of the people of the Book that drew censure. Allah Most High said:

وَ مِنْهُم أُمِّيُّونَ لَا يَعْلَمُونَ الْكِتَابَ إِلَّا أَمَانِيَّ

"And among them are some unlettered ones who do not know the Book but see (therein, their own) desires." (Al Baqarah, 78)

The allusion is to a person who recited without knowing the meaning of it, unlike a believer who understood something or the other of the meaning of the Qur`an and then lived by it. As what remained unclear to him, he attributed its true meaning to Allah.

وَ دِينُ اللهِ فِي الْأَرْضِ والسَّمَاءِ وَاحِدٌ، وَ هُوَ دِينُ الْإِسْلَامِ، قال الله تعالى: (وَإِنَّ الدِّينَ عِنْدَ اللهِ الْإِسْلَامُ)، وقال تعالى: (وَ رَضِيتُ لَكُمُ الْإِسْلَامَ دِينًا)

وَهُوَ بَيْنَ الْغُلُوِّ والتَّقْصِيرِ، وبَيْنَ التَّشْبِيهِ والتَّعْطِيلِ، وبَيْنَ الْجَبْرِ والقَدْرِ، وبَيْنَ الْأَمْنِ وَالْأَيَاسِ

Allah's religion in the heaven and the earth is one religion. It is the religion of Islam. Allah said, 'Verily, the religion with Allah is Islam.' Allah also said, 'I am satisfied with Islam as your religion.' This religion is (the middle way) between two extremes; between anthropomorphism and denial of Attributes; between free will and pre determination; between self assurance and despair.

the Prophet has said in a trustworthy report transmitted by Abu Hurayrah: "We family of Prophets: our religion is one religion."

And Allah said:

وَمَنْ يَبْتَغِ غَيْرَ الْإِسْلَامِ دِينًا فَلَنْ يُقْبَلَ مِنْهُ

The Islamic Creed

"Whoever sought a religion other than Islam, shall not have it accepted of him." (Āl `Imrān,85)

Although the verse was revealed addressing a specific situation, its message is universal and will remain so through the ages. Only details of law have differed, as Allah said:

$$\text{لِكُلٍّ جَعَلْنَا مِنْكُمْ شِرْعَةً وَمِنْهَاجًا}$$

"We have prescribed a Law and a Way for everyone of you." (Al Mā'idah, 48)

Religion is then that which Allah declared by the tongue of His Messengers through and through the ages. Its main characteristic is that it is as clear as a mirror. Any discerning person, whether he is young or old, Arab or non Arab, can enter into it in no time. Delegates came down to Madinah (in those early days) learnt it in no time and returned to their land. And, what they had learnt sufficed them.

It might also be pointed out in reference to some of the differences that are noted in the instructions the Prophet gave to the delegates from distant parts of the land, that it was because of the needs of the individuals concerned. If they happened to be from a distant land, such as Dumam b. Tha`labah al Najadi, or the delegation of `Abd al Qays of the Bahrayn region, he taught them what would be easily appreciated by even the most ignorant of them. He knew that his religion was going to spread far and wide, and soon, those who had knowledge would visit them teaching them what they needed to know most. In contrast, when the inquirer happened to be someone who could visit oftener, and could gradually increase his knowledge, or, if the Prophet (*saws*) happened to know that the inquirer had already learned the basics, in such cases he replied in accordance with the requirements, needs and situations of the person. An example is the Prophet's words to the young man: "Say, `I believe in Allah,' and then remain steadfast." (The reference is to the incident when a young man came up to the Prophet and asked to be admonished with some words that would free him of asking anyone after him. the Prophet spoke out the words quoted above :tr.).

Further, as Tahawi has said, this religion is between two extremes. Allah Most High said:

قُلْ يَا أَهْلَ الْكِتَبِ لَا تَغْلُوا فِي دِينِكُمْ غَيْرَ الْحَقِّ

"Say, `People of the Book! Do not exceed the limits in your religion other than the truth." (Al Mā'idah, 77)

He also said:

يَا أَيُّهَا الَّذِينَ أَمَنُوا لَا تُحَرِّمُوا طَيِّبَتِ مَا أَحَلَّ اللهُ لَكُمْ وَلَا تَعْتَدُوا إِنَّ اللهَ لَا يُحِبُّ الْمُعْتَدِينَ (٨٧) وَكُلُوا مِمَّا رَزَقَكُمُ اللهُ حَلَالًا طَيِّبًا وَ اتَّقُوا اللهَ الَّذِي أَنْتُمْ بِهِ مُؤْمِنُونَ (٨٨)

"Believers! Treat not as unlawful that which has been made lawful to you and exceed not the bounds. Verily, Allah does not approve of those who exceed the bounds. Eat of the lawful and the clean that Allah has provided you. And fear Allah in whom you believe." (Al Mā'idah, 87, 88)

The *Sahihayn* have a narration of Anas b. Malik. He said: "Some of the Companions of the Prophet (*saws*) enquired about his deeds in private. (Such as his Prayers, recitation of the Qur`an, etc. But they thought little of it and so), one of them said, `I shall not eat meat.' Another said, `I shall not marry.' Another said, `I shall not sleep.' the Prophet heard about them. He responded, `What's the matter with some people who make such and such vows. So far as I am concerned, I fast and eat, sleep and Pray (in the depth of the night), eat meat and have married women. Lo! Whoever showed aversion to my ways is not of me.'"

Tahawi also stated that this religion is between self assurance and despair. This is because a man should always be fearful of Allah's punishment descending down, yet hopeful of His mercy. Fear and hope in Islam are like the two wings of a bird for a slave in his flight towards Allah.

When Imam Tahawi Abu Ja`far Ahmed bin Salamah al Azadi, may Allah show him mercy, reached this point, and had stated the Islamic creeds and its offshoots, he ended his treaties by saying:

فَهَذَا دِينُنَا و اعْتِقَادُنَا ظَاهِراً وبَاطِناً، وَنَحْنُ بُرَاءٌ إِلَى اللهِ تَعالى مِن كُلِّ مَنْ خَالَفَ الذِي ذَكَرْنَاهُ وَبَيَّنَّاهُ ونسأل الله تعالى أن يُثَبِّتَنا على الإِيمان، ويختم لنا به، ويعصمنا من الأهواء المختلفة، والآراء المتفرقة، والمذاهب الرَّدِيَّة، مثل المُشَبِّهة، والمعتزلة، والجَهْمِية، والجَبَرية، والقَدَرية وغيرهم، من الذين خالفوا السُّنة والجَماعة وحالفوا الضلالة، ونحن منهم بُرَآء، وهم عندنا ضُلَّال و أردياء، وباللهِ

264

العِصمة والتوفيق

This is our religion and our faith, the open of it and the secret of it. We absolve ourselves before Allah of everyone who is opposed to what we have stated and explained. We supplicate our Lord to grant us firmness in faith, until the last breath, save us from discordant heretic tendencies, disparate opinions and rejected sectarian attitudes, such as that of the anthropomorphists, the Mu`tazilah, the Jahmiyyah, the Jabariyyah, the Qadariyyah and others of those who deviated from the *Sunnah* and the *Jama`ah* and befriended the misguided. We are quit of them. To us they are the misguided and hence the rejected ones. By Allah is the preservation, and from Him the right inducement.

The reason for the misguidance of these people and their likes is their abandoning of the straight path which Allah has ordered us to tread in the following words:

قُلْ هٰذِهِ سَبِيلِيٓ أَدْعُوٓا إِلَى اللهِ عَلَى بَصِيرَةٍ أَنَا وَمَنِ اتَّبَعَنِيٓ

"Say, 'This is my way, I invite you unto Allah, with sure knowledge   I and whoever followed me.'" (Yūsuf, 108)

`Abdullah ibn Mas`ud said: "Once the Prophet drew a line and said: `This is the path unto Allah.' Then he drew several other lines (running out of it) towards the right and the left and said: `These are (other) paths. On everyone of them sits a Satan inviting to it.' Then he recited:

وَأَنَّ هٰذَا صِرَاطِي مُسْتَقِيمًا فَاتَّبِعُوهُ وَلَا تَتَّبِعُوا السُّبُلَ فَتَفَرَّقَ بِكُمْ عَنْ سَبِيلِهِ ذٰلِكُمْ وَصَّكُمْ بِهِ لَعَلَّكُمْ تَتَّقُونَ

"This is my path, follow it. And do not follow other paths, that will take you off His straight path. Thus He admonishes you, so that you (may learn to) fear." (Al An`ām, 153)

It can be deduced from the above that to seek and supplicate for the straight path is the need that overrides all other needs. That is the reason why Allah has ordered us to recite *Surah Al Fatiha* in every cycle of the Prayers. He told us to say:

اِهْدِنَا الصِّرَاطَ الْمُسْتَقِيمَ (٦) صِرَاطَ الَّذِينَ اَنْعَمْتَ عَلَيْهِمْ غَيْرِ الْمَغْضُوبِ عَلَيْهِمْ وَلَا الضَّالِّينَ (٧)

"Show us the straight path. The path of those whom Thou favored, and not of those who were angered upon, nor of those who went astray." (Al Fātiha, 6,7)

The Prophet explained the verses by saying: "It is the Jews who were "angered upon," and the Christians are those "who went astray."

Trustworthy reports also say that the Prophet said: "You shall surely follow the ways of those who went before you: exactly, identically. So that, if they entered a lizard's hole, you will enter it also." They asked, "(Who do you mean) O Messenger of Allah? The Jews and the Christians?" He replied: "Who else?"

Some of the earliest scholars have said: "Whoever of the scholars (of this *Ummah*) deviated, will resemble the Jews in some ways, and whoever of the common people deviated will resemble the Christians in some ways."

We seek Allah's protection and security. Gloried is your Lord, the Lord of Power, far above what they ascribe (unto Him). Peace upon the Messengers. And praise be to Allah, the Lord of the worlds.

Notes :

1. This *hadīth*, numbered 6702 in *Musnad Ahmed*, is an authentic one. Reports of this meaning are found in the same collection, such as under *hadīth* no. 6668. Bukhari has also narrated something near about this in his collection, under ch., "Allah's Creation of Men's Deeds", p. 78, as has Muslim in vol. 2, no. 304 in a shorter form (Ahmed Muhammad Shakir).

2. Dara Qutni has narrated this *hadīth* in its full (no. 185) as has Bayhaqi in his *Sunan al Kubra* (4/19), apparently taking it from Dara Qutni. It is one of the narrations of Ibn Wahab with Mu`awiyyah, al `Ula b. al Harth, Mak-hul and Abu Hurayrah in the chain. Dara Qutni himself adds his remark that Mak-hul didn't hear from Abu Hurayrah. But subsequent narrators are trustworthy. And, after reporting Dara Qutni's remark, Bayhaqi added his own remarks saying: "Several traditions of the Prophet (*saws*) have been reported on the subject of validity of Prayers behind the virtuous as well as the corrupt of those who testified to Allah's oneness. However, all of them carry some weakness or the other. Closest to being trustworthy is Mak-hul's report which he narrates from Abu Hurayrah. Abu Da'ud has given it a place in his *Sunan*." The report is of course is the same as the one narrated by Ibn Abi al `Izz. But, it can be noticed that a narrator is missing between Mak-hul and Abu Hurayrah. Otherwise there is no other problem with this report. And, as I have pointed out in my notes on *Musnad Ahmed*, under *hadīth* no. 5724, whatever has been said about Mu`awiyyah b. Abi Saleh, is, truly speaking, a bit out of proportion (Ahmed Muhammad Shakir).

3. This however applies to a ruler who rules by the laws of Islam but adulterates it with oppression of some kind. In contrast, if he declares the lawful as unlawful, the unlawful as lawful, then the above text does not apply to him, rather, what the author and his commentator have said earlier is applicable.

Index

A

`Abbas (ra) 74, 79, 105, 114, 127, 130, 136, 148, 176, 181, 196, 199, 235-237

Abdullah 36, 78, 84, 94, 117, 126, 132, 155, 160, 168, 170, 182, 190, 199, 232, 234, 236-239, 244, 245, 261, 265

Ablution 184, 192

Abyssinian 188

Adam 54-56, 96, 101, 110, 115, 173, 200

`Adāwah 171

Adhān 259

Adultery 156, 161, 181

Āhād 168, 170

Ahādith 63, 68, 77, 99, 137, 170

Ahzāb 53, 78, 91, 147, 148

Anas 81, 100, 107, 109, 110, 163, 182, 195, 206, 264

Anbiyā 2, 4, 8, 49, 55, 64, 140, 146, 203, 221

Anfāl 45, 162, 167, 171, 174, 214, 251, 256

Aqsa 100, 106

`Arafah 141, 182

`Arsh 31, 34, 36, 37, 54, 84, 98, 108, 113, 126, 129, 134-138, 141, 143, 146, 147, 151, 199, 201, 206, 207

Astrology 254

Atheist 204, 256

Awliyā 248

A'isha (ra) (66, 78, 88, 99, 106, 161, 201, 202, 233, 238, 239, 241, 245, 253

B

Badr 214

Barzakh 196, 197

Beliefs 84, 85, 120, 124, 152, 153, 158, 182

Bilqis 64, 135

Bridge 163, 199, 202, 203

Buraq 100

C

Caliphate 233, 235-237, 239, 241-243

Caliphs 190, 241, 244

Christians 15, 59, 73, 110, 153, 169, 266

Cosmos 126

Curse 123, 155, 180, 189, 229, 261

D

Dajjal 252

Da'ud 94, 126, 182, 186, 199, 209, 267

Dinar 142, 157, 224

Dirham 44, 142, 157

E

Egypt 59

`Eid 182, 259

F

Fāsiq 157

Fiqh 26, 66, 95, 184, 259

Firdaws 135

Furqān 20, 41, 129, 249

G

Ghāfir 16, 134, 140, 141, 147, 148, 160, 198, 226

Gharqad 116

Ghazali 84

Gospels 51

H

Umm Habibah 42, 43

Hajj 83, 163, 182, 193, 211, 222, 223, 225, 241

Hanafiyyah 165, 185, 235

Abu Hanifah 26, 66, 95, 98, 112, 150, 166, 184, 222, 225, 254

Honey 104, 108

Hour 198, 228, 245, 249, 252

I

Iblis 120, 121, 218

Idols 1, 4

Idris 102

Ihsān 174

Ijtihād 184

Ikhlās 48, 92, 218

Imān 146, 150, 156, 166, 174

Injil 73, 149

Intercession 4, 54, 59, 96, 108-111, 113-115, 163, 180, 186, 208

Israfil 85, 146, 147

Isra'il 104, 105

Istawā 31, 32, 84, 134, 136, 137, 141

J

Jabariyyah 22, 35, 119, 213-215, 265

Jabir 127, 245

Jahannum 119, 247

Jawhari 25

Jerusalem 159

Jews 54, 59, 73, 142, 153, 266

Jibril 65, 68, 69, 85, 100-104, 106, 121, 146, 151, 174, 175, 199, 206

Jihad 54, 121, 122, 175, 182, 193

Jinn 29, 30, 45, 58, 66, 70, 88, 119, 121, 125, 196, 209, 253-255, 257

Jizah 248

Jubayr 136, 233

Juwayni 85, 143

K

Kāfir 252

Kāfirūn 9

Kahaf 18, 192, 204, 212

Kalām 84

Kawthar 107

Khadijah (ra) 50, 51

Khalid 100, 232

Khalq 40, 216

Khattab 160, 234-236, 238-240

Khawarij 110, 152-159, 165, 242

Khawlah 138

Khidr 256, 257

Khilafah 242

Khudri 78, 111, 144, 207, 232

Khullah 56, 144, 145

Khyber 243

Kingdom 8, 30, 46, 73, 94, 135, 178, 242

Kubra 267

Kursiyy 18, 134-136

L

Laduni 256

Lahab 24

Law 23, 66, 165, 170, 178, 241, 259, 262, 263

Lawh 44

Light 34, 43, 58, 64, 73, 76, 79, 90, 121, 131, 142, 147, 149, 164, 167, 169, 203, 204, 246, 251, 260

Love 13, 16, 54, 56, 57, 113, 119, 121, 144, 145, 189, 191, 217, 229, 231, 238, 251

Luqmān 4

M

Madinah 165, 237, 239, 241, 263

Maghāzi 138

Magic 254

Mahfūz 44

Majuj 252

Makkah 99, 106, 109, 112, 169, 232

Mankind 25, 29, 45, 54, 58-60, 70, 88, 118, 119, 121, 196, 209, 252, 255

Maqdis 105, 107

Martyrdom 237, 242

Maryam (asws) 148, 202, 252

Mika'il 85, 146, 147

Miswak 204

Muddaththir 70, 109, 167

Muhaddithun 79

Muhammad 2, 7, 12, 13, 15, 42, 49, 52, 53, 55, 65, 66, 70, 78, 84, 101-104, 108, 110, 124, 133, 143, 148, 149, 151, 152, 171, 176, 180, 186, 195, 222, 226, 232, 235, 253, 257, 267

Mujtahid 185

Mulk 30, 130, 141

Muntahā 104

Murji'ah 153, 155, 158, 160

Musa (asws) 3, 51, 54, 58, 60-62, 74-76, 79, 100, 103-105, 110, 135, 141, 142, 144, 148, 149, 166, 200, 243, 256, 257

Mutawātir 168, 169

N

Najashi 51

Nile 104

Nisapur 85

Nūr 79, 128

O

Oaths 62, 64, 181, 254

Oceans 85

Oneness 1, 4, 12, 91, 92, 130, 131, 180, 186, 208, 267

Optimism 164

Orphan 181

P

Pagan 4, 6, 7, 39, 53, 67, 90, 110, 149, 192, 214

Palm 21, 84

Pearls 206

Persia 59

Philosopher 7, 20, 26, 30, 84, 90, 130, 200

Poverty 173

Prey 132, 250

Pride 54-57

Purify 57

Q

Qadariyyah 7, 22, 35, 118, 119, 130, 155, 205, 210, 212-215, 265

Qadīm 21, 22, 27, 29

Qadr 22, 213

Qahhār 121

Qayyūm 28

Qiblah 143, 150, 152, 153, 155, 160, 164, 169, 181, 186, 237

Qiyāmah 72

Quba 169

Qudsi 251

Queen 64

Quraysh 107, 238, 246

R

Rahmān 22, 94, 98, 133, 204, 232, 236, 238-241, 245, 246

Ramadan 175

Rebellion 3, 118, 188, 189, 212, 231, 242

Ruku` 178

Rūm 5, 6, 15, 39, 111, 217

Rushd 84

S

Sabā 18, 58, 255

Safiyyah 114

Sahih 5, 43, 56, 109, 114, 204, 235, 241, 244, 245, 252, 253

Sahw 259

Salaf 10, 23, 68, 139, 225

Shams 216

Shaytan 19, 66, 83, 218, 235, 257,

258

Shirk 4, 172, 181

Siddiq 161

Siffin 242

Smoke 252, 254

Sufi 112

Suhrawardi 250

Suicide 185

Sunan 244, 267

Sūr 147

Suraqa 127

T

Tabuk 185

Tadhkirah 109

Tahrīm 206

Takbirāt 259

Tamhid 118

Tawakkul 128

Tawassul 113

Tawhīd 2-11, 19, 130, 167, 172, 178, 179

Tawrah 73, 149

Ta'wīl 88, 89

Tūr 20, 53, 135

Turkey 4

Tyrant 52, 182

U

`Ubadah 126

`Ubaydah 245, 246

Uhud 160, 199, 204, 245

Ummah 67, 78, 108-110, 156, 188, 190, 213, 226, 233, 245, 253, 258, 266

Uqayl 227

`Uqbah 146, 183

W

Waham 25

Wilāyah 171, 172

Wasf 92

Wasilah 113, 114

Womb 117

Y

Yajuj 252

Yasīn 21, 61, 62, 96

Yūnus 5, 55, 71, 73, 171, 172

Z

Zabur 149

Zajjaj 171

Zakah 168, 175, 184

Zayd 94, 175, 246

Zaynab 138

Zindiq 155

Zubayr 238-240, 242, 245, 246

Zuhri 83

The Author

An Indian, he did his Diploma in Mechanical Engineering, and Masters Degree in English Literature from Mysore University.

He worked for 12 years in various Industries in Bangalore, during which time he also took courses in Arabic language and *Usul al-Hadīth*, *Usul al-Fiqh*, etc.

In 1978 he entered Saudi Arabia and has been there since then, now working as Supervisor for Design Engineering.

He has six children all of whom studied in Arabic schools and then at Islamic Universities of Islamabad (Pakistan) and Malaysia. Four of his children hold Master Degrees in Islamic Studies and Engineering.

He has been the Chief Editor of an English magazine published from Bangalore called Young Muslim Digest. This is popular among the youth for the articles regularly contributed by him. The magazine is now in its 36th year of publication.

He is an active Da`wah worker. He delivers regular lectures at Da`wah centers in Dammam-Khobar and nearby towns. He also co-operates with WAMY of the Eastern Province.

His literary works are all original well-researched works (not the 'cut and paste' type).

Books by the same author

1. Tafsir Ishraq al-Ma`ani:

In 14 volumes. A quintessence of commentaries of the *Qur`an*, old and new. It endeavors to present the *ahādīth* of context (with the Arabic text), and then presents opinions of scholars of first few generations, taking the material from Ibn Jarir Tabari, Ibn Kathir (who supplies sources of *ahādīth* in Tabari) and Shawkani (who gives sources of the statements of the Companions).

The commentary based on the above three sources, is then proceeds to take non-conflicting material from sources such as: Zamakhshari, Razi, Qurtubi, Alusi, Al-Manar, Sayyid Qutb, Sabuni, etc. It also draws from authentic English and Urdu commentaries.

It also states the majority opinions of the commentators throughout Muslim history.

Finally, it has *Fiqh* points (from *Al-Arba`ah*), anecdotes, etc.

It does not use any *hadīth* which has been evaluated as less than Hasan. Every quoted *hadīth* carries the reference, as well as evaluation by Haythamiyy, Albani, Dhahabi, and others.

It is a unique work, the like of which does not exist even in Arabic, and hence it has been suggested that it should be translated into Arabic.

2. Muhammad the Unlettered Prophet Who Changed the World in 23 years.

With introduction by Abul Hasan Ali Nadawi, it is an extremely simple, but comprehensive biography of Prophet Muhammad in 100 pages. Re-printed 8 times in India, as also printed in Canada. Translated into Hindi.

278

3. A Biography of the Prophet in the Light of the Original Sources

Originally in Arabic, by Dr. Mahdi Rizq Allah, translated into English. An authentic work in 2 volumes. Published by Darus Salam, Riyadh. The Arabic version is included as course material in some of the Saudi Universities.

4. The Fundamentals of Islamic Creed

What are the fundamental articles of faith, without which a man cannot be a Muslim. Translation of Imam Tahawi's text and selected Ibn abi al-`Izz's commentary – 300 pages.

Printed in India, Dammam, Riyadh, and Canada. This is being used as course book by the On-line American Islamic University.

5. Islam, the Religion You can no longer Ignore

A very successful short introduction to Islam. 60 pages. Repeatedly reprinted in India, Dammam and Canada, and used by Da`wah people. It has foreword by Dr. Zeghlul Najjar. One of the re-prints was in 100,000 copies, 50,000 of which were sent to the Saudi Embassy in Washington to handover to Visa applicants.

6. Fake Pearls

A collection of 200 *ahādith* taken from 5 different *hadīth* collections, that are either fabricated or very weak, with notes on reasons of such evaluation. Reprinted in Canada.

7. Bilal, the Abyssinian Outrunner

Life of Bilal b. Rabah. 100 pages. Reprinted in Canada.

8. A Short History of Israel

With introduction by Abul Hasan Ali Nadwi, it presents the history of the Jews from the Abrahamic times until the end of the last century – 100 pages. Reprinted in Jeddah.

9. An Introduction to the Arabic Language through Islamic Texts

In two volumes, 700 pages, and two DVDs, it teaches the Arabic language with the help of *Qur'an*, *Hadith*, and other Islamic source books; being used as text-book in a British School.

The DVD carries audio explanation of the lessons. Reprinted in Riyadh, Canada.

10. Life of Abul Hasan Ali Nadwi

A short, but comprehensive biography in 110 pages.

11. *Hadith* of the Night Vision

A translation of Ibn Rajab's book in Arabic, on one of the dreams of Prophet Muhammad – Pocket-size, 130 pages.

12. The Splitter of the Dawn

A collection of *Qur'anic* verses that deal with the fundaments of Islam, meant for non-Muslims as an introduction to the *Qur'an*. Useful for Da'wah purposes – Pocket-size, 130 pages.

13. I Would like to Repent .. But

Translation into English of a short work by Sheikh Muhammad al-Munajjid. Reprinted several times.

14: An Educational Encyclopedia of Islam

A comprehensive work in 2200 pages, 3 volumes, covering all aspects of general need and interest. It is first of its kind in English. With some 45-50 maps and illustrations, it is an extremely interesting work to read and refer. In color, it is filled with interesting epigrams from the Islamic literature.

15: The Inimitable and Physical Sciences

Reviewed and authenticated by no less than four scientists, each of them holding PhD's in physics itself, this admirably done work deserves careful reading. The *Qur`anic* verses quoted, do not need any interpretation to be related to modern day findings. That they are directly related to some of the latest scientific findings should send a reader thinking.

16: Kitab ul *Imān*

A collection of 123 *ahādith* in 190 pages which uses the words, *Imān* of *Mu`min*, with commentaries by well known doctors of *hadith*.

Books available at

1. Al-Attique Publications,

11-Progres Ave.

Unit #7

Scarborough ON

M1P 4s7,

Canada,

Tel.: 416-335-1179, 416-615-1222

al-attique@al-attique.com

2. East West Educational Tools

c/o, Inst. of Higher Learning,

Next to Hasanat College,

Darus Surur Building, Basement,

43, Dickenson Road,

Bangalore 560 042

Tel. 080 / 41133 504

9845 694 683, 9845 301 422, 9902 527 012.

mzaki05@yahoo.com

shareefhusain06@yahoo.com

aft_77@yahoo.com

3. Young Muslim Digest, No. 332,

1st Floor, Darussalam Bldg.,

Queen's Road, Bangalore, 560 052,

India,

Tel. 2228 9305, 9886 858 400

mzaki05@yahoo.com

shareefhusain06@yahoo.com

aft_77@yahoo.com